# ROME
# WAS
# MY BEAT

# ROME
# WAS
# MY BEAT

## REYNOLDS PACKARD

LYLE STUART, INC. / SECAUCUS, NEW JERSEY

Queries regarding rights and permissions should be addressed to
Lyle Stuart, Inc., 120 Enterprise Avenue, Secaucus, New Jersey 07094

Published by Lyle Stuart, Inc.

Manufactured in the United States of America

Published simultaneously in Canada by
George J. McLeod, Limited, Toronto, Ontario

**Library of Congress Cataloging in Publication Data**


Packard, Reynolds, 1903-
    Rome was my beat.

    1. Packard, Reynolds, 1903-        — Biography —
Journalistic career. 2. Rome (City) — Social life and
customs. I. Title.
PS3531.A2156Z52        070'.92'4 [B]        74-31665
ISBN 0-8184-0216-4

TO MY WIFE'S LOVERS
*with appreciation and friendship*

# CONTENTS

# ROME
# WAS
# MY BEAT

# PART I

# THE POPE
# AND
# MUSSOLINI

# CHAPTER I

There were two vice-presidents, the general European manager, and the UP president himself as well as the Paris bureau chief at the Gare de Lyon to see us off. They were waiting for us by the sleeping-car section of the Rome Express. When they saw us, a murmur of subdued cheers went up. Pibe and I never felt so important before.

"That's Pibe who flew with Count Ciano," J. I. Miller, vice-president for Latin America, said to Hugh Baillie, the president of the United Press Association, who had never met her personally. "If anybody can reopen the Rome office she can." Then turning to Pibe he said: "That's right isn't it, Mrs. Packard? You did fly with Count Ciano during the Ethiopian war?"

"Well, it didn't take much courage to do that," Pibe said. "The Ethiopians didn't have any antiaircraft guns worth a damn. What was more important actually was the bottle of White Horse Pack and I had with us the night Addis Ababa fell."

"The tickets, Mrs. Packard . . ." Ralph Heinzen, the Paris bureau manager said, interrupting her. He knew about the White Horse incident and didn't think it was a fitting subject to discuss with company brass as one of the reasons Mussolini might eventually allow the UP to file again from Italy. The bureau had been shut down just three days before because Bud Ekins, the new Rome manager, had sent a story in baseball slang to

3

fool the censors, saying that Il Duce had suffered a stroke while reviewing troops, fallen to the ground, and been taken to a military hospital where he was still as senseless as a vegetable. Heinzen was wild on a typewriter, but a puritan in conversation with UP executives. You would have thought that he and his colleagues never drank, smoked, nor screwed to hear him talk at such times.

"Tickets?" Pibe echoed. "Pack has them."

I started going through my pockets and looking between two books I was carrying, but I couldn't find them.

"I've lost them," I said.

"Don't be silly. You've never lost any tickets in your life," Pibe said. "You have them somewhere in your pockets. Go through them again, quietly and calmly, and you'll find them."

I almost blew my top. That was Pibe for you. Always bossing me around in front of other people and, in this case, the very ones who had named me the new Rome bureau chief. I didn't resort to marital bickering in front of my company peers but just thought to myself: You bastard you, Pibe, you are just a goddamn Xanthippe with no more respect for your husband than she had for Socrates. I thought of the reputation Pibe had made in covering the Italian invasion of Ethiopia, the woman reporter up front with the troops, but in reality I had to be there to prevent her being raped. She couldn't even squat in the bushes alone to answer a call of nature; I had to stand guard over her with a Beretta to keep off sex-starved Italian soldiers and officers. "The toilet sentinel," the other correspondents used to call me, but I didn't mind because I was proud of her as a woman war correspondent.

"Well, goddamn it, I have lost them," I said after going through all my pockets again. "You see, I can lose tickets." I sounded as though I were scoring a point.

"They were in a big envelope, Pack," Heinzen said. "I gave them to you in the office just before noon. When you arrived from Madrid."

"It was a big manila envelope," Pibe added. "Too big to go into any of your pockets. You were carrying it with the two books."

An official in a plum-colored uniform came over to our group and asked if any of us had two sleeping-car reservations for Rome. He said the train was leaving in a few minutes.

By this time I wasn't the only one who was panic-stricken. Even President Baillie lost his cool.

"Will you take a check for the tickets?" he asked the Wagons-Lits man.

"No, but I can give you a receipt for cash."

"Let's take up a collection," Baillie said, and we all began frantically counting our money.

"We can travel second class without any sleeper," I volunteered.

"No, no, not that," J. I. Miller objected. "I know Latins. You must arrive there in style. No second-class travel for UP executives in Latin countries."

"M'sieur et Madame Packar," somebody was yelling.

We all looked around. There was a young Frenchman, panting and repeating our names.

"Les billets, les billets," he gasped and, recognizing me, handed me the package. "You must pay me for the taxi to get here on time."

Now I remembered him. He was behind the counter in the bureau du tabac on the Boulevard des Italiens when Pibe and I bought two cartons of Chesterfields just before taking a taxi to the station.

Heinzen handed the young Frenchman enough money for four long taxi rides. The Wagons-Lits man took the tickets and our passports. There was a whistle and the train jerked forward. "Vite, vite," a conductor shouted. Then Miller, despite his age, bolted toward Pibe and myself as we scrambled aboard the moving train and continued to run alongside it.

"Don't talk too bohemian in Rome," he shouted as a farewell order. "Italy is a Roman Catholic country, so don't brag about being atheists and believing in free love. And don't . . ." The train carried us out of hearing range of the rest of his counsel.

We collapsed in one of the adjoining sleeping compartments reserved for us. The beds hadn't been made up yet. We sipped our favorite White Horse, brought to us in miniature bottles by the same coach attendant who had been on the platform. There was barely a slug per bottle for drinkers like us. We sat back, feeling relaxed, hardly noticing the French countryside as we passed through it on our way to Italy and Rome.

The Eternal City! For us a new city of adventure; another label on a suitcase; another dateline to be added to our list that already included Paris, Geneva, Papeete, Pago Pago, Shanghai, Peking, Prague, Asmara, Addis Ababa, Guadalajara, Oviedo, and Madrid. But the United Press was not sending us to Rome for adventure or reporting. It was sending us there as smart operators who could wangle those Fascist bastards into letting us reopen the UP office. They were counting on the contacts we had made while covering Musso's take-over of Haile Selassie's empire.

I had already forgotten Pibe's bossy manner at the station, probably because I favored women's lib and liked tough, dominant Amazon types.

"I resented the way Miller warned us not to talk too bohemian in Rome," I said.

"Why not? He thinks we are crackpot bohemians. They don't think we are typical Unipressers."

"Who wants to be?"

"We don't but they expect us to be. If we hadn't met all those Italian VIPs in Ethiopia, they wouldn't have decided to send us to Rome. They sent Ekins because they thought he was the real type of Unipress bureau manager. Always smartly turned out, smooth-talking, and a good salesman. But he let them down when he tried to be a reporter."

"Well, I didn't like Miller's crack. I don't get it."

"Well, I do," Pibe laughed. "It was all for you, dear. You're the loud-mouthed extrovert on this team. You're always telling everybody how you lived with me for a year before marrying me in the Vienna Rathaus and that we still don't believe in marriage and that we are atheists. And now we are going to cover the Vatican."

"I get it. You don't need to draw a diagram."

"And you might also stop telling people when we get to Rome what a whoremonger you are and how promiscuous you think I am but you don't give a damn, or we will be back on the battlefields again."

"Okay. I won't even recount the time you knocked out five Peruvians in a bar fight when they were knocking hell out of me. You kicked them adroitly in the balls — remember? — one after the other. I like people to know how great you are."

During the night I went into Pibe's compartment and squeezed into bed with her just so we could say we had made love on the Paris-Rome Express. The jolting movement of the train made it almost as exciting as the time we screwed in an outrigger during a hurricane in Tahiti. We had breakfast and lunch in the restaurant car. Everybody seemed to be Italian. Most of the men wore a Fascist button in their left lapel.

We knew when we crossed into Italy because suddenly the French and American newspapers we had in our compartments disappeared. Fascist officials were either making sure they wouldn't get into the hands of other Italians or else were taking them home for their own edification.

# CHAPTER II

As we got off the train in the Rome station, two chubby young men, both wearing horn-rimmed glasses and reminding me of Tweedledee and Tweedledum, greeted us. They looked like twins, but one brother was two years older than the other.

They were Ralph and Aldo Forte, Italo-Americans, who held American passports but were regarded by Mussolini as Italian citizens and subject to the Italian draft. They were the backbone of the outgoing service of the UP that was filed in English. They were always under an undiluted American as bureau manager, and they didn't like the setup. They were very polite to both Pibe and me, but their resentment of us glinted through their courtesy, especially in the case of Ralph, the elder.

"Benvenuti a Roma," Ralph called out to us in a mock American accent. He and his brother were bilingual and spoke both Italian and English perfectly. We had never met them before.

When we got settled in a small car, luggage piled on top, Ralph began explaining what he had arranged for us. It was his car, but Aldo was driving it.

"I have gotten you a suite in the Ambasciatori Hotel on via Veneto," said Ralph, who was about thirty-one. "It's right across from the American Embassy and Consulate, and it's the favorite spot of Count Ciano. He has cocktails in the downstairs bar and eats lunch in the grill room as a rule. But I haven't made any appointments for you with Ciano or the ambassador. J. I. Miller, who seems to be running the show, phoned us to say only to make reservations for you and leave everything else up to you, Mr. Packard.''

"Pack, is the name," I said. "If I may call you Ralph and Aldo. And Mrs. Packard is Pibe to both of you."

"I know your by-line as Eleanor Packard," Aldo said. "Why are you called Pibe?"

"It's a nickname," Eleanor explained. "Pack gave it to me when we first met in Paris, and he had just come from Buenos Aires and was always talking Spanish. He thought I was so unsophisticated that he called me the Kid — *Pibe*. It's really an Argentinismo."

"You are a very guapa Pibe," Ralph complimented.

As Aldo drove through the streets of Rome on the way to the Albergo Ambasciatori, I noticed that he frequently banged the flat of his hand against the side of the car. Soon I realized other motorists were doing the same thing.

"What's with the hand, Aldo?" I asked.

"I have to do something to get these pedestrians out of the way," he explained. "If I hit one I could lose my driver's license. Rome is not only the Eternal City, it's the Silent City. No honking of horns is allowed. Even autobuses use their airbrakes instead of horns."

"And jaywalkers are given tickets," Ralph said. "See, there's one paying a fine to a cop over there."

"A Mussolini idea?" I asked.

"That's right, Ralph said. "Some dictator!"

I couldn't tell whether he approved of the strongman or not.

"Did Musso get over that stroke Bud Ekins reported?" I asked Ralph.

"What!?" It was both an exclamation and a question. "He never had a stroke," Ralph said. "Nothing happened to him at all. He appeared on the balcony of Palazzo Venezia the day after the report was published, just to show the public he was all right. He waved both arms to prove it and shouted out some of his slogans in a good husky voice. You know, like 'Many enemies, much honor.' "

"What did you do about it?"

"The UP was already closed down. I couldn't even send the fact it had been wrong — fortunately."

# CHAPTER III

The next day we were received by Ambassador William Phillips. He had already become known as America's envoy to Italy for life because his successor would have to be accredited to Victor Emmanuel, King of Italy and Emperor of Ethiopia. Washington had never recognized the Fascist take-over of the country and so was reluctant to send a new ambassador to Rome.

I told Phillips that we wanted to express the appreciation of the United Press for all he had tried to do in diplomatic channels to help get Ekins's expulsion order revoked and for whatever help he might give us in our efforts to reopen the office.

A tall, slender man with gray hair and pointed features, he looked very much the scholarly statesman and talked like one.

''Well, I must say,'' he said, ''I was taken aback when I went to Chigi Palace to protest the expulsion and told Count Ciano that Ekins had assured me he had never sent such a report and that it had never come from your Rome office but had been picked up in London from anti-Fascist sources. Count Ciano very politely interrupted me, saying, 'Excuse me a moment and listen to this.' He then turned on a recording of the telephone conversation between Ekins and a news editor of the United Press in London. I could hear Ekins, whose voice I know, saying, 'This is Bud here.' He then went on to say that the pitcher of Italy's national baseball team had collapsed on the ground and was carried off the field, and it was quite clear to me, and I am not a baseball fan, that the pitcher was obviously Mussolini.

"I was convinced then that Ekins had not told me the truth and that there I was out on a diplomatic limb, defending a correspondent who had misrepresented the facts to me and thus compromised me and the embassy. So I am not disposed to do much more about the incident nor do I have the impression that the State Department would want to push this matter."

"But I thought the Fascist government denied it had censorship," Pibe pointed out.

"Well, this is not exactly censorship," the ambassador said with a wan smile. "Rather, it was punitive action taken after the dispatch had been sent from Rome. It had been recorded but not stopped.

"As I see it," the ambassador continued, "most of the Anglo-Saxon correspondents here are anti-Fascists, but they aren't expelled unless they break one of the three cardinal rules of the regime. They are: never hint that the lira isn't sound; never cast doubt on the courage of Italians as soldiers; and never hint that Il Duce doesn't enjoy excellent health. This last was the rule your colleague broke."

Looking down pensively at his long, thin hands, the ambassador said as though just having thought of it: "Yes, there are two Italian authors who are overtly anti-Fascist in their writings but who have not been molested. One is the philosopher Benedetto Croce, and the other is Trilussa, who writes in trasteverino dialect."

"Why is that?" I asked like a good straight man.

"Because only a few intellectuals can understand Croce and Trilussa is too popular to touch."

We listened a bit longer to the ambassador, but it was quite clear he did not intend to do anything to help us.

"Well, thanks anyway," Pibe said. "We will try to see Count Ciano ourselves. I guess that's about all we can do."

"I guess so," he answered.

We needed a drink after that negative meeting and went across via Veneto to the Albergo Ambasciatori. Like all the hotels that used to call themselves hotels in Italy, it was now known as an *albergo*. Under Mussolini's nationalism, esperanto terms were Italianized whenever possible: *restaurant* became *ristorante; football, calcio; sandwich, panino;* and a *cocktail, una coda di gallo.*

The Fascists, however, were defeated by some international words such as *bar, tennis,* and *polo,* but tried to avoid their use.

We walked up to the bar and asked the barman — excuse me, the barista — for a Scotch and soda con ghiaccio. It still came out British.

The bar was crowded with men wearing black shirts and gray-blue uniforms with a lot of braid on the sleeve. Most of them sported snappy, spade-shaped beards. Pibe whispered to me that they looked like handsome actors in a musical comedy — more sexy than military. Two of them were staring at her.

"They're undressing you with their eyes," I told her. "It's like Ethiopia again."

Suddenly, everybody snapped to attention and even those seated at tables near the bar jumped to their feet. Pibe nudged me.

"You see who it is," she said. "Let's go over and speak to him."

"Okay, but just wait for the right moment."

When the newcomer Fascist-saluted a man next to us at the bar, he noticed us and said: "And what is my favorite white woman of Ethiopia doing here? And always with her husband."

Count Ciano smiled disarmingly at me as he made the lecherous innuendo, which after all was a compliment, I suppose, Italian style. Besides I was here in the guise of a diplomat and did not intend to start off my mission by getting sore at a casual wisecrack by the dictator's foreign minister and son-in-law. While I was still thinking of something to say, Pibe spoke up: "We would like to have a talk with you."

Ciano was clean-shaven as usual. He also wore a black shirt and uniform, but he seemed to be weighted down by less braid than the others. His thick-lipped, sensual mouth bore its characteristic smile.

"Excuse me a moment," he said to the uniformed men at the bar. "I'll be right back."

He put an arm around both our shoulders and led us off into a corner, where he pushed us down into big leather chairs. He sat down in one himself. The barista brought over our drinks.

"You are both here for the United Press? To reopen the office?" He asked and answered the questions himself. "Good. I am a busy man these days, much too busy to receive you formally at Chigi Palace. But what's wrong with right here? The last time we met, the charming Pibe was hostess in her bedroom (he had a fantastic memory for names) in the Imperial Hotel in Addis Ababa and served me White Horse. Here's to that night. I became foreign minister shortly after that. Now I have the chance to pay you back for miraculously producing Scotch amidst the flames of a burning city.''

He raised his glass and clinked it with ours.

It seemed to me unnecessary for him to refer to Pibe's bedroom. It had been given to her because she was the only woman correspondent on the wild dash into Addis, and General Pietro Badoglio wanted to pay tribute to her as such. I shared the double room only as her husband — a sort of correspondent consort. The other correspondents slept in tents.

Ciano thought a moment.

"When did you arrive in Rome?"

"Yesterday," I said.

"Now, let me see. We have to respect protocol and foreign policy. We have to be severe with British and Americans because they aren't too friendly and use baseball slang to report that Il Duce had a stroke he never had. So. Today is Wednesday. You must kick your heels a few days more. Let's say next Monday, the beginning of the week. You open on Monday. That's a decree from the Foreign Ministry. I'll fix it up with the Ministry of Popular Culture and Propaganda. You come directly under that ministry.''

"Do we need anything in writing?"

"Not a thing. My decree is enough. Il Duce will initial it. So all the best.''

He rose, smiled and Fascist-saluted. He then rejoined the men at the bar.

A bottle of Scotch had helped to reopen the UP office.

# CHAPTER IV

At nine o'clock on Monday morning, Pibe and I arrived at the bar of the Foreign Press Club, where Ralph Forte was waiting for us. The UP office was on the fourth floor of the same building. He was going to take us up and introduce us to the staff.

The Foreign Press Club occupied the first two floors of the five-story building. On the ground floor sprawled the bar with access to a vine-covered terrace on one side. A ping-pong table, a piano, and small tables and big leather chairs were scattered around the huge room wherever there was space. On the walls, Italian and other pro-Axis newspapers hung attached to wooden rods. There was also an adjoining bridge room.

In the bar you could get real coffee even though Fascist clubs could not obtain more than a surrogato made from roasted barley and peanuts. Eggs, fried in butter, could be had at the bar every morning for breakfast even though the Italian ration for ordinary people at that time — 1939 — was one egg a week and one quarter of a pound of butter a month.

Upstairs on the mezzanine floor, looking down on the bar as from the rim of a big eye, were the workrooms, the reference library, and a series of soundproof phone booths for international news calls. On the mezzanine floor were issued the latest news bulletins, communiqués, and official announcements.

If you were a foreign correspondent in Rome, you had to belong to the associazione whether you wanted to or not. The dues were about five dollars a year. There was a total of ten or twelve clerks — known in Italian as *uscieri* — who worked in shifts to run errands and help out the correspondents in general, such as by mailing letters, sending telegrams, taking phone messages, and fetching cigarettes.

There were all kinds of foreign drinks at the bar from bourbon and Scotch to Pernod and gin, including vodka and rum. And they were to be had cheaper in the Foreign Press Club than any place else in Rome. All members were entitled to cards giving them a 70 per cent reduction on all railway fares inside the country. And free opera tickets, six at a time, were given out in alphabetical rotation.

The Club was really a Fascist-subsidized institution. It was Mussolini who thought of the idea. He had been a newspaperman himself at one time, having been a reporter and then editor of the Socialist newspaper *Avanti* before becoming a Fascist. He believed that good communications and cheap drink would cajole correspondents into serving Fascism. He was a sort of Black Shirt Machiavelli.

The Club also served another purpose. It greatly simplified the work of the OVRA — the Fascist secret police — one of whose duties was to check on the activities of foreign correspondents. News calls from the Stampa Estera went through faster to foreign cities than they did from private homes. So correspondents, anxious to make deadlines, usually phoned from the Club. The reason for the speed was simple: the OVRA had carefully tapped all the phones and was prepared to listen in at a moment's notice, with the aid of expert linguists.

The only thing odd about the Club was the dark-skinned barman. Ralph said he was an Ethiopian who had joined the Italians during the Abyssinian invasion and was one of the few natives granted permission to come to Italy. His name was Ali.

Ralph nodded and spoke to about ten or twelve members in the Club. They included Spanish, Swiss, German, Austrian, Japanese, American, and British.

"Let's go and see the zoo," Ralph suggested when we had finished our coffee. "There's only one outspoken anti-Fascist in the lot. Don't be baited into agreeing with her and saying something against Musso, because it may be reported by somebody."

The three of us — Ralph, Pibe, and I — got out of the elevator on the fourth floor. Ralph led the way. They were all standing in the newsroom as we entered. Ralph introduced them one at a time: Palcinelli, a paunchy, gray-haired, amiable old man who wore a Fascist badge on his lapel; Woody, whose nickname came from *Boschetto* — meaning little forest or wood — who was dressed in a Fascist uniform; a young college student named Elvezio Bianchi; and la Signora Grace Coppi, who, Ralph smilingly said, did not mind being called Signora Grace. Ralph's brother, Aldo, was also there standing in front of his desk.

"I hope you are both going to be as anti-Fascist as Mr. Ekins but that you don't get expelled," Signora Coppi said in English.

"I am not even sure he was anti-Fascist," Boschetto put in. "I think he had bad advice from somebody in sending such a stupid story."

"Well," I said, "Mrs. Packard and I have come not with the intention of getting expelled but of keeping the office open and functioning. If you have any complaints about anything, feel free to come and talk to me about them. I hope we can all get along on the basis of the good fellowship of newspaper work. I am not going to make any speech. I just want to say I am glad to meet you all, and I hope for your cooperation and that you won't find me a tough boss. I like to think of myself as a friendly person, but I can be tough if necessary."

Remaining silent, Pibe just managed to produce a smile. She found it difficult to listen to bullshit. My reference to being tough was intended primarily for Ralph, who despite his helpfulness, oozed disapproval of the fact that I had been sent in over him, and he wasn't even sure of the position of Pibe. Nor was I, for that matter. That was typical UP procedure. My reference to toughness was also aimed at the uniformed Boschetto.

Ralph showed me my office which was quite impressive with a pillar in it and the sun streaming in through two huge stain-glass windows. There was a big executive-style desk with two phones on it and a smaller desk for the secretary off in a corner. There was a case full of reference books. An autographed photo of Mussolini hung on the wall behind the desk. On it was written: "To Tom Morgan in appreciation of his journalistic work, (signed) Benito Mussolini."

I thought to myself: I'll have to find a way to take that down. Morgan had been in charge four bureau managers ago.

I went back to the big newsroom, which was really two rooms knocked into one.

"I want a desk for Pibe, Ralph," I said. "Where can she sit?"

One section of the room was fenced off with a wooden rail. Inside the corral were two desks, those of Woody and Palcinelli. I noticed that Woody also had a big filing cabinet near his desk and that it was closed with a padlock. They represented the incoming service which was translated into Italian from English and sent to the Italian newspapers, all of which were UP clients.

Bianchi had a small desk off in a corner where he worked for both the incoming and the outgoing service. The latter consisted of sending news about Italy to the rest of the world in English. There were three other desks. I asked about them.

"One is mine, and one is Aldo's, and the other is for the bureau manager when he comes in here to write news stories and edit copy."

"Okay," I said. "Pibe can have that desk, and I'll bounce her out of it when I need to work in here. I am counting on you, Ralph, to handle most of the outgoing news until I get the hang of things here. Okay?"

Aldo showed me the outgoing file, which included six innocuous messages about traffic accidents, the derailing of a passenger train without anybody being killed, and a slight increase in the volcanic activity of Naples's Mount Vesuvius. But there was one other item that was about Pope Pius XI. It made me go cold with apprehension. I didn't feel quite ready for the biggest story that Rome can offer.

"It's mostly just crap for Latin America," Aldo said. "Wordage-tonnage. No real news except the illness of the pope."

"Did you see, Ralph, about the pope?" I asked.

"No, let's see it." I handed him the file. He read the item over twice. "It's lucky you got the office open is all I can say."

Aldo's message, which had been phoned to London for world-wide distribution — otherwise it would have gone direct to Buenos Aires or New York for regional relays — read as follows:

> Pope Pius XI, who has been ailing the past six months, was stated in Vatican quarters today to have suffered "a set back."
>
> A Vatican announcement said the Pontiff has cancelled all audiences for the time being on advice from his doctors, who also recommended that he remain in bed for at least a week.
>
> Close friends of Pius XI said he had been depressed recently because his efforts to ease the

16

international tension did not have the results he had
hoped for.

The dispatch also recalled that Pius had been the pope who had worked
out the agreement with Mussolini that regulated all State-Church relations
between Italy and the Holy See. Called the Lateran Accord, it was signed
by Pius's Secretary of State Pietro Gasparri and Il Duce on February 11,
1929.

Ralph and I talked the situation over with Eleanor listening in. Ralph
called some UP contacts but in talking to them he used code names that
were meaningless to me. When he got through he said: ''Most of the
tipsters think he won't last the night.''

I decided to send Aldo out to the Vatican immediately and have Ralph
remain in the office. Eleanor could phone the stuff to London and write it
up for newscasts to North and South America as it was passed on to her.
I'd be around as handyman.

Ralph was very good at taking down the gist of Vatican broadcasts in
both Italian and Latin.

''If it comes to a long siege,'' I said, ''you and Aldo will do the
overnight trick, and Pibe and I will do the daytime hours. I'm not trying to
be tough, but in the daytime we can call on plenty of people for assistance
and advice including those in the Stampa Estera. But in the nighttime we
would be somewhat isolated.''

Ralph reluctantly agreed.

''Come on, Pibe, let's start reading background in the files on this
Achille Ratti.'' (Achille Ratti was Pius XI's name before becoming
pope.) ''I understand he was a great mountain climber. I also remember
he sent Cardinal Spellman to Paris when Spellman was a young man in the
Secretariat of State with a document criticizing Fascism. In fact,
Spellman handed it to me in the UP Paris office when he brought it there
after smuggling it out of Italy.''

''So you are a Vatican expert yourself,'' Ralph said, somewhat on the
sarcastic side.

''Not at all, and that's why, Ralph, I'd like to have the names of those
UP Vatican tipsters you just called up and their phone numbers.''

He looked pained.

''Well, it's kind of complicated. You see these fellows work in the
Vatican, and they would lose their jobs if it were known they were acting

17

as tipsters for the UP.''

''That's an awkward position, but I can't imagine who allowed you to develop such a setup. Why the bureau manager doesn't even know his own tipsters! So write out their names and telephone numbers, and you'd better tell them I may be calling. If they don't like that, then they can quit. I told you I could be tough.''

He looked both hurt and furious. He turned pale, then deep purple as though he might be having a heart attack. Then he wrote out a list of names and numbers on a piece of paper and handed it to me.

''Please be careful with this. Don't let anybody else see it.''

I let that pass. I noticed out of the corner of my eye the Fascist of the incoming service was listening. I thought: and you're the next to be told there are no Mafia secrets in this office. You with your padlocked files.

# CHAPTER V

The line had been open to London for more than half an hour. We were waiting for Aldo to call again. The pope had suffered two serious heart attacks in the afternoon. The last time Aldo phoned he said: "It looks as though death will come at any minute. He's already had the last sacraments." He waited until we got that news off, then he said, "I found a phone that nobody knows anything about. Only trouble is I have to climb over a wall to get to it."

Aldo hung up. I decided to keep the line open to London. Every ten minutes the London night editor would object to the expense of such a procedure and beg us to hang up and call again.

Pibe relayed what London said to me.

"Tell them to hell with expenses. This is the biggest story of the month. I'll take responsibility for it."

I gave Pibe some new obit material I had written up, to be released when he died. We had a lot of good personal stuff in the files.

"That will keep them quiet," I told her.

It worked for a while, but the budget-minded London office was always for cutting us off, saying the open line was too expensive. Then finally Aldo, panting from his fatman's sprint and fatman's climb over a wall, announced breathlessly and haltingly that the Vatican Press Office — which was really the Osservatore Romano office in those

19

days — announced the pontiff had died. The official time of death was 5:31 A.M.

After we sent all of Aldo's details, we flashed the service message: "Release advance story of Pius XI's death."

That contained the colorful bit about the camerlengo, as part of the papal death ritual, hitting the newly dead pontiff over the head with a silver hammer. Each time the silver mallet struck the pope's skull, the camerlengo would ask in a deep voice: "Are you alive, Achille? Answer, are you alive, Achille?"

Receiving no answer after the third bang on the head, the camerlengo pronounced the pope officially dead. Immediately the machinery for the election of a new pope was set automatically in motion. The camerlengo was in charge of the church until the new leader of the half-billion Catholics in the world was elected.

Cardinals and newspapermen from all over the world began converging on Rome.

Before Pibe and I left for home, a message of congratulations from the New York office came in by wire. It read:

> 10012 PACKARD AND TEAM YOU SCORED ONE MINUTE WORLD SCOOP ON DEATH POPE CONGRATS
>
> BAILLIE

"Listen, Aldo," I said, "tell me the story of the hidden phone and the climbing over the wall. What's your weight and height, and I'll write a box about the fat reporter who scored a world scoop." He obliged and my little story got good sidebar play in most American newspapers.

During the next two days, I was surprised to see all the warm, sympathetic condolences and eulogies sent by Mussolini, Ciano, and the Fascist Grand Council. After all, Ratti had been a fairly outspoken pope. Although he was responsible for the historic Lateran Accord, he did not kowtow to Mussolini and various times had criticized both Fascism and Nazism.

Ciano, garbed in his Black Shirt uniform, personally paid homage to the body of the pope as it rested in state in the Sistine Chapel.

All the condolences were addressed to Eugenio Cardinal Pacelli as camerlengo. Pacelli also had been secretary of state for the past nine years.

The Fascist press didn't mention any of Pius XI's anti-Mussolini and

20

anti-Hitler pronouncements but recalled what a great alpinist he had been in his youth and how he had broadened the diplomacy of the Vatican throughout the world.

The Fascist press also stressed how close Pius had worked with Il Duce on drawing up the historical Lateran Accord. It never recalled that Mussolini as a socialist had proclaimed himself antichurch and an atheist.

Reading the obituaries in the Italian newspapers, you would certainly get the idea that Pius thought the dictator was a great guy, the Fascist Council a benevolent society, and that the pope himself would have been a Black Shirt if he had not first become a prelate.

# CHAPTER VI

There is one thing good about a big news break: it brings all your old colleagues together, some you haven't seen in years. As soon as the flash of Pius XI's death sped around the world, cardinals and newspapermen began to foregather. In a few days Rome was full of a lot of old friends like Bill Shirer and Alex Small, both of whom we had known in Paris. They were still with the *Chicago Tribune* covering affairs in Europe. The AP sent some extra men over to help out, as did the INS in the form of Frank Gervasi. Among the arriving cardinals were O'Connell of Boston, Dougherty of Philadelphia, and Mundelheim of Chicago. The UP, however, didn't send anybody extra to help out. I guess they figured that in having both Eleanor and myself to replace Bud Ekins, the office was already overstaffed.

Even Alfred Noyes, the poet laureate of England, showed up. He was too late for the death, but he was to put the election and coronation of the new pope into epic iambic pentameter — for newspapers.

The UP office suddenly became full of bewildered correspondents who represented client newspapers. They all considered they had the right to call on the UP for any kind of help, running from reading the news file to getting hotel accommodations and introductions to high government and Vatican officials. They also wanted the names and addresses of all the good restaurants, especially the good cheap ones, and some of the younger males asked the office to help them get laid at reasonable prices and without any danger of catching clap or syph. Americans always struck me as being more erotic when abroad than back home.

It was a busy period. The Sacred College of Cardinals decided that the conclave to elect the next pope should begin in the traditional Sistine Chapel on March 1, exactly eighteen days from Pius XI's death. The Sacred College estimated that with modern transport being what it was that would give most of the sixty-two cardinals time to reach Rome somehow by train, car, boat, and airplane.

But even so there wasn't too much to write about during those eighteen days. After the burial of the pope beneath Saint Peter's Basilica three days after he died, there was hardly anything left to say. The Italian papers were back to talking about the Fascist Grand Council achievements, the doings of the Duck, as the American correspondents generally called Il Duce among themselves, and Count Ciano's trip to Berlin.

Alex Small was a legend in Paris. He used to sit at a table in the Cafe Flore near Place St. Germain des Prés, and in two minutes it would be crowded with hypnotized listeners. He was the philosopher of the Left Bank. He and Pibe and I had long been good friends. I had heard that they had been lovers once, but I never tried to check on it. You couldn't hope for a better lover for your wife.

"You see that fellow over there?" Alex asked us as we were sitting at a sidewalk table at a cafe near St. Peter's.

"You mean that slight, wispy-haired fellow?" I asked.

"That's right. He's here for the *Chicago Tribune* just for one story. That's all. I am covering all the crap for the paper, but he is here for just one Vatican story."

"You're mad," Eleanor said. "I think I know who he is. He's Arch Ward, the chief sports writer on your paper."

"That's right. Well he is going to get the first exclusive interview with the new pope."

"Impossible," I barked. "Everybody's trying to get it, including myself."

"Yeah, but he has Mundelheim behind him." George William Cardinal Mundelheim was archbishop of Chicago in those days. "Have you anybody like Mundelheim behind you?"

"Nobody like him," I admitted. "Just a lay tipster."

After a week of pressuring by the young buck correspondents and photographers sent over from America for the conclave and coronation, I decided to find something to slake their sexual urges. The conclave could take days, weeks. I wanted to get them off my back as quickly as possible. Ralph or Pibe and I had already taken them all at different times around to the Foreign Press Club and had made them temporary members. That was some help, but they still persisted in their intentions to get fucked while in the Eternal City.

I tried to turn that part of the task over to Ralph as an old Rome hand, but he adroitly brushed it aside saying snootily: "I never have to go with whores. I just don't know any whorehouses."

His brother Aldo was less arrogant but said, "I'm engaged and I just don't know any girls I could lend out like that. You must understand, it would be insulting to them. Of course, there are the brothels run by the government which are slightly like department stores of sex they are so crowded with customers, but I never go to them. Then there are the card carrying streetwalkers who are slightly more dangerous. Gee, I'm sorry, Pack, I can't help you in that respect."

I thought of the Black Shirt staffer, Woody. He would probably know. He knew about everything practical, but I didn't want to get friendly with him on an intimate subject like getting UP clients fixed up.

Oh, hell, I thought. I'll just ask the hotel porter. He ought to know.

"Say," I said, rather embarrassed. "I've got a lot of friends in town right now who want to have a good time. Meet some girls they can . . . well, you know, go to bed with."

"Certainly, sir." He replied very courteously as though I had asked him how to get to the Colosseum. "The American Embassy is right across the street, right? Well take the via Boncompagni which runs between the embassy and the Albergo Excelsior and turn left on the first street after via Veneto. That's via Marche. Well you can't miss the place, it is the middle of the block on the far side of the street. The doorway is arched and inside you go up the staircase on the right to the next floor. The name: Signora Francesca, Aesthetics, is on the brass plaque on her door. You ring and say I sent you."

I thanked him and slipped him in lire the equivalent of a five-dollar bill.

I looked at my watch. It was almost lunchtime. I called up the office and told Pibe that she had better eat near the office as I was going out to find a call-girl house or something for some of the UP client youths who were here for the conclave and that I wouldn't get back until late afternoon.

"You always pick the choice assignments for yourself," she said

24

sarcastically, "and be careful. I don't want any secondhand VD."

"Don't worry, I'm just going to look it over. I'll tell you all about it later."

It was this understanding between the two of us that made the UP wary about appointing us to executive jobs, above all in Rome. But Pibe and I were very proud of our understanding. We called it the goldfish-bowl philosophy. We had no secrets from each other, and we believed in sexual freedom for both of us. As I already said, we only got married to make freedom of living less cumbersome and awkward. We didn't expect our marriage to last long, but we expected to remain good friends after a divorce. However, it lasted forever and ever.

I rang the bell outside the door bearing the name Signora Francesca. A small, rather pretty girl, dressed like a maid, opened the door. I said I wanted to see Signora Francesca. She invited me to follow her into the apartment. She led me into a living room that resembled a doctor's office the way it was filled with uninteresting magazines and there were no pictures on the wall.

"Un momento," the girl said and disappeared.

In a few minutes, a tall, thin woman with a very pronounced goiter appeared.

"Buon giorno," she said. "What may I do for you?"

I decided not to mention the Albergo Ambasciatori porter as it might increase fees in general.

"I understand you go in for aesthetics. I am a bit overweight, as you can see," I said in Italian.

"You want a massage? A general massage?"

I only learned later that general massage meant play massage — the sex organs receive the masseuse's ministrations, also. I nodded and then she led me into a very medical-looking room with a rather high table covered with a spotlessly white sheet.

"Get undressed and stretch out on the massage table, and I'll be right in. I want to put on my white jacket."

I got undressed, hanging my clothes on a chair that seemed there for the purpose, and hoisted myself onto the table. I leaned back and rested my head on a pillow. It brought my eyes in focus with a magnifying mirror tilted toward me from the wall in front of me. It transformed my little tallywacker into a gargantuan instrument of sex. It reminded me of one of the dictator's tricks.

The Duce insisted that all pictures of him be taken from below knee level so as to make his dwarflike stature appear huge in perspective. This must be a Mussolini mirror, I thought and laughed at the flattering reflection.

The woman with the goiter, wearing a white coat over her dress, came in and started to massage my arms and torso. She called out: "Polvere, Pina."

Pina came in dressed as before, carrying a box of talcum powder. Pina sprinkled the powder all over my chest, stomach, groin, and legs, then started massaging my feet. Every so often, she took off a bit of her clothing saying that it was warm and kept on massaging. As I looked in the mirror I saw that both the hands of the goitered woman and Pina were together close to my penis which began to erect until I had never seen such an enormous lingam as in the mirror. I began to feel proud of myself, even knowing it was an optical illusion. Pina by this time was completely nude and suddenly started sucking me while the older woman stroked my scrotum with her silk hands.

"Eh, Cristo! Io vengo! Vengo," I cried out. At the same time I thought what a strange thing that it's the same word in Italian, English, and French.

Finally the older woman asked: "Basta?"

Pina lifted her head and slipped away, picking up her clothes as she left.

The older woman dabbed me with some tissue, then put a sheet and a blanket over me.

"You rest. I'll bring you a whisky," she said.

In a few minutes she was back with a bottle of Black and White and poured me a slug into a glass. She even had a bowl of ice with her.

As I sipped the whisky slowly, she handed me an album.

"I think you are a gentleman, and I can trust you. Look at the pictures in this book. If you see a bel pezzo you would like to try, just tell me which one, and I'll get the girl here in twenty minutes. They are all good clean girls. They have to be because they are married, and their husbands would kill them if they ever contracted a venereal disease. Their husbands don't know they do this. You owe me five dollars for the massage and ten dollars if you take one of the girls in the book. That's reasonable, è vero?"

I looked through the pictures. They depicted all kinds of types: blondes, brunettes, tall and petite, willowy and buxom, serious and laughing.

I pointed to the photo of an impish-looking girl, saying: "Prendo quella."

"That's a good choice," La Goiter said. "She takes it in the rear. Most of them do, but she seems to really like it."

I gave her the equivalent in Italian lire of fifteen dollars.

Pina came back fully dressed and ushered me into a bedroom across the hall. She then brought my clothes along and showed me the bathroom. I took a quick shower and used prophylaxis because of Pina's oral play with me.

I had hardly finished when the new girl arrived. She was fully dressed in a smart-fitting but not flashy blue suit. She wore no hat. She looked very much the proper young housewife.

"Io sono Assunta," she said, holding out her hand, which I shook. "And you?"

"Io sono Ford," I said, "like the automobile."

We laughed, knowing we were both lying.

"You are all ready for me," she said, looking at my nakedness.

"Yes, I just had a shower."

"I won't be long."

She immediately started getting undressed. When she was entirely nude, she sat on a bidet in the room and washed her intimate parts. She then turned off the light so that I couldn't see what she was doing, but I could hear her dabbling with something. I quickly turned on the light.

"We don't need darkness with a beautiful girl like you."

She laughed and put the tin of cream she had been using on the bed table. We played around on the bed for a time until I recovered from my adventure with Pina, and then she slipped under me and aided me to get into her.

"Lower, lower," she said. "Now push hard. I'm like a virgin there."

It was rugged going, but I pushed down and she shoved up and finally I penetrated.

"You see how nice and tight it is, caro, tighter than a virgin's fica. Only nicer." She cooed and tongued my ear until I was again yelling: "Io vengo, io vengo."

She groaned and muttered: "Oh che bello." I assumed she was pretending, but it was a great act and just about as good as if she had been sincere.

We lay there for a while and then she said: "You use the bidet first. I'm in no hurry."

I went to the bidet and started washing my penis. To my horror, I saw excrement floating off it. I suddenly wanted to vomit and washed myself like mad. I rinsed out the bowl and washed myself a second time. Then I reached for my packet of prophylaxis and used another tube of it.

In the meantime she went to the bidet and washed leisurely.

"Well, I won't take somebody else's baby home to my husband. See how thoughtful I am. It was your first time that way, wasn't it?"

"Yes."

"Did you like it?"

"I guess I did, but I was a little shocked seeing it afterwards all speckled with merda like that."

She laughed. "You'll soon get used to it in Italy. It's one form of birth control used here. And young girls do it that way to keep their virginity."

"I've already paid, but here's something extra for you." I slipped her five dollars in Italian money.

"Grazie, tante. Non dimentica mio nome è Assunta."

We shook hands. She lingered behind as I left the bedroom. I spoke to La Goiter once more and asked her to give the same hospitable treatment to my friends.

"Ford is the name," I said, "Signor Ford. They'll mention it when they come."

I went back to the office where everything was under control. Aldo was at the Vatican. Eleanor was working on a list of papabili in which she pointed out that with the imminence of war, the question was whether a pastoral or a political pope would be the choice of the cardinals. Some favored a pastoral pope, others argued that the Vatican could not remain aloof and needed more than ever a political leader. If this thesis prevails, Pibe wrote, then the favorite is Eugenio Cardinal Pacelli, the former secretary of state. If a pastoral pope is chosen it may well be Elia Cardinal dalla Costa, seventy-year-old archbishop of Florence, noted for his piety and aloofness from politics.

On the other hand, she recalled the ancient Vatican proverb: a cardinal who enters the conclave as pope comes out a cardinal.

She also stressed there was still no chance of a non-Italian being elected.

"Good cud-chewing," I told her after reading it over. "You can't be wrong no matter who is elected."

Ralph was working on a Fascist Grand Council story, and I didn't bother to read it, letting him know that whatever he wrote was all right with me.

Woody, without looking up from his fast touch-typing, said hello and I answered back. My secretary had already gone home. Palcinelli was off duty.

"Say, could I see you a moment in your private office?" Pibe asked.

Oh boy, I thought, here it comes. But I replied for the benefit of the others, "Sure, come on in."

"How was it?" Eleanor immediately demanded. "The whorehouse I mean."

"Wonderful and cheap."

I then proceeded to tell her all about it in accordance with our goldfish-bowl philosophy.

"That was the first time you ever buggered, wasn't it?"

"Yes," I said.

"Was it as good as the Italian men say it is?"

"I don't know, I don't think tightness is all that thrilling, and it will certainly take some doing to get over seeing my cock smeared with shit."

"Well, don't get any Italian ideas about me." She laughed and that was the end of my confession. Except that I kissed her passionately and said: "You are really wonderful, and I love you for understanding."

"And I love you for understanding that I like sex, too."

# CHAPTER VII

That same night and the next day I met most of the young correspondents who had asked me for special information. I told them about the apartment on via Marche.

"Just tell Signora Francesca that Signor Ford sent you," I said.

Months later I happened to meet the goitered madam on via Veneto. She stopped me and thanked me for all the customers I had sent her. It seemed the ones I told about the place passed the word on to other correspondents who also mentioned Signor Ford as a reference.

"Any time you want a play massage, Signor Ford," Francesca said, "Pina and I will oblige and it will be on the house. Grazie tante."

I didn't accept her offer for fear I'd feel like a pimp.

The UP offices in New York, London, and Buenos Aires wanted at least two stories a day on the forthcoming conclave. To meet the requests, we pulled out of the mothballs all the old stuff that had ever been sent on papal elections in the past. We recalled the conclave at Viterbo, seventy-five miles north of Rome, in medieval times when after a year had gone by and no pope had been elected, the townsfolk first began rationing the food sent into the conclavists and then started tearing down the roof, letting in the rain. A pope was soon elected. We wrote about the three sizes of papal robes: big, medium, and small, which were being made by a Vatican tailor for the new pontiff. He was to wear the best-fitting one on his first public appearance forty-five minutes after being elected. That would be on the central balcony of Saint Peter's Basilica. In the case of husky Pius XI, the biggest was too small and in the case of diminutive Benedict XV, the smallest was too big and had to be pinned up so that he wouldn't trip over it.

On the day before the cardinals entered the conclave with their assistants, the correspondents were allowed to walk through the Sistine Chapel, see the voting arrangements and even the adjacent apartments where the various cardinals would sleep. Some of the beds were stuck in between coats of armor or alongside priceless tapestries in the Borgia apartments. We even examined the bathing arrangements for the American cardinals. That's how hard up we were for material.

Then the next day on March 1, 1939, sixty-two cardinals, each with his two assistants, were sealed into the conclave area by Prince Ludovico Chigi Albani della Rovere, marshal of the conclave and grand master of the Order of Malta. The voting began on March 2 and would continue daily until a new pope was elected. The Holy Ghost was supposed to descend on the gathering and give the cardinals special enlightenment to select the right man.

Alex accompanied Pibe and me on the tour. He was always critical and ruminative. We were in the Vatican, so he rambled on about the Vatican.

"I've been trying to get some of the cardinals to admit that when a man is elected pope, he must have a sex examination, but they just refuse to admit it," he said. "It's a well-known fact, however, that as soon as a new pope is elected, he takes down his drawers and sits on a rimmed stool without any seat, and the camerlengo puts his hands up between his thighs to make sure he has testicles and a penis. He squeezes them and then intones in Latin: 'He has them and they are well hung.' That's to prevent there being another woman pope. Pope Joan is the only woman who made the grade, and that was way back in 855 when she ruled as John VIII until she gave birth to a baby during a public ceremony and was lynched by the mob and killed. The baby was trampled to death."

Then he suddenly changed the subject. "You know," he said, "the more I come to Rome, the more I see that the Catholic Church is just like an Italian male. It treats women like inferiors. There can't even be a woman priest. The Virgin Mary is only a divine incubator who gave birth to Christ. And the only other woman I can remember from the New

Testament was Mary Magdalene, the prostitute. The Church made a saint out of her. So you can see how both the Italian male and the Catholic Church look at women: either as incubators or whores.''

We did not, however, let his ruminations interfere with our note-making, and Eleanor interrupted him to stretch out on William Cardinal O'Connell's bed to see if it was comfortable. It was.

There were to be four votes daily: two in the morning and two in the afternoon. After each inconclusive balloting, black smoke, produced by using brush as fuel, issued from the periscopelike chimney of the Sistine Chapel to inform the world that nobody had been elected. In the case of a new pope being chosen, the smoke would be pure white — without any brush being used to make the fire.

That was the only signal the outside world would get for forty-five minutes: that a new pope had been elected. There was no announcement by loudspeaker or radio giving such an important detail as the name of the successful papabile. His identity would be known only when he appeared on the central balcony of Saint Peter's wearing one of the three ready-to-wear robes. Then the people of Rome, seeing him, would shout out his name. They were the first to know who he was. This was their privilege because the pope is also the bishop of Rome. Then he would announce the Latin name he had chosen for his reign.

The UP was beaten by forty-five minutes on the identity of the new pope. The British Exchange Telegraph scored the world scoop, even if I do say it myself as one of the losers, by gun-jumping.

As soon as the white puffs of smoke came curling out of the Sistine Chapel chimney on the third balloting of the first day of voting a roar went up. ''The pope is elected. Viva il papa.''

All anybody knew officially was that a pontiff had been chosen. All the agencies except the Exchange Telegraph flashed that brief, unadorned fact. But the Exchange Telegraph carried much more in its first urgent dispatch:

> FLASH EUGENIO CARDINAL PACELLI FORMER
> VATICAN SECRETARY STATE WAS ELECTED POPE
> THIS AFTERNOON FIVE OCLOCK PARA HE WILL
> APPEAR SAINT PETERS CENTRAL BALCONY WITHIN
> FORTYFIVE MINUTES TO BE PROCLAIMED BY
> THOUSANDS ROMANS TOURISTS PILGRIMS IN
> COBBLESTONED SQUARE BELOW STOP HIS

ELECTION BREAKS OLD TRADITION THAT
WHOEVER ENTERS CONCLAVE AS POPE COMES
OUT A CARDINAL MORE

RABACHE

And so it went. When all the other agencies, including the UP, got.
rockets for not saying flatly it was Pacelli, we who were beaten, as usual
in newspaper reporting, called the scoop a phony and a fake.

What happened was that the Exchange Telegraph correspondent, a
young Frenchman, André Jacquqes Rabache, reasoned, and logically so,
that on the third ballot only the favorite could obtain enough votes for
election, and there was no doubt that the outstanding papabile was Pacelli.
Rabache just took a chance and flashed the flat statement.

Finally, we trailed along by adding to our original undetailed bulletin
that well-informed Vatican circles generally believed that the new pontiff
was Eugenio Cardinal Pacelli and gave a thumbnail sketch of his life.

Pacelli appeared in the middle-sized robe and after accepting the
acclaim of the throngs in the square below him, announced he had chosen
the name of Pio XII — Pius XII — because of his respect and admiration
for the preceding pope whose secretary of state he had been for eight
years.

It was also Pacelli's sixty-third birthday.

Trying to recoup a bit on the story, I patiently waited in front of the
elevator in the Ambasciatori Hotel, where Cardinal Dougherty was also
staying. I tipped the elevator boy in advance to make sure that I got into
the cage along with the cardinal. Finally, around 10:30 P.M., Dougherty
came with his clerical assistant and went up to his room. I was right beside
him. He knew me by this time as I had spoken to him in the hotel before,
introducing myself as a reporter.

"Your Eminence," I said, "would you give me a statement on what
you think of the new pope?" I knelt down and tried to kiss the cardinal's
ring.

He pulled me to my feet and smilingly said, "That's not necessary. I
know you are not a Catholic."

"Well, Your Eminence, all Americans want to know what an
American cardinal thinks about the new pope."

"All right," he said, "come along and I will write out a statement. I
want it to be given to everybody."

"Don't worry about that, Your Eminence, the United Press has more than two thousand clients. It will reach everybody.''

I went into his living room and waited about ten minutes while he and a monsignor who was acting as his secretary on the trip typed out the final statement.

"This is for all newspapers,'' the cardinal repeated. "I want you to see that everybody gets this statement.''

I pocketed the typed statement and dashed to my room to phone it to the office. I noticed the monsignor had not made a carbon copy. I phoned it to Pibe.

"Take this down for me will you, and send it urgent through London.'' I then dictated the message.

> 02225 EXCLUSIVE DATELINE ROME DENNIS CARDINAL DOUGHERTY OF PHILADELPHIA DECLARED TONIGHT NEW POPE IS MAN OF VAST EXPERIENCE GREAT ABILITY AND OF SAINTLY PIETY PARA IN EXCLUSIVE INTERVIEW DOUGHERTY SAID QUOTE FROM TIME HE WAS YOUNG MAN HE WAS REGARDED AS FUTURE HOPE OF CHURCH STOP HE HAS REMARKABLE COMBINATION OF THE HIGHEST QUALITIES OF BODY AND BRAIN STOP HE IS REMARKABLE LINGUIST HAS CHARMING MANNER AND HIS DISPOSITION IS GENTLENESS PERSONIFIED UNQUOTE MORE

PACKARD

I sent two more takes on my interview. Two hours later Eleanor and I met in the Stampa Estera bar to celebrate at least a partial scoop on a story we had already been beaten on badly. We were still sipping White Horse and soda when in came a crowd of U.S. correspondents headed by Frank Gervasi. They started to beat me up.

"Dougherty's statement was a handout for the American correspondents here,'' Gervasi yelled at me. "He told me so himself. You deliberately kept it for the UP. You goddamn skunk, you.''

Even worse epithets were hurled by some of the other correspondents I hardly knew.

I would have had a bad time of it if Eleanor hadn't helped me out by punching and kicking some of them. European club members, shocked at such a brawl in their midst, intervened, and it finally ended up with me buying whisky for everybody and admitting I had pulled a fast one.

But even so, nobody was very friendly.

Gervasi said the cardinal complained my conduct had not been very Christian.

I felt like saying: what do you expect? I am not a Christian. I am an atheist. I am also a tough reporter. But I remembered Miller's running lecture at the Gare de Lyon and kept my mouth shut.

# CHAPTER VIII

Ralph didn't come to the office one morning. The Black Shirt and Palcinelli were also missing. Only Aldo, the English secretary, and the cub reporter Bianchi were there when Eleanor and I came in at 10 A.M.

"Is there a strike, Aldo?" I asked.

"No, not a strike, just a discreet leave of absence," he tried to explain. "You know how you have a very positive way of doing things, and I think that for certain people today there are reasons why you might insist on them doing things your way. So they stayed away."

He was whispering all the time he was talking to me. Eleanor couldn't even hear him.

"Let's you and I go down to the Press Club bar, Aldo, and have a beer or coffee off in a corner and talk this over."

"Okay, a good idea."

Being more Italian than American by training and background, Aldo didn't like to discuss delicate matters in front of a woman. So I left Pibe behind.

It had been quiet in Rome since the coronation of Pius XII, and that was only pageantry stuff. All the old friends of ours had gone back to their respective posts, including Alex Small. He turned out to be right about Arch Ward, the sports writer, getting the first interview with the new pope, but it didn't matter because the pontiff said nothing political or important in it, and actually the interview was only a benediction to the people of Chicago.

Off in a dark corner in the Press Club, Aldo ordered a caffè doppio, and I ordered an Italian beer. As soon as Romeo, the Italian barman on duty, had gone back to his precinct of bottles, I asked Aldo to tell me what it was all about.

"Well, officially," he began, "Ralph is home with a touch of flu and high fever, and Boschetto has been called up for some emergency work at Venice Palace. You know, of course, he is one of the four official stenographers who take down Mussolini's speeches. And Palcinelli had to remain home with a sick wife. Now, that's what I can tell you. The secretary is here because she doesn't know anything about anything, and young Bianchi is in the same boat. I am here so that you aren't alone, and maybe I can advise you, if you want me to. But it has all got to be your own responsibility, one way or the other, whatever you decide to do."

"Well, for Christ's sake, Aldo, after all this mysterious buildup, what's it all about?"

"An attempt on Mussolini's life!"

He blurted it out fast. As though wanting to get rid of the statement as quickly as possible before somebody heard part of it.

"Did they get him?"

"No."

"Was he wounded at all?"

"No."

"And the assassin, the would-be assassin, I mean. Who is he?"

"I'm not sure, but he's been arrested."

"Then the police have the facts. We can talk to them about it."

"No, because they haven't told anybody about it yet. They would just have to deny it until the Duce says when they can release it, or maybe it will never be released."

"I see. Then how did you get it, and how did the others in the office know about it?"

"It came from one of Ralph's police tipsters."

"Have I got his name?"

"Yes. It's on that list Ralph gave you some weeks ago."

I pulled it out of my inside coat pocket.

"Which one?"

He pointed to a name as though afraid to mention it aloud.

"That one. He's in the OVRA. He wants to be paid for the story."

"How much?"

"About twenty dollars."

"Is that all? Secrets and whores are certainly cheap in Fascist Italy."

"Well, he works for us anyway, and it's just a sort of bonus."

"How do I meet him?"

"I'll phone him and he will tell us where to meet him."

"Okay."

"Let's make the date."

"We better phone from a pay station outside."

I followed Aldo out to the main post office, which was right across the street, and where there were a lot of public phones. He talked so I couldn't hear him. He finally hung up and said: "We'll meet the fellow casually at the Caffè Greco. He hangs out there. I'll go in first and start talking to him. Then you come in and I'll introduce you to him."

We went over to the Greco. It was a long, narrow establishment on the via Condotti with a bar in the front and tea tables in the next room and then two long corridors that ran way back to the kitchen and the toilets. There were comfortable, padded banquettes against the gray walls. As planned, Aldo went in first and I followed two minutes later.

Way in the back, in a rather dark spot where a light bulb was missing, I found the two of them talking.

Aldo introduced me to the plump, middle-aged man with graying hair, adding: "I've told the boss everything you told me. He just wants to hear it from you."

The man quickly gave me the same story, more or less as Aldo had related it to me. At the end of the quick summary, he rose and shook hands indicating our talk was over. Aldo gently pulled me away, and we went out into via Condotti, which was full of beautiful girls and seemingly no political intrigue. We walked back to the Press Club building.

"Do me a favor, Aldo. Send Pibe down to me when you get to the office. I'll be in the Club bar. You know, Pibe and I are a sort of man-and-wife team. I like to consult her about such things."

He looked at me as though he thought I was crazy to want to consult a woman, but said, "Okay, Pack," and took the elevator. While I was waiting, in came an old friend of ours. She was Betsy Mackenzie of the *News Chronicle* of London. We had met her at the old League of Nations in Geneva. She was now stationed in Rome. Betsy had been raised in Italy, her father having been British consul in four or five Italian cities. He was now retired and lived in an old-fashioned Rome apartment. She spoke both romanaccio and the patrician tongue: *toscana in bocca romana*. I invited her to a drink. She took a Campari and I ordered two whiskies and soda, "one for my wife, who is coming," I explained.

"Can I trust you?" I asked Betsy bluntly.

"We trusted each other in Geneva, didn't we? So I guess you can trust me here. What's the problem?"

"Well, I'm told by a UP tipster — police tipster that is — there was an attempt on Mussolini's life early this morning, and I would like to send it. What do you know about it?"

"I'm patiently waiting for the story to be released. Then I'll send it to the *Chronicle*. It will be released at about 8 P.M. Rome time, if at all."

"Do you think I'd get expelled if I jumped the gun on the release? Flash it now? We haven't had a good story since the coronation."

"They'll probably expel you even though it would embarrass them to kick out the chief of the same bureau twice in rapid succession."

Eleanor came in.

"Listen, Pibe," I said. "All this mystery is about an attempt on Musso's life. I am wondering if I dare send it. I might get expelled like Ekins." Turning to Betsy, I asked: "Could you give us any facts? That UP office upstairs is so screwed up with Mafia codes and signals, I don't know what to believe."

"My tipster, who is probably the same bloke as yours, phoned me this morning to say that a crazy man had tried to shoot Mussolini to death from a window behind the main railway station," Betsy said. "The OVRA was on to it and let the man set up his gun and everything before arresting him just as the Duck arrived to speak to a group of railwaymen. Musso stopped the crowd from lynching him. The police said the man had just been released from an insane asylum." Betsy gave us a few more details.

"Oh, hell, send it," Pibe said. "It's fairly safe to send, since the would-be assassin is a nut. He can't represent any serious move to overthrow the Duck."

"I'm convinced," I said. "We'll send it. Thanks, Betsy. Aren't you going to send it, too?"

"No thanks, Mr. Bud Ekins, Jr. Not until it's released. Ciao."

Eleanor and I rushed to the elevator.

"Of course, the gimmick is that the half-ass assassin is just out of a nut house. You saw it right away." I patted Pibe on the back in congratulation.

Aldo jumped up when we came into the office. "What's the decision?"

"I'm sending it."

"I was afraid you would. If you don't mind, I'll invite the secretary and Elvezio out for lunch, so there's only you and Pibe here when the story is sent. Fair enough? Ralph is against sending it and so are Palcinelli and Boschetto. Ralph thought I ought to tell you and let you make up your own mind. We can't hold back tips from the bureau manager, but we do advise you not to send it."

"Have lunch on the expense account. I hope we are still around when you come back."

"In bocca al lupo," he said and they all cleared out.

"Let's get cracking, Pibe. I'll write the story and you phone it. Okay?"

"Okay."

It was 12:30 P.M. I began writing a series of telephone bulletins. Pibe put in an urgent call for the UP office in London. I batted out the messages:

> FLASH ROME Mussolini escaped attempt on his
> life early this morning by a man described by
> police as crazy more

> reynolds packard

There was a break with London. A voice in Italian said, "Repeat that slowly."

Eleanor read it over very slowly and then continued with the messages that I had piled up at her elbow in the meantime:

> 25123 ADD FLASH Rome police caught the man
> as he was aiming his sharpshooter's gun set up in a
> railway shed behind rome's central station at il
> duce para The man suffered minor injuries as
> police bowled him over in a mad rush to knock him
> down before he could shoot para Although the
> commotion inside the shed could be heard by
> workers outside mussolini plunged into his speech
> stop The theme was that railway workers were vital
> because of the part they played in national and
> international communications aiding the axis
> countries para quote Our trains run on time and we
> are proud of the men who make them punctual

unquote mussolini said more

reynolds packard

25124 THIRD FLASH ROME As police brought the man out of the shed comma workers tried to lynch him but mussolini cried out quote let him have a fair trial stop Don't kill him now unquote para The police captain told il duce that investigation of the mans papers indicated he was released from a rome insane asylum only four days ago on probation stop mussolini then joked with the crowd saying quote you see only a crazy man wants to kill me stop unquote There was wild applause more

reynolds packard

I sent a few more takes, listing other assassination attempts on the Duck.

In less than half an hour correspondents began calling saying they had been queried on my story. They added that they knew about it but that the custom in Fascist Italy was to wait for government confirmation before sending such a story.

"That's what you think," I said. "If I'm sure of a story I send it."

One correspondent said, "I hope, Packard, you are not going to give us trouble by beating the government handouts."

An hour later an official communiqué was released confirming my story. The next day I received a summons from Minister of Unpopular Culture Alessandro Pavolini. A handsome young man, he was a tough veteran Fascist and had written some fairly good poetry, which had been published.

"I called you in to say that you were very nearly expelled, Signor Packard, for sending that attempted assassination story before it was released officially for publication," he said.

"I am sorry, Your Excellency, I could see nothing wrong with the story. I am a newspaperman. I must get scoops. There was nothing wrong with the story from your point of view, so I sent it."

"I don't approve of such tactics. It's risky to have correspondents here trying to beat the official releases. You may go now, but this is a warning,'' he said. ''It's a good thing for you that the would-be assassin was crazy.''

I wondered if he was really crazy.

# CHAPTER IX

The frequently held belief that Italians cannot keep military secrets from being bruited about was certainly true in Fascist times. Not only in the Foreign Press Club but even in the cafés of via Veneto, the word was going around that Mussolini was planning to invade Albania, just across the narrow Adriatic, within a few days. That was in the beginning of April of 1939.

Even the Black Shirt in the office who always was suggesting enterprise assignments that would take me out of Rome away from the military secrets, said it might be a good idea for me to go to Albania and cover the liberation of that country by Italy. He said Il Duce was tired of the way King Zog was flirting with Britain. Feeling very much like a louse, I sent Eleanor. She managed to catch what turned out to be the last commercial flight to Tirana before the invasion started.

As she arrived in Tirana, the Italian civilian population was being evacuated by boats from the port of Durazzo and from the capital, twenty miles inland, by a military airlift. The Duck was clearing the decks for action.

Eleanor had been told by those who knew Tirana that she should stay at the Hotel Carlton. But when she got there by horse and buggy, she found the proprietor was Italian, and he and his family were leaving by airlift that same afternoon and the hotel was closed down. She went to an

Albanian-run hotel and then, still keeping her horse-drawn carriage, she called at the U.S. Legation and had an interview with American Minister Hugh G. Grant. He had just come from a call on King Zog.

Two days later, the Italians landed at four Albanian ports: Durazzo, connected by direct highway with Tirana; Valonga, shipping center of the Albanian oil fields; San Giovanni di Medua, the port for the commercial center of Scutari; and Port Edda in the south, near the Greek frontier. Most of the scanty resistance was made at Durazzo.

American-born Queen Geraldine slipped away from the Royal Palace in a closed limousine, bearing with her her two-day-old son, who already was losing the throne he was to have inherited. She found refuge in Greece.

The next day King Zog, a self-made monarch, announced he was taking to the mountains to lead his toy army of thirty thousand troops against the Italians but instead also escaped to Greece.

There was some gunfire during the first few days Eleanor was there, but mostly by Albanians shooting at the highly armed Italian Legation with rifles and being repulsed by machine-gun blasts.

At the same time twenty-one Italian airplanes appeared above the capital and, sweeping low over the rooftops, dropped leaflets, written in Albanian, that called on the people not to resist.

"Albanians," the leaflets said, "Italian troops landing today in your country belong to a people who have been your friends throughout centuries. Do not oppose them with useless resistance.

"Soldiers of His Majesty, King-Emperor of Italy, have come and will remain only for the time necessary to restore order, justice, and peace."

The morning after King Zog left, Count Ciano flew into Tirana piloting his own plane. He landed at the airfield at 11:00 A.M. smiling broadly and wearing a trench cap at a jaunty angle. He swung a swagger stick. He was greeted by a delegation of Albanian quislings who had come to welcome him. He then got into an automobile and was driven at the head of a parade through the main thoroughfare of the town and smiled and Fascist-saluted whenever a few Albanians cheered or applauded him. The streets were already bedecked with pictures of King Victor Emmanuel and the Duce. There were also banners that read: "Our hearts overflow with gratitude to the Italian nation which has rescued us from the hands of a tyrant."

Ciano ended his drive through the city at the Italian Legation, where a great reception was being held. Eleanor, as a correspondent, was admitted. She managed to get Ciano off to one side for a moment.

"What? It's you again," he laughed. "The most beautiful white girl of Ethiopia following me here." Then he suddenly shaped up into the sedate foreign minister. "But you want something you can print.

"You have seen there has been practically no resistance. The Albanians have welcomed us. We do not anticipate that King Zog's army will give us much trouble and even if they try guerrilla tactics, the country is disgusted with Zog.

"Probably we will establish an Albanian Fascist Party so that the country can be governed by sound Fascist principles that will put it in harmony with Italy.

"That's all I can say now. I have so many people to see." He gave her another of his facile smiles and was gone.

Eleanor quickly typed up the interview as part of her dispatch on the Italian take-over of the country. She then ran down at the cocktail bar an Italian correspondent she had known in Ethiopia. He had come over with Ciano and was returning the same afternoon. He promised her he would deliver her dispatch to the UP office in Rome as soon as he returned. He handed it to me at exactly five past eight of the same evening.

The UP had a field day with the Packard by-lines for three consecutive days. It played up the husband-and-wife angle for all it was worth with Eleanor datelined Tirana and Reynolds in Rome. Our dispatches were generally published side by side and complete with our respective photos. The impression was that the two of us were slugging it out personally — more like a marital row than a miniwar. We hoped our dispatches, however, gave newspaper readers some idea of a typical Fascist take-over of a small independent country with blitz tactics. Victor Emmanuel was now king of Italy, emperor of Ethiopia, king of Albania, and the regal puppet of Mussolini.

# CHAPTER X

With the German invasion of Poland, the conflict in Europe began to snowball, and almost before we knew it, Mussolini was preparing to declare war on England and France. When we arrived in the Union Club alongside the Spanish steps — it was ultra-British — we knew that something was wrong. Women were drinking in the bar for the first time in the Club's history. It was a momentous date: June 10, 1940. Practically the entire British colony was jammed into the bar and spread out, holding drinks in hand, into the library, waiting room, and hallway. Besides newspaper people, there were bankers from Barclay's, Imperial Airway executives, British Institute officials, and those ubiquitous retired British colonels who make the most of their pensions in all parts of the world.

Ian Munro, the British press attaché, soon explained the excitement. He told us that British Ambassador Sir Percy Loraine and French Ambassador François-Poncet had been summoned to the foreign ministry at four-thirty that afternoon.

"There's no doubt about it now," Munro said. "Ciano is going to hand them Italy's declaration of war on both England and France. And the Duce is going to announce the declarations from the balcony of Venice Palace at six this evening."

"And that means," Betsy Mackenzie said to us, "that you two will have to leave the Ambasciatori Hotel and take over our place. We are going to be evacuated within the next few days, and then there will be nobody to look after our apartment.''

''What?'' said Pibe. ''That place is enormous and it takes up the whole top floor and the roof as well!''

''Don't forget how I've given you two plenty of news tips. Now you can reciprocate.''

''We'll do it,'' said Pibe. ''I have been wanting to get a crack at cooking again. Isn't it great, Pack?''

''I'm not so sure about that, but we'll have to take it.''

''You get a comfortable apartment, and you don't even thank us for it,'' complained Betsy.

''Don't pay any attention to Pack,'' Pibe said. ''I do thank you and Phyllis. We'll take good care of it until it's our turn to be at war with Italy.'' Phyllis was Betsy's sister and worked in the British Embassy.

At four that afternoon, gendarmes and infantry began moving into strategic points around the piazza Venezia. An hour later thousands of uniformed Fascists, including students, began gathering in the square. At 6:01, Mussolini, garbed in his uniform of a corporal of honor, suddenly appeared on the balcony. The one hundred thousand persons jamming the area broke into tremendous applause, probably the most enthusiastic he had received since he announced the end of the Ethiopian War. Little did they realize the tragedy they were applauding. They thought the war would be over in several weeks and that Mussolini was making a brilliant move in terms of history. They believed he would obtain the Fascist revindications on France.

Before the crowds dispersed, Black Shirts all over Italy pasted up announcements that Italy, beginning that very night, would have blackouts until the war was over.

Actually, in his notes to the French and British envoys, Il Duce stated the war would not go into effect until midnight and in fact train service between Italy and France continued until that time with many Frenchmen in the north taking advantage of the service to get back home.

Three days later, the diplomatic train bearing the British official party left from Rome's central station at 10 P.M.

One of the great mysteries is why the Italians, who entered the war to gain their claims on such territory as Nice, only forty miles away, and on nearby Corsica and Tunisia, didn't start an attack.

At the same time, Mussolini called up more men for the draft and stated that Italo-Americans were regarded as Italians. Ralph arranged with the

London office to be transferred to Zurich, which had been developed into a UP communications center. I was ordered to hire somebody local to replace him but only on the basis of a stringer. By chance, a few days later, an American walked into the office asking for a job. He was tall, wiry, and aristocratic-looking except for a straggly beard. I used to grow beards in my Paris days, much to the bureau chief's disgust, so I was immediately inclined toward him.

He said he knew Italian. I had him translate some Virginio Gayda for me. Gayda was known as Mussolini's journalistic conscience. He was the only Italian editorial writer who could come right out in print and criticize or praise a given event from the Fascist point of view. The idea was that he thought like Mussolini — or vice versa.

I finally asked the job-seeker his name, and he said it was Livingston Pomeroy, and his brother Eugene had known me in Ethiopia.

"Oh, that crackpot," I let slip out. "I mean he was a brave but very reckless reporter. I remember him, indeed. He came to Ethiopia for the old *Brooklyn Eagle* and was determined to walk from the Italian side over to the Ethiopian side as a journalistic stunt. He was finally arrested out in no-man's-land by Starace's Black Shirt column. He had a close call. Starace wanted to shoot him as a spy."

Livingston didn't seem to have much money at the moment, so I said he could temporarily sleep in a spare room in our new home.

Eleanor took over running the apartment. She didn't think much of the cook the Mackenzies had nor of their maid, so she hired a cook recommended by some of the wives in the American Embassy. It seemed she was a real gourmet cook, having established a reputation while running the kitchen for a Scandinavian embassy. We got a new maid through the Cianfarras — Camillo Cianfarra was the second man in the *New York Times* office. We called her the Pig Misery behind her back because that was the phrase she used the most in Italian: porca miseria. She was good natured and could open beer bottles with her strong white teeth.

One day Eleanor and I came home rather late for lunch and asked the cook why the meal wasn't ready and the dining room table not set.

"Oh, I don't know what's happened to Lucia." That was the Pig Misery's real name. "I didn't send her out for anything."

We yelled but got no answer. Finally I went up on the roof which had flowers, awnings, and a turtle. I found Pomeroy painting the shapely Pig Misery in the nude.

48

"Get some clothes on and start serving lunch," I ordered the maid.

"I'm sorry," Pomeroy said. "I forgot all about the time." He also showed a smart commercial art sense and began painting small canvases completely black. They were all labeled: "Rome during a Blackout." He actually sold a few.

A few weeks later Pomeroy moved into the home of his sister, the Baronessa Josephine Marincula. Life at our place seemed dull without him.

Lucia wasn't politically minded, but she had a Communist lover from whom she took her views. She used to give me the clenched-fist salute when nobody was around.

Pibe began entertaining at dinner parties, mostly American Embassy people. Even Italians who liked us didn't want to fraternize with Americans too much. It could get them in trouble.

Romeo, the barman at the Stampa Estera, was fired because he had shown more attention to Americans than to Germans in the Club. He frequently came out with English phrases when he addressed Axis correspondents. The Club council fired him without notice. He came to Pibe and me looking for a job. He was a bit punch-drunk, having been a professional boxer before becoming a barman. He limped badly and his nose had been flattened and pushed over to the left side of his face.

We asked what he could do, and he said he could be gardener, butler, and barman. We hired him.

# CHAPTER XI

Guido Rocco, head of the foreign press section of the propaganda ministry, who had the title of ambassador without the post, announced at one of his daily news conferences that Il Duce would show the foreign correspondents how he keeps fit in wartime. Rocco said that the foreign correspondents would meet in front of the Stampa Estera at seven the following morning to be transported to Villa Torlonia, a spacious walled estate with the villa turned into an armed citadel. The women journalists, however, were excluded, he said without any explanation.

"It will probably be difficult for the American correspondents who are not accustomed to the rigors of Fascist living to get up so early, the ambassador cracked. All the Axis correspondents laughed.

We reached Villa Torlonia by 7:30 the next morning. The Duce was already warming up on a finely trained chestnut mare that had been given him by Hitler. Musso wore blue-gray cavalry trousers stuffed into stiff black boots, a white singlet that showed off his muscular arms, and a white Fascist cap. Finally warmed up, he started to take the jumps: brush jumps, fences, and hurdles. He was followed by a young cavalry captain. We had to admit that the Duck was a good horseman. He cleared all the hazards in perfect style, but the young officer following behind him knocked down several rails just to show how good Benito was by contrast.

Then the foreign press corps was presented to the head of state one by one. Members of the Axis group were the first in line. They stepped up in front of the chestnut mare, on which Musso was still astride, as each name was called. Mussolini gave the Fascist salute which was smartly returned by the person presented in accordance with the established protocol of Fascism. They also called out: "Viva Mussolini." I heard my name called and I walked up in front of the mounted Duce and received his salute. I then raised my right arm. My hand got as high as my head and then I began to ruffle my hair with it, before pushing it up higher into a sort of schoolboy's request for permission to go to the toilet. "Good morning, Mr. Duce," I said.

Later I was told at the embassy that I should have placed my right hand over my heart and merely stood at attention. That, apparently, is the way a trained U.S. diplomat answers an unwelcome form of salute. Well, live and learn.

The Duce then rode off, and we were escorted to a table in another part of the rambling estate which was located right in the city itself. The table was heavy with all kinds of hors d'oeuvres and liquor, ranging from Scotch whisky and French Courvoisier to Italian Strega and grappa. Our host was Capt. Camillo Ridolfi, in Fascist uniform, who was Musso's riding master and fencing instructor. The Americans particularly plied him with questions about the Duce's horsemanship, fencing skill, his early rising habits, and even his diet. It was our first opportunity to get some firsthand information about his private life. The press officers moved in quickly, ready to interrupt Ridolfi if he said anything that might not be according to propaganda standards. Although he rattled on, seemingly pleased to talk about his favorite subject, he didn't make a single slip.

"I have been with Il Duce as his equerry and fencing instructor for twenty years," Ridolfi said. "He never drinks coffee nor anything stronger than orange juice. He is a vegetarian and eats very little. I have never known him to eat any meat, for many years.

"Oh, yes, he eats lots of spaghetti but only with butter and cheese," he continued. "No meat sauce. His favorite vegetables are broccoli and zucchini. But he likes fruit more than anything else, especially grapes, which he eats at both lunch and supper. Oh, and he likes peaches too."

Ambassador Rocco then interrupted and said the group had better be leaving as we would be coming back in the afternoon at three. As I was getting into the bus, Rocco called me aside and said, "Your wife is invited to come this afternoon."

Later it was reported that Musso was angry that no women had been present that morning to watch him show off his vaunted masculinity. As there were only a few women correspondents, Rocco drafted female secretaries and file clerks in the Ministry of Unpopular Culture to come along.

The afternoon's spectacle turned Eleanor and me more than anything else against Mussolini as a man. We had long been opposed to his political and foreign policy, but we did think he must possess certain personal qualities in order to remain chief of state of forty-four million people. As the press group was being conducted toward an old jousting field which had been converted into a modern tennis court, Pibe and I, as well as Allen Raymond, of the *New York Herald Tribune*, saw Mussolini slip out of the back door of the villa and bicycle over his private path to the tennis court. We were not supposed to see him. Five minutes later we arrived at the court in a more roundabout way. The doubles game was in full progress and the referee, who was Propaganda Minister Pavolini, informed us that the Duce had been playing for nearly three-quarters of an hour. He announced that Il Duce and his partner, Lucio Savorgnan, former university champion, had already won the first two sets, the score being 6-4, 6-3. He said the present score was 5-1 in favor of the leading team.

The dictator wore a beige polo shirt and white shorts which revealed the scar of a World War I wound. He served underhanded like a girl novice at the game and violated one of the main tennis rules by walking at least two or three steps beyond the base line to serve.

His opponents, Mario Delardinelli, Rome's number one professional tennis player, and Erlado Monzogoio, a member of Italy's national soccer team, were consummate actors. They pretended to miss Musso's shots, and when they did return some of them, they floated over the net so slowly that even a lame man with a broken arm could have returned them. Il Duce lobbed, smashed, and smiled, pleased with his pseudotriumph. Finally he and his partner allegedly won the third set 6-3. The Facist officials thronged around him, congratulating him on his victory.

"Thanks," he said, "I am proud to have won."

It was a terrible shock to see a man in his position really fooling himself into believing that he had given a good performance and taking as sincere the false congratulations he received. Needless to say, we didn't try to send our personal opinions through Fascist censorship when we wrote up his daily program for keeping fit in wartime.

# CHAPTER XII

For the sake of the record, I might as well put in here exactly how Pibe and I met and became joined together in a marriage to end marriage with our own private pact of mutual freedom. Otherwise our private lives, tied up with our reporting, would make little sense. Or the other way around.

One night in the summer of 1930 I was standing at the bar of the Café Select in Montparnasse when Charlie Ferlan, a founder of the Overseas Press Club, came in with a girl with the most wonderful legs. They sat down at a table and ordered Scotch. I was sipping a Porto Flip and looking for what is commonly called a piece of tail on my night off. Charlie finally recognized me, despite the red beard I had grown, and called out: "Hey, Pack, you old bastard you, come over and join us for a drink. I want you to meet the girl with the million-dollar legs."

"I'll be right over," I said and ordered another Porto Flip to take with me. "I noticed the gams all right. That's why I didn't notice you."

He introduced me as the wildman of the UP Paris office and the girl as a graduate of the Columbia School of Journalism looking for a newspaper job.

"I find it best not to mention the School of Journalism," she said. "Editors think we are already trained the wrong way."

A literary guy came in named Homer somebody and wanted to have a game of chess with me. I was supposed to be good in those days and knew he was. A waiter brought an échiquier and we started to play. A small group gathered around to watch. We must have played for nearly two hours. As Hemingway would have said, the sun was also rising, and the Select was being closed down for an hour. Homer and I jotted down the positions on the board. I suggested we continue the game at my hotel. He agreed and we all went to pay our bills. Then we were outside by the taxi rank and I found myself and Eleanor in a cab by ourselves.

"Allez vite," I said to the taxi driver. "Vite, vite." He took off as though for a fire and then I gave him my address, the Hotel Dacia on the Boulevard Saint Michel. When we got out, I told Eleanor the others would be along shortly, and we would go up to my room.

To keep up the subterfuge, I got out my chessboard, put it on the table, and arranged the pieces from my notes. I also gave Pibe a shot of Courvoisier, which was all I had in the room. She said she played chess, and I suggested she take Homer's place, and we would finish the game.

She was already suspicious by this time.

"I don't think they know where you live. They would have been here by this time, if they did."

I looked out my window which looked down on the Boulevard Saint Michel, and there was no sign of any chess enthusiasts.

"I think this is outrageous," Eleanor exploded. "You've tricked me. I'm leaving."

Then she suddenly found she was missing her purse.

"Where's my purse?" she demanded. "I'm not going to let you keep me here that way."

"Your purse?" I went over to the door, locked it, and put the key in my pocket. "You're not going to leave here until you produce that goddamn purse. I don't know what you're up to."

"I'm not up to anything, but there's about a thousand dollars in cash in that purse."

"Well, let's start looking."

After about five minutes of not-too-sober searching, I found it. It had fallen behind the bed, on which she had thrown it.

"Now, count that money before you get out of here."

She counted it.

"It's all here," she said, somewhat sheepishly. "But you must admit it looked bad. I don't really know you."

"I'm sorry I was a bit rough. Let's have some more Courvoisier and drink to a better understanding."

We drank more straight cognac and still more as we became more and more friendly.

When I woke up it was morning. We were both in bed. Naked.

"I can't remember whether we screwed or not," I said, kissing her on the cheek and pulling her toward me. She didn't resist. I kissed her on the mouth and she responded. "Let's make sure," I said and pushed myself into her.

"Kerhist that was good," I said.

She didn't answer but breathed heavily. We finally got up and took showers. By this time it was 3 P.M. I suggested lunch, and we went to Harry's Bar at Sank Roo Dough New as anglicized for tourists, and had hamburgers and beer.

"This is a helluva place in the gourmet capital," Eleanor complained. "And with an American too. I ought to be with a Frenchman, eating in a real French restaurant, dining on snails or Chateaubriand and drinking Chablis and Bourgogne."

"I thought Charlie said you were looking for a newspaper job."

"That's right, but one doesn't interfere with the other."

"Okay. I like you. I'll give Eric Hawkins a ring at the *Herald Tribune*. I hear he is looking for a reporter. Not a sob sister, a real reporter, who can cover riots and politics."

"Give him a ring and I'll dash around."

I went to the phone booth and got Hawkins almost immediately. He was the English editor who made the *Herald Tribune* an American journalistic success. He said, "Send her around and let me talk to her. About five this afternoon."

And by God, she got the job.

We did a lot of eating and drinking our way around Paris, and the experiences we had brought us close together.

The first episode was the time I was playing chess in the Café Regence with one of the professionals there. I always lost to him but it was good practice. Maxwell Bodenheim, the author of *Replenishing Jessica*, had just arrived in Paris after some girl had committed suicide because he told her she didn't have enough talent to become a writer. It was my day off. About ten that night, Eleanor came in to join me. I introduced her to Bodenheim, who was watching the game. He soon began trying to feel her legs and put his hands up her skirt. She slapped him, but I couldn't tell whether she really minded. Then we adjourned to the Café Coupole on the Left Bank to eat, and Maxwell kept on with his ever more carnal advances. Suddenly Eleanor picked up a wine bottle and threw it at him. It missed him, hurtled into an after-theater group — and hit one of the elegant ladies smack in the face. She crumpled to the floor unconscious. Two husky Frenchmen stalked angrily over to our table and demanded to know who had thrown the bottle.

"C'est moi," I said. "Je vous demande pardon."

"Pardon?"

Wham. They plastered me with punches and kicks before I knew what was coming, and I lost consciousness. When I came to, I was in the gutter outside La Coupole, and Pibe was holding me to her breast tightly, muttering, "You are really wonderful. Taking the blame for me." Bodenheim had disappeared. She got me to my feet and took me home in a cab.

A few nights later, we were in Johnny's Bar just off the Avenue de l'Opéra. There were six drunken Peruvians at the bar, reciting the line: "Y que piernas hermosas tiene la señorita americana."

"Listen," I told them. "I know Latin American poets myself. I have worked in Argentina, Uruguay, and Chile. My favorite is Reuben Dario. I especially like his ' . . . La princesa está triste. Que tendrá la princesa?" . . . I recited a few more lines.

Without any warning they began attacking me. I was socked on the chin, somebody got a hammerlock on my right arm, and two of them began punching me in the stomach and face. I fell on the floor. One Peruvian held me down with his knees while another tried to strangle me with my necktie and still another kicked my ribs. I began to think this was really the end when the men, one by one, stopped kicking and punching me, and the Lima Strangler let go of my necktie while the one holding me down, suddenly was no longer on top of me.

Eleanor pulled me up and as we ran for the door, I saw all six of them bent over in agony, holding their balls, so adroitly had they been kicked by La Pibe. We hailed a cruising cab and got away before they came out of the bar.

"I love you, I love you," I said, "You marvelous amazon." Then thinking of myself as a philosopher who didn't believe in love, I added, "In the sense of liking something: I love coffee, I love tea."

"You would have to spoil it," she said. "But now we're even."

We kissed and went to the Hotel Dacia for the night.

Then I inherited some money. Not much, but enough to let me tell off Heinzen. He was annoying me by constantly ordering me to take off my beard. I said I liked it and wanted to keep it.

"Then why don't you quit?" he said. "And do what you like."

"Okay, I quit."

And I did.

I went to Juan-les-Pins to write a philosophical novel. Eleanor didn't want to go with me so I went alone and worked there for more than a year. With the book still unfinished, I went back to Paris and succeeded in persuading Pibe to quit the *Herald* and tour through Europe with me. She did and we took in all the European capitals and a lot of big and small towns. Sometimes, particularly in Holland, we had difficulty getting a room together because we weren't married.

We ended up in Vienna, where we stayed nearly a year. Our favorite haunts were the Café du Louvre, frequented by foreign correspondents, and the Café Edison, which was a gathering spot for medical students, including those majoring in psychoanalysis.

One day one of Pibe's admirers in the Café du Louvre, who wrote about opera and art, said he would like to have a long talk with me. Would I have lunch with him?

"Perhaps if you tell me what it's all about."

"It's about Eleanor and what you are doing to her."

"Oh. I'm not sure I want to discuss that."

"I insist that you do, otherwise I'll knock the shit out of you."

"I don't think you can."

He hit me on the jaw. I went reeling and fell on the floor. We were in a café where I spent hours playing chess every day.

I got up and knocked him down. The waiters grabbed us both. Suddenly feeling ashamed of myself, I held out my hand and said, "Okay. Let's be friends. You are fond of Pibe and so am I, so let's talk about it." We shook hands.

The next day we lunched together. During the first part of the meal, we talked about Pibe and how brilliant we both thought she was. Then with the coffee and digestifs he came to the point.

"You think of yourself as a sort of primitive philosopher, a half-ass Socrates, or something, and I like you for that. But you are not living in a philosophical world. We are living in a bourgeois world in which marriage is the molecular unit of society. And you, by living in open sin — not to me it isn't sin, but to most others it is — are doing Pibe great harm. It could interfere with her getting a good job, for example. It ruins her socially and her chances to marry somebody else."

"You really believe that?"

"Of course. She is your mistress and everybody knows it. You live together openly. It's very unfair to her as a woman. You ought to be ashamed of yourself."

"Jesus H. Kerhist. I never thought of it that way. I thought we were pioneers in this brave new world and that people admired Pibe for her courage in doing what she is doing."

"A damn small minority. To the majority of people, she is just a kept woman even though I understand she pays her share."

I collapsed as though he had hit me in the solar plexis. I immediately realized I had been thoughtless and egotistical. After a long silence I said, "What do you suggest I do?"

"Marry her. You can always get a divorce."

We were married a few weeks later in the Vienna Rathaus. What an appropriate place for a wedding, you rat, I thought. We were actually married twice because the first ceremony was marred by some of our drunken friends laughing and because I said *nein* at one point when I should have said *ja*. So we came back in the afternoon without any guests except the necessary witnesses, and we were married with the aid of an interpreter.

Our American newspaper friends, including news-agency correspondents, decided to make a story out of it, and the wedding of two unknown persons was converted into a rather interesting news item. The ceremony was described as a "marriage to end marriages." All the stories stressed that neither the bride nor the bridegroom believed in the marital institution and only decided to wed in order not to expend all their energies in fighting convention. In one of the agency stories, we were both quoted as saying, in effect, that we believed in free love, but in order to make a living and not be treated as lepers, we bowed to the antiquated custom of marriage, but under protest.

We then set out, as legal man and wife, to see the rest of the world. First we took a French freighter to Tahiti, where we wrote feature stories about the South Seas for the Hearst news agency — INS. That lasted about a year. Then we went to China, where we got jobs with the United Press in Shanghai and stayed more than a year. All of a sudden I had a row with the boss and we came to a nonamicable agreement that I be transferred to Paris and Pibe could remain at her job in Shanghai. She decided, however, to accompany me — without a job.

Shortly after we returned to Paris, Fascist Italy invaded Ethiopia. I immediately volunteered to be a war correspondent, but my offer wasn't accepted until Webb Miller, the UP's star reporter of those days, was taken ill with altitude sickness in Asmara, the Eritrean springboard for the invasion. I was immmediately sent to replace him. I left Eleanor behind in Paris.

The day I arrived in Eritrea, General Emilio De Bono, who had been replaced as commander of the Italian forces in Ethiopia by Badoglio, was leaving for Rome. I watched De Bono embark in the harbor of Massawa.

Badoglio was anti-Mussolini but he came out of retirement because he had confided in friends, he didn't want to see Italy make a brutta figura of herself in a war with natives. The day after my arrival Badoglio gave a press conference at which he said he was going to reorganize the entire military campaign as carried out by De Bono and that in the meantime correspondents would be confined to Asmara, allowed to send only communiqués.

"I regard the life of any one Italian soldier as more important than a newspaper dispatch," he concluded.

I found it pretty dull in Asmara: socially, sexually, and journalistically. It was the wrong kind of man's town. There were men everywhere. Men, men, and more men. Soldiers, truck drivers, contractors, and road builders.

The only women to be seen on the streets were a few elderly Eritreans. As one correspondent said: "These women look younger and whiter every day. I'm dying of sex hunger."

Later I learned there was a brothel full of Italian women, run by a madam especially imported from Milan's biggest bordello. It was open to soldiers in the afternoon and officers in the evening. Correspondents were rated as officers.

Even in the whorehouse you rarely saw women. There was no display room where the girls sat about and you took your pick. No. Here, you stood in line in front of a door and when a man came out another popped in. You waited your turn. It was a carnal assembly line. When you finally got into the room yourself, the girl would be using the bidet and call out to you to take off your pants. The girls weren't so bad looking, only slightly on the hard side, but the mass fornication system put me off them.

I decided to try to get Pibe to join me. It wasn't easy because of Mussolini's military restrictions and because the UP didn't want to pay the salaries of two correspondents to cover the same story. It's motto was: "The AP outnumbers us but we outreport them."

The Rome bureau manager at the time, Stew Brown, was an old friend of ours. He also had worked with me in the UP bureau in Paris. I wrote him to try to get Eleanor accredited as a correspondent without saying anything to the UP because I was sure the London office would veto it. To my surprise, he got her accredited, and a week later she arrived in Asmara to join me.

After one week I was called up by Colonel Branca, one of the chief press officers, and asked when Mrs. Packard was going to file. He said there was no record of her having sent a story since her arrival. I tried to explain that I covered the spot news for the UP and she covered the think pieces for which it required a certain amount of time to collect material.

"Bene," he said. "I will give your wife two more days to start filing. Then if she doesn't send any dispatches, I must ask her to leave."

I told her the bad news.

"Well," she said. "I'll just send a story to the UP and see what happens."

She sent a story about Mussolini's two sons, Bruno and Vittorio, who were pilots, including interviews with them. She sent another story about a flight she made in an army plane which fed scouting parties of Askaris by dropping food cushioned in bales of hay. The hay was fed to the mules.

Harry Flory, the European manager of the UP wired me, saying:

> 19174 PACKARD ELEANORS STUFF GREAT STOP
> NEWSPAPERS WORLDWIDE FEATURING IT STOP
> THEY LIKE IDEA OF WOMAN WAR
> CORRESPONDENT STOP TELL HER WIRE LEASTLY
> ONE STORY DAILY STOP SHE BACK ON PAYROLL
>
> FLORY

And so Eleanor stayed on, and her stuff was used more than mine. I was proud of her success. I decided I was neither a jealous husband nor a jealous correspondent.

# CHAPTER XIII

Hitler was doing so well that Mussolini began worrying about getting some of the war loot himself. He feared that it might all go to Hitler if Italy didn't engage in actual battle. First he declared war on England and France and then later invaded Greece from Albania.

The non-Axis foreigners immediately melted away in Italy as times became hard and unpleasant. The huge American colony shrank to only those with actual work in Italy deemed necessary by Washington.

If other U.S. citizens tried to continue on, they soon found they couldn't get their passports renewed except to go home.

A couple of exceptions were Ezra Pound, of Idaho, the expatriate poet, and beautiful Teddy Lynch, the fourth wife of Paul Getty, Sr. She was studying opera in Rome and was determined to continue with her singing lessons. Pound was doing anti-Roosevelt, pro-Fascist broadcasts for the Italians.

It was clear to most correspondents that what Hitler really wanted out of his pact with Italy was that she remain a non-belligerent, thus acting as a buffer state for Germany against the Allies. But Mussolini was as much a born dictator with dreams of territorial aggrandizement as Hitler. He wanted to get in on the spoils of war. And at that time there were rumors everywhere that Germany was about to invade England.

Panic-stricken, Mussolini ignored Hitler's wishes that he keep out of the war so as not to enlarge the conflict area. Also, Hitler was always convinced that once the Italians started fighting, he would have to intervene and help them out.

As soon as Il Duce plunged into the war by invading Greece, rationing began on a rigid scale in Italy. The Fascist government rationed rice, flour, cornmeal, butter, lard, and even spaghetti and olive oil. The first olive oil quota per person per month was fixed at eight hundred grams but was soon reduced to four hundred grams, or slightly less than one pound. These measures worried the Italian public as to how badly the war was going and at the same time resulted in a mushrooming of the black market.

No wonder bootleggers during American prohibition were generally Italians, I thought.

The Italians took to bootlegging rationed products with such aptitude that it showed almost a national characteristic. And nobody seemed to have a guilty conscience about buying black-market products, including the Fascists themselves.

Shortly after it had been forbidden by decree to serve meat except on Saturday, we went to one of Rome's leading restaurants on a Wednesday night. The menu mentioned only vegetarian dishes, but the headwaiter without any hesitancy recommended that we have a meat dish — saltimbocca alla romana. At a table near us was a bemedaled Black Shirt officer in uniform, a red stripe around his left cuff to show he had participated in the march on Rome. I asked if it wouldn't be rather risky to serve meat right under the eyes of such a high Fascist official.

"Oh," laughed the headwaiter, "he just ordered a steak himself. That's why he comes here regularly — because he knows he can always get meat."

In another restaurant a week later we were served steak on a meatless day. This time it was cleverly hidden beneath a huge lettuce leaf which the waiter suggested we use to cover the contents of our plate whenever a new customer came in.

"We don't think anybody cares, but it's best to be careful, and it's simple to hide it with a lettuce leaf."

In several deluxe restaurants, until the United States got into the war, it was possible to have real coffee though it had been banned since January, 1940. Almost every morning two or three bootleggers would come to our home and offer us leg of lamb, ducks, eggs by the dozen, and butter. It was just a question of paying more. At first prices were double but slowly mounted as the rationing became more and more strictly enforced to as much as five times the legal price. And, typically Italian, the bootleggers and their customers never felt they were doing anything wrong or unpatriotic. The war was unpopular; Italian families needed to eat; there was a good chance to make big profits; so what was wrong with bootlegging?

As soon as the OVRA learned about the house-to-house peddling of contraband produce, it began to search farm wagons coming into the capital from the country and even to examine the packages and bags carried by people traveling on suburban trains. The bootleggers soon found the answer to this and would hand their bundles of contraband over to soldiers and officers, who came from the same small town, and had them carried through the station under military protection. The OVRA seldom dared to search men in uniform.

But a limited amount of food was only part of the hardships the Italians had to suffer. Lack of adequate heating was one of the worst because so-called Sunny Italy is far from warm in wintertime. In Rome, during 1941 — 42, heating of apartment buildings, hotels, and houses was permitted only between 2 P.M. and 9 P.M. and that only for one hundred days beginning December 10. Office buildings and stores had even greater restrictions on heat. In fact, the only warm establishments in the big cities were the official brothels which were heated from nine in the morning until midnight to keep the scantily clad inmates warm and to enable their customers not to catch cold while making love. Sometimes men just sat in the display rooms of brothels to keep warm. The irate madam eventually would point to them and order them to take girls upstairs or get out.

The Italians could not make up for the lack of heat by bundling themselves up in warm clothes because clothes rationing had already been imposed. But on the evening of September 30, 1941, a Rome radio broadcast unexpectedly announced that all clothing stores and shops would be shut down for one month. During that period, the broadcaster said that a careful inventory of stocks would be made and that when business resumed, clothing could be bought only with coupons. Shoes were almost impossible to buy and on the black market brought as high as forty dollars a pair.

One of the worst hardships at the time was the restriction on transport. The absolute elimination of private cars and the drastic reduction in the number of taxis swelled the numbers already using the already overcrowded public conveyances like buses and streetcars to such an extent that a ride in one of them was to be dreaded. The buses stopped running at ten o'clock at night, so that all social activities in the evening — even going to the movies — had to be foregone unless one lived in the center of town. Most places of amusement accordingly closed down before 10 P.M. Dancing, whether public or private, had been forbidden ever since Italy entered the war. It seemed to me that all this had a bad effect on Italian morale, since the Italians, instead of being able to forget their troubles in harmless amusements, had nothing to do but go home and grumble to neighbors about how many more sacrifices they would have to endure before the war was over.

There was more freedom in the Fascist press than most people realized abroad or maybe it was the Fascist way of making light of hardships. For example, jokes began to appear in many newspapers and magazines, poking fun at the shortage of fuel, food, clothing, and the closing down at early hours of cafés and other gathering places. The humorous magazines like *Marc' Aurelio, Il Travaso*, and *Il Bertoldo* devoted entire pages to wisecracks about wartime difficulties.

A typical cartoon in *Il Travaso* showed a man bounding along the street on his head. He explained to a curious friend: "What do you expect? The hat is old, the shoes are new."

In another cartoon, in the *Bertoldo*, two policemen were questioning a man with a basketful of eggs demanding to know how he obtained them. "I laid them myself," he explained.

Turin's daily newspaper, *La Stampa*, contributed its bit of critical witticism with a sketch of a beggar standing in the street with outstretched hands. He was practically naked except for a pair of brand new shoes. "Why should you beg?" a passerby asked. "You've been able to buy shoes." The beggar answered: "That's why I am bankrupt."

The handshake was frowned upon as a foreign importation and un-Roman compared to the open-hand Fascist salute. Orchestra conductors in summer were ordered to wear white linen Fascist uniforms instead of the usual tails with stiff-bosomed shirts and collars which were considered British style.

The Fascist youth took particular delight in the edict against women wearing shorts or long trousers which were supposed to be a mode imported from "plutocratic America." The great sport of young Fascists was to find a girl so dressed and then chase her down the street or along the beach trying to remove the offending piece of apparel.

During the year preceding the United States' entry into the war, we were besieged with well-to-do Italians who wanted to sell us lire for dollars at a rate considerably higher than the official one. They offered twenty-four lire to the dollar as against the official exchange of seventeen. Since Italian-American transactions had been frozen, they did not want nor expect to be paid for their lire until after the war was over. What they hoped was to have a stake with which they could start life again no matter how badly Italy was beaten. It was insurance against a very rainy day. They always seemed to be very disappointed when we explained that our delicate position as correspondents under constant surveillance of the OVRA made it impossible for us to enter into any such transactions, besides all the other reasons.

It was economic evidence early in the war that even the Italians themselves favored America against the Axis as the winner in the final outcome of the conflict.

# CHAPTER XIV

I was having dinner with Ezra Pound on that Sunday evening when all hell broke loose. We were eating in the San Carlo Restaurant on the Corso Umberto, now called Il Corso. The establishment has changed, too. It was a gourmet restaurant with old-world service. Now, it's a snack bar.

Ezra was quite a mephistophelian figure in those days. He sported a red, pointed beard, wore his collar open, Lord Byron style, and outdoors in wintertime draped a black cape over his shoulders. He covered his head with a ten-gallon hat. His letterhead was impressive. It was composed of a woodcut of himself and the Mussolini epigram: "Many enemies, much honor." Whenever he came to the Mackenzie apartment to see Eleanor or me, he frightened the women servants with his emphatic Fascist salute and his stentorian cry of "Viva Il Duce," as either of them opened the door. He had become a caricature of the Fascist leaders themselves. He might have been Il Duce except he was tall and slim.

Pound had long been an expatriate, seemingly nonpolitical, writing his poetry while traveling widely in England, France, and Italy. In Rapallo, where he finally settled down in a modest house, he seemed to have been impressed by Fascism but mainly, judging from what he said to me, he was disgusted with Roosevelt. He found that the Italian radio would give great prominence to his harangues against the president of the United States. Then he started becoming the American Voice for Fascist Italy.

He not only gave pro-Fascist broadcasts but also wrote books explaining and praising Fascist economy. When I told him once — before America entered the war — that he had better lay off the broadcasts or he would be regarded as a traitor, he came back at me: "But I believe in Fascism." He gave the Fascist salute to emphasize his belief. "I want to defend it. I don't see why Fascism is contrary to the American philosophy. I am only against Roosevelt and the Jews who influence him."

"What does Pavolini pay you for a broadcast?" I asked him.

"Ten dollars for a fifteen-minute broadcast. Otherwise it's less."

"Jesus. That's peanuts."

"That's right. It's not much but you don't think I do it just for the money, do you? I tell you I want to save the American people."

There was no way to reason with him.

We had known him in Paris in the old days of Hemingway, Elliot Paul, and Gertrude Stein, when he was more poet than politician, more literary than political

Eleanor and I often discussed the transformation that had come over him since he settled in Italy. We decided it was because he had never received acclaim in his own country, as he did in Fascist Italy. Although he had published forty-one volumes of poetry, essays, stories and, treatises in the United States, they had brought him little in the way of fame or wealth. What fame he had achieved was limited to small literary and scholarly groups. He wanted to become great somehow or other, while still alive and fairly young. He was about fifty-five at that time. So when Fascist Italy showed interest in his talents, he went along. Although he wasn't paid much, his name was in the Italian press almost every day, mentioning something about his broadcasts or his books on Fascist economy. In fact his acquaintanceship with us was based on the fact that he liked a couple of stories that I had written about him for the UP which had been published in the American press.

A waiter came over to Pound's and my table in the San Carlo and said that I was wanted on the phone.

"The signora said it is urgente," the waiter said.

It was Eleanor on the phone.

"The Japs have just bombed Pearl Harbor. It seems they've knocked hell out of the U.S. Navy. I've already informed the embassy. They didn't know a thing about it. Get back here quickly will you. I am having a Pearl Harbor here in the office, and I need your help."

"I'll be right over. Ciao."

As I rushed back to the table, I grabbed the headwaiter and told him I must pay immediately.

"Il conto subito. É urgente."

"What's the trouble?" asked Pound.

"The Japs have bombed Pearl Harbor, and according to my wife they've knocked the shit out of the U.S. Navy."

"My God!" gasped Pound. "I'm a ruined man."

He paid his bill, too. We dashed out into the night, going different ways. I didn't see him again until years after the war. In the meantime, he had become the American Lord Haw-Haw of Italy and a traitor. Finally put into an American insane asylum, he became all poet again and won a number of literary prizes.

Rushing into the office, I found Pibe having a hassle with seven aggressive little Japs.

"Get the hell out of here, you goddamn bastards," Pibe was yelling. "You are no longer clients. You have stabbed us in the back, and you aren't going to see a single dispatch." Then, seeing me, she added, "Now get out before my husband knocks you out."

"Very please, Mr. Packard, to see you. Please explain to your esteemed wife we are clients of the United Press and have right to see the report you have from Pearl Harbor. We pay you much dollars for the service."

"Mrs. Packard is right," I answered. "You fuck off immediately, or we'll have a Pearl Harbor here — but in reverse."

I grabbed two of the diminutive Nippons and dragged them to the door. Pibe hauled out two more and the other three scampered out after the others.

"Now stay out. Your contracts are busted. They are no longer valid. We are at war with you."

One of the correspondents, named Maida, who had always been friendly with Eleanor and me, tried to shake hands with both of us.

We grabbed our hands away from him and I said, "We are at war with even you, Maida, so fuck off."

He looked hurt and walked away with the others.

The other members of our staff — there were only Italians working that Sunday evening — seemed not to be aware of the Japanese incident.

They went on with their typing, only a bit faster than usual.

# CHAPTER XV

Ever since England and Italy were at war, the UP in Rome could file by uncertain radio to New York and Buenos Aires or by phone to fast and more expensive Press Wireless in Zurich, which, being located in neutral Switzerland, could relay our messages to both Axis and non-Axis countries. But within half an hour after the news of the Pearl Harbor attack, the American correspondents found they couldn't communicate with any point outside of Italy. We were incommunicado.

The next morning we were informed by the press ministry that we could not leave Rome until further notice. On Tuesday morning the uniformed Fascist in the office gave me a personal tip that he would be busy taking down an important speech by the Duce that afternoon. Elvezio, the student apprentice in the office, said he had received notice to join his university group that was to assemble in a specified section of piazza Venezia. Then the Rome radio announced that Mussolini was going to speak at 5 P.M. on a subject of international magnitude.

Eleanor looked at her watch. It was 3 P.M.

"Let's go and have a good lunch at Libotti's," she said. "If we hurry we can just make it, and then we'll go and listen to the Duck declare war on the United States." We locked the office. What else was there to do? Even the incoming service couldn't function.

Libotti, the owner of the restaurant, was a diehard anti-Fascist, who had lost two sons in Musso's attempt at conquest. He insisted on our having Strega on the house at the end of the meal. It was always a beautiful Italian drink, a golden fluid in a bottle with a label featuring a witch riding on a broomstick. The distillery had just been converted into a munitions plant. That's how potent the drink was.

"Here's good luck to you," he said, sipping the Strega. "The evil eye on the Black Shirt bastard. Now he is going to war against the United States. What a bloody fool!"

"To victory over the Black Shirt bastard," we said as we drained our glasses in one gulp.

By the time we came out of the restaurant, the streets were already in a festive spirit with hundreds of groups in uniforms converging on piazza Venezia. Many of them sang Fascist songs like "Giovinezza." After each song they broke into shouts of "Viva Il Duce. Viva Il Giappone. Down with America."

Many of the groups were in civilian clothes, but wearing the Fascist insignia. They carried obscene posters caricaturing both FDR and Mrs. Roosevelt. One of them depicted Mrs. Roosevelt wearing a toilet seat as a necklace. Another had crossed canes on a field of dollars as the U.S. president's coat of arms. Other banners read: "Roosenfeld the Jew President," and "Down with Pluto-Democracy."

We slipped down a side street to get into a corner of Venice Square, where seventy thousand people were already massed and more flowing in. The balcony was prepared for the occasion being draped with Italian and Fascist flags. A microphone was raised above the balustrade.

Soon Mussolini, dressed in the uniform of a corporal of honor of the Black Shirt Militia and a field cap that covered his bald head, popped out on the balcony. The Fascist claques let out a roar of "Duce! Duce! Duce!" The German ambassador to the Quirinale (Italy's equivalent of the White House), Hans Georg von Mackensen, towering above Mussolini, then appeared on the balcony. He was followed by the tiny Japanese Ambassador, Zembei Horikiri.

Musso looked smaller than ever beside the huge German diplomat. And suffering from a small-man complex, he tried to look fierce and mimicked his own conception of a warlord with fierce gestures and expressions.

It was one of the shortest speeches the Duce had ever made. It was less than three hundred words long. Between each sentence he paused lengthily and gave his professional cheering squads an opportunity to arouse the crowds. In front of each group of claques was a loudspeaker that amplified the applause and cheering tenfold. Over the radio it must have made an impressive sound; but to us who could see motionless hands and lips on all sides, the noise seemed as unreal as offstage sound effects breaking in at the wrong time. Certainly most of the people we saw didn't find anything in the speech to acclaim.

It was a declaration of war against the United States where most of them had relatives who sent them financial assistance either regularly or from time to time.

"The powers of the Steel Pact — Fascist Italy and Nazi Germany — participate in this war as from today on the side of the heroic Japanese against the United States," Il Duce roared. "I say to you it is a privilege to fight with them. . . . The Tripartite Pact becomes a military alliance which draws around its colors two hundred and fifty million men, determined to do all in order to win. . . . Italians once more arise and be worthy of this historic hour. We shall win."

Suddenly we realized we were at war with the people around us. We began speaking to each other in our peculiar Italian. Already the kiosks we passed were displaying newspapers that contained the text of the Duce's speech. We could see the bannerline: "Duce Declares War On U.S." It was like a nightmare: hearing a speech, then almost simultaneously reading it in the newspapers. We ran into a Swiss correspondent from the Press Club. He always spoke his impeccable English to us, but this time he resorted to Italian.

"You have heard," he said in a most impersonal tone, "that the Italian police are arresting all American correspondents. Bye-bye. Hope to see you one of these days."

"Grazie," we chorused and slid into a taxi that was cruising slowly down the street.

"To the American Embassy. Subito," I directed and we sat back to grope for our bearings.

They were difficult to find. The Italians were such a likeable people. Almost anybody who had lived in Italy found them so. Yet here they were being lined up against the United States, the land of their prosperous relatives, and this, apparently against their own will. Somewhere along the line Mussolini had run off the track and now was dumping his followers into a wreckage of war.

The cab came to a halt in front of the embassy. The walled buildings and grounds were surrounded by a cordon of carabinieri in greenish-gray uniforms with steel helmets. They were not wearing full dress but were wearing fighting equipment.

"You know what to do," I said to Pibe. "We both run interference and right through them and straight into the entrance. Let's go."

I handed the taxi driver a handful of coins more than enough to pay double the fare.

With football tactics we managed to dodge and slip through the carabinieri ring and kept running through the small gardens. We didn't stop running until we were inside the embassy building itself.

We almost knocked down Colonel Norman Fiske, the U.S. military attaché, as we entered. George Wadsworth, the chargé d'affaires, was still in Chigi Palace, where he had been summoned by Ciano. Everybody was awaiting his return. There was an odor of smoke as secret documents were burned in different offices. An American businessman was ruefully sending up in flames a check for ten thousand dollars for fear he would compromise an Italian associate if it were found on him by the OVRA. Six American priests who planned to reside in the Vatican for the duration of the war were having their passports renewed. A number of Italian clerks, both men and women, were crying. Some of the American staff were laughing with nervous relief that the war had finally come after all the months of uncertainty.

We were surprised to find ourselves the only correspondents inside the embassy. I phoned Herbert Matthews, of the *New York Times,* and suggested it might be a good idea for him and his assistant, Cianfarra, to join us. Cianfarra was an Italo-American but with an American passport.

Matthews pooh-poohed the idea and said he and Cianfarra had to clean out their desks. Suddenly he changed his tone and said, "I have to hang up now. Call me later."

"Don't you think you had better try to come to the embassy? You could probably crash the cordon of carabinieri the same as we did."

"No," Herbert replied with exasperating aloofness. "I must finish sorting out my papers. Since they didn't arrest me along with Cianfarra, I guess I'm all right here."

Half an hour later Herbert managed to phone to the embassy one brief sentence: "They've come for me, too."

We phoned our house to tell the cook that we wouldn't be home for supper just to see what was happening. She was clever enough to warn us by saying, "That is too bad, there are two gentlemen here waiting to see you," before the phone was banged down.

Reports came into the embassy that all the American correspondents except Eleanor and myself had been arrested. After Wadsworth returned from seeing Ciano he had a long conference with the counselor of the Swiss Legation which was going to look after American interests. Then he had a series of conferences with practically everybody else in the embassy before it was our turn. Then it was about midnight.

He received us in his private office. We had expected to find him looking tired and worried. Instead, he was thriving on the excitement. We had never found him in a better mood. He even told us about his visit to the foreign ministry.

"I received a summons this morning from Chigi Palace saying that Count Ciano wanted to see me at three-thirty this afternoon about a most urgent matter. The count received me most brusquely, so unlike his usual promiscuously friendly manner. When I walked into his office, he halted me halfway to his desk by rising, making it clear I was not to sit down. With a scowl on his face, he recited his piece as though he had learned it by heart, saying in one sentence that he must inform me that Italy considered herself at war with the United States. I bowed my head and said, 'I'm very sorry to hear it.'"

Eleanor asked, "Well, why did you say that?"

"Protocol, my dear lady, protocol. One is always sorry when war is declared on one's country. Then as I was leaving the office, he said, 'Good-bye' and gave me the suspicion of a friendly smile."

We then got down to the problem of ourselves.

"Now I must tell you something you aren't going to like. According to my information, you are the only two American correspondents not arrested. So I am going to give you very sage advice: Don't be special cases. Go out there and get yourselves arrested. If you want to stay in the embassy you can, but then you would be special cases. Have yourselves some food and some more drinks and then go out and get arrested."

We got up from our chairs.

"Well, thanks for the rugged advice," I said. "I'm sure it's sound."

We shook hands with Wadsworth and left his office. We had a few more whiskies with the second and third secretaries and then zigzagged out into the arms of the police.

# CHAPTER XVI

There was a police car near the curb by the side entrance of the embassy on via Boncompagni. The two policemen who had taken us into custody politely asked us to get into their car, saying they would take us to the Questura as a matter of routine. There was the usual Italian inefficiency at the Questura. Nobody seemed to know what to do with us. We sat on a bench and watched police bring in two drunks, a disorderly character, a burglar, and a streetwalker whose papers weren't in order. In between these cases we could hear the night chief and detectives discussing what to do with us. The chief said he had received written instructions to send me to Regina Coeli (Queen of Heaven) prison, but that it was closed for the night and that Eleanor was to be booked and sent home under police surveillance.

At 4 A.M. it was decided to take Eleanor to our apartment and four detectives got in the same car with her after assuring me that they would not molest her in any way despite her beautiful legs. They were quite proper and as far as Eleanor could make out, two of the detectives only went along for the ride because it was on their way home.

Eleanor was handed over to still another detective who was stationed in the portiere's lodge. He permitted Pibe to go alone into the apartment where she found the cook and maid still up and in a fine state of nerves as a result of frequent police visits to search the apartment to make sure we hadn't slipped in at some time or other. Pibe just wanted to go to sleep, but the servants insisted on cooking some of our hoarded spaghetti and eggs as a gesture of sympathy.

Hours later I was taken to Queen of Heaven jail. The two detectives asked me whether I wanted to go by bus or taxi.

"What's the difference?" I asked.

"The bus is free but the taxi you pay for."

I didn't relish being escorted in a crowded bus by police. I agreed to pay.

We reached the Queen of Heaven jail about 9 A.M. I was immediately fingerprinted and then, for some unknown reason, was locked up in a smelly toilet which kept flushing automatically. Through the keyhole I saw prisoners, handcuffed with huge wooden blocks and their legs chained, go clanking by. An hour later I was taken before another official, who took my passport, about three hundred dollars in lire, for which I was given a receipt, and next I found myself in a big office where two wardens ordered me to strip naked. They then examined my clothes carefully, including the coat lining and trouser cuffs. My garments were returned to me except for my belt, tie, and scarf. I was given two pieces of bread and handed over to a guard who marched me through endless corridors. My unbelted trousers kept falling down, tripping me like a hobo. I was finally locked in a cold cell with concrete walls, one heavy wooden door, and a barred window facing a dark courtyard.

An hour later a gray-haired Italian who had a two weeks' beard was shoved in with me. He told me he had been arrested for safecracking but that this time he was innocent.

"Just because I was caught cracking a safe once, I am arrested every time a safe is cracked and they can't find the man who did it."

The old lag taught me tricks of prison life. How to pile up our two iron cots so we could walk in a straight line. He suggested I remove my overcoat, saying, "It will be colder tonight. Then you can put it on and feel warmer." There was one wooden bucket in our cell for corporal needs, but he warned against using it except just before 6 P.M. and 7 A.M. when a trustee came to empty it. Later we were each given a bowl of soup which I was unable to stomach, but the old lag consumed mine as well as his. We were also given wooden spoons and forks.

"So we cannot kill each other or commit suicide," he explained.

The old lag frightened me when he used the wooden bucket to urinate. He made no effort to conceal his penis, which he shook after he finished voiding and then caressed with one hand after the other. When he finally put it back in his trousers, he left his fly open so that I could see it dangling inside.

"Do you go in for buggery or cocksucking?" he asked me.

"No," I said. "This is my first experience in jail."

"You'll learn," he said. "If you're fussy we can just toss each other off. What about it? You're a sexy-looking ragazzo."

"Well, maybe if I'm here long enough, we'll try it, but just now I am pretty well satisfied."

He took out his lingam and waved it at me. Then he put it back into his trousers, but left the fly open.

"Just remember, any time you want it, you can have it. And I'll be glad to suck you off any time."

"Thanks. I'll bear that in mind."

For the next three days I had trouble with the old lag. Whenever I would go to the bucket to piddle, he would come over and watch me.

"Don't hide your cazzo," he said. "It's nothing to be ashamed of. Not so big as mine, but a nice one."

On the third afternoon, a warden came and took me out of the cell. We walked through a labyrinth of steel corridors to an empty room where two wardens seemed to be in charge. They then ordered me to drop my trousers. While they frisked me for hidden objects, Livingston Pomeroy came in and started laughing.

"What's so funny?" I snapped.

"I always wanted to catch my boss with his pants down."

After we dressed and were leaving, Dick Massock of the AP and Herbert Matthews came in. Matthews said: "I think the embassy has got us paid cells."

This proved right. Pomeroy and myself found ourselves in a cell as small as the one I had been in but with sheets, better mattresses, and clean blankets.

"Am I glad to see you, for once," I said to Pomeroy. "I was stuck in with a sex maniac."

"You were lucky. I was all alone. Nobody even to talk to. Hey, listen to that."

I listened. We heard tappings on the concrete wall. Pomeroy soon guessed our neighbors were using the Morse code. He began tapping back. They said they were political prisoners and asked us why we were in jail. Pomeroy replied: "We are Americans. Musso has declared war on

America.''

''Sorry to hear that,'' came back the reply. ''That's news to us.''

That evening we were permitted to buy against the money taken from us a can of bully beef and a glass of red wine each. It was good fare after the slop I had had with the old lag.

Lunch the next day was even better with chicken and a whole carafe of wine.

The warden said he had a brother in Chicago and liked Americans. He hinted that he was in a position to get us bootleg food that would make us forget we were in prison — if we were willing to pay for it.

The next three days, he kept his word and we had meat, beans, and broccoli with both red and white wine as well as a jigger each of sambuca complete with three coffee beans.

''If we stay here long enough,'' Pomeroy said, ''We will be able to have the warden's daughter.''

But after about a week in prison, the warden came to us one afternoon and whispered in half English, half Italian: ''You leave carcere.''

Later, he returned and ordered us to follow him. We trudged through more steel corridors to the inception office where we had all left our valuables and forbidden bits of clothing. Here all the other American correspondents were gathered. Detectives were also there and laughed and joked with us for leaving the hospitality of the Queen of Heaven jail so soon.

''Now you are real Romani,'' one of them said. ''You have spent time in Regina Coeli.''

After putting on our ties, belts, and scarves, we were led out by the detectives, who asked us whether we wanted to travel by bus or taxi. They refused to say where we were going, but we all opted for taxis.

We ended up at the Pensione Suquet, which had once been a brothel on the Corso Umberto. There were three rooms with one bathroom for the six correspondents who had been arrested. The bedroom of Pomeroy and myself was also the dining room and lounge, but it seemed deluxe after the prison. Detectives sat in the hallway guarding us. We were sealed off in the back section of the third floor of the pensione away from the regular boarders, who seemed to include a number of displaced Italian diplomats of the second and third secretary category. The six Americans comprised Matthews, Cianfarra, Pomeroy, Massock, Robert Allen-Tulska, and myself. Allen-Tulska, an American who had lived in Como for many years, was taken on by me just six weeks before Mussolini's declaration of war as a replacement for Aldo Forte, who was transferred to Switzerland. Allen-Tulska's wife, an Italian, was the first visitor at the Pensione Suquet. She took a message to Eleanor for me.

The next day Eleanor, who arranged through the Ministry of Unpopular Culture to visit all six of us twice daily at mealtimes, brought along our cook and maid. The Italian detectives, who liked the looks of them, permitted them to act as food bearers and waitresses. The combination of our black-market provisions and the Suquet fare resulted in fairly substantial meals.

On our third day at the pensione, the glamorous Teddy Lynch, who had sung at the Stork Club before coming to Rome to study opera, was brought in by the police. She was still trembling with her harrowing experience. She had been arrested on December 11, suspected of intelligence activity, and had been held in the Women's Prison of Rome for five days in the same cell with an abortionist and an Austrian Jewess accused of espionage. Tall, stately, and titian-haired, she still had sex appeal despite her bedraggled appearance. Everybody called her Teddy Lynch, including herself, although she could have kept the name of her former husband, millionaire J. Paul Getty.

"I hope prison life hasn't ruined my voice," Teddy said.

She soon had the Italian detectives running errands for her and by the next day an amazing amount of luggage and clothes, all kinds of games, and a collection of stuffed Donald Ducks and teddy bears filled her room, which was on the same floor as ours but separated by a long hallway. She was allowed to eat with us.

"I do hope you don't mind my spending most of my time in your room," she said to Pomeroy and me, "but I don't feel safe with those detectives who keep knocking on my door all the time and asking the stupidest questions like, what do I think of Latin lovers."

Two days later, Count di Sorbello, one of the lesser-ranking officials of the Ministry of Unpopular Culture, paid us a visit. Speaking as always with an Oxford accent, he apologized for our imprisonment, saying the authorities had heard on the radio that Italian correspondents in the U.S. had been arrested, and so we were given reciprocal treatment, "Now we know that wasn't true," he said.

"The day after tomorrow you will be leaving for Siena, where you will be lodged in the best hotel, the Excelsior."

"But you might have confirmed the facts first," muttered Matthews.

"What about Teddy Lynch?" asked Pomeroy.

"She is a special case," Sorbello said. "It has nothing to do with the press ministry."

We were all allowed several hours at our homes to get packed for the trip to Siena, and the next day the seven correspondents were off on a regular passenger train guarded by about ten detectives, Eleanor having joined the six of us who had been in Regina Coeli jail.

Just before New Year's, Teddy Lynch was brought to Siena, too, and put into the Excelsior with the rest of us where we were very comfortably installed. Eleanor and I each had a single room with bath, but we converted one into a living room and used the other as our bedroom. The other correspondents all had single rooms with bath, and we were given an enormous room as sort of clubroom where we could play cards, chess and lounge around without being watched by the Italians. It also had a fireplace where we broiled bootleg steaks and baked potatoes in the ashes.

As far as Teddy Lynch could make out, she was finally made a correspondent on the basis that she had an old letter from Allen Raymond while he was still in Rome, authorizing her to send interesting news items to his paper, the *New York Herald-Tribune,* by mail for consideration by the editor. In that way, the Italians were able to drop the spy charges and make her a member of the Fourth Estate.

In mid-February of 1942 David Colin, who had been appointed NBC representative in Rome just a short time before Mussolini declared war but had not been officially accredited, was also brought to the Excelsior. He completed the group and contributed to upsetting everybody by winning consistently at bridge.

To cope with the boredom of internment, the group of nine took up one hobby after another. First it was visiting the historic monuments of Siena, including the zebra-striped Siena Cathedral, the fourteenth-century Palazzo Pubblico, art galleries, various churches, the home of Saint Catherine, and mounting the many towers of the town. Many of the group became collectors of antiques and spent hours poking around in dusty, rubbishy antique shops, hoping to find genuine Renaissance masters. A number of spurious paintings were purchased by the more enthusiastic shoppers. Next, there was a bicycling craze, and to everyone's astonishment no objection was made by the police to long, cross-country excursions during which contraband eggs, butter, and flour were bought from farmers.

The detectives, who undoubtedly got a cut like the good pimps they were, insisted on taking the men to the local bordello. I must say it was a pleasant change from the hotel. It was warmly heated and the girls didn't hesitate to show preference for the Americans as more carefree spenders than the locals or the soldiers who had to be taken on by the girls at the equivalent of twenty-five cents. But Italian brothels were not like those in France. There was no drinking nor sitting around in the display room with the inmates. The girls, who wore bathing suits, evening gowns, or just scanty undies, were never naked. They didn't mingle with the men but stood on a staircase waiting for customers to make a choice. The prostitutes waggled their tongues lasciviously or bent over and stroked their own buttocks to indicate their specialties. Talking and laughter were frowned upon by the madam. She sat behind a high desk and gave each girl a token coin as she went upstairs.

As for myself, I generally paid the girl I took upstairs three times the regular price in order to have a little time to chat with her. I learned that the German militaries in the area had their own private brothels and that the prostitutes in them were paid better than in the Italian establishments. The girls in the Italian houses were fairly well fed, mainly on spaghetti, and were strictly checked against venereal disease.

As part of our goldfish-bowl philosophy, I always told Pibe when I went to a casa chiusa — so called because of shuttered windows — and she immediately would make me shower, gargle, and use a prophylaxis.

"This being married and interned is double internment," she complained.

I finally arranged with the hall porter to get a masseur. He turned out to be a queer. He gave both Pibe and me titillating massages, and as soon as he left, she and I would make fantastic love. We both admitted he had a maestro's touch.

What impressed us most about internment was how friendly everybody in the town was to us. At one cinema the girl ticket-seller wouldn't let us pay because she said she was engaged to an American in Newark, N.J., and all Americans could enter free.

One time Pomeroy, Pibe, Teddy Lynch, and I were laughing at some of our own jokes during a very dull film in another movie house. Two Italian men behind us timidly said: "Scusi. Would you mind making less noise so we can hear the dialogue."

Count Chigi, who sponsored chamber music, invited our group to his Sunday afternoon concerts. We finally stopped going for fear he would get in trouble for fraternizing with the enemy.

"When people listen to music," he said, "there are no enemies."

In honor of Pibe's birthday, the group decided to give a little dinner party at the best restaurant in town. It was located in the main square where in peacetime the Palio — a race by local youths on bareback farm horses — is held. Matthews had called and reserved nine places in a private upstairs room. As we were mounting the steps, we ran into a harangue by a Black Shirt colonel who was yelling at the maître d'hôtel: "I don't care if this room is already reserved. I want it. I insist on having it for my guests. I am the head Fascist in this town. Do you understand?"

The waiter humbly replied: "Yes, sir, but here come the people now."

The Black Shirt colonel looked around at us.

"Oh, Americans," he said. "That's different. Of course you can have the room. Have a good time."

He gave us an energetic salute and smiled as he walked down the stairs.

All this friendliness toward us while we were interned as enemies made me think that perhaps every Italian is born with a built-in computer which tells him well in advance who is going to win the war. Or, perhaps a little friendliness is always good insurance.

# CHAPTER XVII

On a Sunday afternoon a detective came into the bar and tobacco shop where Dick Massock and I were playing Russian billiards and informed us that we were to appear with the rest of our group at the Siena Questura at 8 P.M. The questore, who was officially stern, tried to talk to us like enemy aliens. He announced that we would be leaving for Rome on Tuesday morning for eventual repatriation. His reserve broke down, however, when Massock shouted out, "Yipee."

Then he smilingly said: "I am as glad to get rid of you as you are to go."

We left Siena by train at 6:50 A.M. In Rome we were met by the police who took us in their official cars to the luxurious Grand Hotel. It was quite a triumphant return to Rome, where we had been kept behind prison bars and put up in a third-rate pensione that once had been a third-rate whorehouse.

The police this time were much more relaxed than before with regard to our liberty of action. Allen-Tulska, for example, was permitted to go out in the custody of his Italian wife, and Pomeroy in the custody of his sister, who was married to an Italian baron. We made the most of the eight days we spent in Rome and although we were always accompanied by an Italian detective or two, went to all the best restaurants and even to the livelier underground cafés where there were music and singing. In one nightclub we were nearly arrested when drinking with a group of B-girls, who were curious that we spoke English among ourselves.

"How is that?" one of the girls asked. "We are at war with England and America."

"We are American paratroopers in disguise," Pomeroy whispered in a conspiratorial tone. "We just dropped in and are hiding out here until it's time for the attack."

"Paracadutisti americani!" two of the girls shrieked.

We were grabbed by both civilian and military Italians and had a bad time until our own detectives came in and identified us as American internees being exchanged for Italian internees in the United States.

It cost us a half-dozen bottles of spumante at champagne prices to get ourselves out of that mess.

Every night, very late, Pibe and I would have a nightcap at the Grand Hotel bar which is just off the lounge. We used to drink with Pietro the barman. On our last night he bought us an Italian brandy — Vecchia Romagna — and toasted our return to Italy.

"That will mean the end of Fascism and the war. Here's to your return," Pietro whispered.

"Here's to our return," we whispered back.

Probably to make our departure as unobtrusive as possible the foreign office had arranged for our leaving to take place at the siesta hour, and at 2:45 P.M. on May 13, 1942, a big red bus slipped away from the side street beside the Grand Hotel and took us on a half-hour ride to the rarely used Ostiense station on the outskirts of Rome. The station had been specially built to receive Hitler when he made his 1938 visit to Italy.

Even at the station we continued to find evidence of Italian regard for America. Right in front of the foreign office officials, a number of the carabinieri who were on guard at the railway platform asked us to look up their relatives in the United States. One, who gave us the address of his brother, said: "Tell him I will join him in Brooklyn as soon as this war is over."

Then the train began moving and several wives of embassy officials, who had been playing at Betsy Ross, pulled out little American flags they had made and waved them as the train moved out of the station, headed for Lisbon where we embarked on the Swedish exchange ship *Drottingholm* for New York.

Before the *Drottingholm* even docked, two intelligence officers, one British and one American, whom I had known as correspondents in

Czechoslovakia during the Sudeten crisis, knocked on our cabin door.

Ralph Izzard, of the *London Daily Mail,* was one of them. He did most of the talking and right in front of Pibe, whom they both knew.

"Listen, Pack, old boy, we've got a lot of people to talk to today on important matters," Izzard said. "You know you have the reputation of being an expert on whorehouses — excuse me, Mrs. Packard, but your husband is one of the few reporters who ever writes about them — and I want you to give me a quick rundown on the best bordellos in Rome where we can place spies to get ship and troop movements."

I told him the best I could about the fact that the Germans ran their own brothels, but he didn't seem interested.

"We are more concerned about the Italian houses because Italians talk more freely. They have no sense of security like the Germans."

I gave him a list of the ones particularly patronized by Italian sailors, including two on via Mario dei Fiori and one on via Capo le Case. They made notes and left.

"I am glad to know you are an expert on something," Pibe said sarcastically. "So even British and American intelligence services know you are a whoremonger."

When we reached the New York office of the UP, Miles Vaughn, the day editor, said: "Now you can really tell us what a son of a bitch Mussolini is. There's no censorship here on running down the enemy. If you think he has syphilis and it's eating up his brain, just say so. Just use plenty of purple ink and make him look like a real bastard. Do it under a joint by-line."

"Okay," I said. We'll try our best."

We wrote what we considered a fairly strong story about Mussolini being a womanizer, making promiscuity a Fascist principle; how he would seldom give interviews to a girl reporter unless he laid her; and how he had seduced the very young Clara Petacci, daughter of an accredited physician to the Holy See. We recalled how he insisted on official cameramen taking his pictures from below knee level in order to make him look big because he had a dwarf complex.

Vaughn read it over. I could see he didn't like it very much.

"I don't know. It doesn't make him look bad enough. We'll have to use it, though, as we are filling the wires with all the inside stories of you returned correspondents. And we've got to get something off early on Musso."

The next morning, although we were supposed to have several days rest, Vaughn called up and wanted us to write a more vitriolic story about the Duce.

"Can't you think of something terrible about that half-ass dictator?"

"Okay, we'll try again."

"I've got it," Eleanor told me. "Let's write about the day the correspondents spent with Mussolini. We'll make his tennis game the lead."

"You genius," I cried. "Let's get it written and rush it around to Vaughn."

We sat down and dashed it out together, always a harder job than you think, two persons writing the same story and generally disagreeing with each other on the details. But we pieced it together on the typewriter. Vaughn was pleased with it, and it was given a big play in most of the newspapers in America and England under the general headline of "Il Duce Cheats at Tennis."

# PART II

# THE POPE
# AND
# GENERAL
# MARK CLARK

# CHAPTER I

After our return home from internment, the UP didn't seem to know what to do with Pibe and me. She was sent out on wartime stories in the New York area, involving warship launchings and airplane production. I was sent to the Caribbean to write a series of feature articles about U.S. bases established there against German submarine attacks and to arrange for stringers to report on any U-boat activities after I left.

Then Eleanor was sent to Turkey while I was still away, and a month later I was dispatched to North Africa. There was a backlog of air transport because of the forthcoming Casablanca conference between Churchill and Roosevelt along with their leading political and military advisers; there was no way for mere correspondents to travel by plane. The preparations for the conference were top secret, of course, and nobody in the UP knew why its reporters weren't being allocated places on planes. I heard of a Portuguese steamer that was leaving from Hoboken, New Jersey, and decided to take passage on that. It took twenty-eight days, zigzagging from its course at the radio commands of German submarines and Allied warships — the Germans wanting to conceal their attacks in the mid-Atlantic and the Allies to keep the whereabouts of their convoys a secret.

Finally, reaching Portugal, I caught the last plane from Lisbon to Tangiers and from there made it to Gibraltar by a cockleshell motorboat.

The motorboat was supposed to be safe because it was too tiny to waste a torpedo on. From Gibraltar I flew by a U.S. military plane to Algiers where Allied Force headquarters had been set up. The picturesque city, half Arab, half French, was full of spot news, veteran correspondents I knew, and luscious French girls I wanted to know. Many of them were very generous with their carnal treasures once they were certain of receiving a petit cadeau afterwards — and not too petit at that.

Their most-favored customers at the time were American airmen who were trying to get in all the screwing possible before being shot down. Some of the U.S. fliers had been on more than sixty bombing raids over enemy territory and were beginning to think their luck was running out. I felt a bit the same way after I had made only ten runs, including a rugged flight over Budapest during which one crew member of the Flying Fortress I was in was killed and two others were wounded by flak. I was really scared that time. Weighing 255 pounds in those days, I couldn't even squeeze through an escape hatch with a parachute strapped on my back. I was five foot nine and seemed to be mostly belly.

I also remember the air raid on Palermo, before the invasion of Sicily. I wasn't permitted to attend the briefing of that one. A public relations captain took me out to a Flying Fortress and intoduced me to the crew. After he had gone the pilot asked me, "Do you know what the target is today?"

"No, I didn't get in on the briefing. It was pretty hush-hush."

"No wonder," the pilot said. "You know what day it is?"

"Sure, Sunday."

"Well, we've been ordered to drop the eggs on Palermo itself just before noon when obviously there will be a helluva lot of Wops coming out of church this bright Sabbath. Plenty of women and children are the target. Well, this crew is dumping its load of eggs on the harbor. I'm not in this war to kill women and children."

"They told us the idea is to give the Itais a helluva scare that'll blast Italy right out of the war. Force them into a separate peace," the bombardier joined in. "Fuck 'em. I'm not doin' it. The harbor's good enough for me."

A signal was given. The crews that had been clustered in groups all over the huge field scampered into planes. I was inside a Fortress and looking out. The engines were being warmed up slowly as if there was no hurry. The planes took off, one after another. It was the first all-American air raid against metropolitan Italy. There were over two hundred Flying

90

Fortresses on the Constantine airfield. They rose gradually, almost reluctantly, like fat birds that had gorged themselves on too big a meal; only this time the meal of bombs would be regurgitated. The planes reached an altitude of some twenty thousand feet and straightened out. The flight to the target took nearly two hours, giving me plenty of chance to worry before running into the ack-ack. I was in one of the lead planes. Below me in the near distance I could see the buildings of Palermo dazzling white in the summer sun before the bombs burst around them.

The ack-ack blossomed into black puffs that resembled black chrysanthemums against the robin's-egg blue of the sky. They made an unpleasant sound like dogs barking at night. From the ground great billows of black and gray rose skyward, toward the planes, slowly, majestically tinted here and there with splashes of saffron from the flames of burning buildings. It was the diabolical artistry of destruction, the beauty and power of it, rising above the anguish it had caused on the earth below, the bleeding and sobbing of the wounded and dying. Then the field of ack-ack was left behind, and the waist-gunners went into action against enemy fighters that buzzed in and out of our formation like wasps.

Back on the ground, the bombardier told me: "I made sure our bombs didn't kill any women and children. I dropped them on water. I just hope we got some ships, but we weren't briefed on the harbor."

The crews lined up for doughnuts and coffee served by pretty Red Cross girls in gunmetal-colored uniforms. Everybody was happy. There was at least another twenty-four hours to live.

The American air force was wonderful at public relations. One of the great phrases coined by the master copywriters was pinpoint bombing. It meant dropping a bomb within one mile of a given target. If you work it out, it comes to anywhere within four square miles around the objective.

I also covered in the field the mass surrenders of German and Italian troops in North Africa and jeeped into Tunis as it fell.

Most of the correspondents stayed in the Aletti Hotel in Algiers, where we had to triple, quadruple, and even quintuple up in one room, some using portable cots. All the beds were constantly warm with the newsmen sleeping or fucking in them in continuous shifts.

As soon as I had reached Algiers, the UP put out full-page ads in trade magazines like *Editor and Publisher* featuring a picture of me in uniform with a gold-braided "C" for correspondent on the cap. The punch line was: "Packard Arrives in Algiers En Route to Reopen the United Press Office in Rome."

It didn't strike me as a very brilliant advertising gimmick but I liked the bit of luster it gave me. It also meant the New York office still regarded me as an executive type.

Little by little I became the assistant to Virgil Pinkley, who held the title of North African bureau manager. When I wasn't in the field or in the air, Virgil and I worked like a team. All dispatches that both he and I sent for morningers were signed by him even though I wrote half of them, and all the dispatches intended for afternooners were signed Packard even though he wrote half of them. With this system we cooperated as well as any agency team there. For example, he would generally write the lead while I, simultaneously, would be writing the add to it. Then he would jump to the third take while I would be banging out the fourth.

Hugh Baillie, the UP president, arrived and genially acted as copyboy, running dispatches from the newsroom to the censors' office down the hall where each message was given a number marking its place in the sending order. Bulky as a fullback, Baillie barreled his way through frailer correspondents who were trying to perform the same service for their colleagues. It was important work because the copy piled up so fast that a gap of five numbers could represent a half-hour's delay in a message being sent.

Then the invasion of Sicily took place. Chris Cunningham, one of the UP staff in Algiers, went with the invading forces. Richard McMillan, another Unipresser, flew over the Sicilian beaches and gave a description which was one of the most enigmatic accounts of the war. He described the thousands of landing craft that hit the beaches as looking like water bugs from the air, but he never made clear whether anybody landed. His vagueness was to get around censorship. Later, the communiqué declared that the invasion had been a success and that the Allied forces had gained a considerable foothold on the island.

A few days later, U.S. Army intelligence reported that the Italian army in Sicily had vanished overnight. There just weren't any Italians left wearing uniforms. They had buried their military attire and borrowed civilian clothes. This defection left entire sectors unmanned and the Allied forces had no trouble in making fantastic advances.

Inside information in Algiers had it that Lucky Luciano, once the rackets king of New York, who was serving a fifty-five year sentence in Sing Sing, was the mastermind behind the mass desertion of Italian militaries in Sicily. He was authoritatively stated to have sent a coded message to Mafia leader Don Calogero Vizzini asking him to help the

Allies and at the same time revive the Black Hand organization that had been driven into dormant undercover by Mussolini. According to the report, the message was placed in a wallet and dropped from a U.S. fighter plane close to Vizzini's house a few days before the Sicilian invasion started in July 1943. The plane had a black initial "L" for Lucky painted on a yellow background. The wallet was wrapped in a yellow handkerchief with a big black "L" on it. The report stressed that Lucky and Vizzini had communicated regularly before the war and that Lucky had done several favors in the United States for Vizzini.

Some correspondents close to high American army sources, including myself, sent the story but the censors killed it. When I objected, one of them looked at me angrily and shouted: "You can't send it because it gives aid and comfort to the enemy. You are telling the world that our heroic advances in Sicily are due to the Mafia and to that arch-pimp of the underworld, Lucky Luciano. It's pro-Fascist, pro-Nazi propaganda."

However, years later, after talking to Lucky Luciano in Italy and to other Italo-American deportees as well as Italian army officers, I am inclined to believe the report was substantially correct. It would also explain why Thomas E. Dewey, who as a young crime-buster sent Luciano up the river in 1936 for compulsory prostitution, turned around ten years later as governor and pardoned him for no clear reason.

# CHAPTER II

On July 25, 1943, high-powered Allied radio stations in Algiers picked up Rome broadcasts disclosing the results of the Fascist Grand Council. They were sensational. Mussolini had been outmaneuvered and bounced out of power. Even Ciano, his own son-in-law, often regarded as a mere playboy, was one of the leaders who dared to speak out against Il Duce.

"You concentrate on the Musso story," Pinkley told me. "Don Coe will take your place with the war communiqués."

Pale and haggard, Mussolini opened the Grand Council trying to explain away the defeats of the Axis in North Africa, the disastrous end of the Italian army in Russia, Italy's pitiful invasion of Greece, and finally the vanishing of the Italian troops in Sicily. Mussolini admitted in his report that an angry Hitler had refused to send any more reinforcements to bolster the Italian defenses in Sicily. It was smooth-talking, spade-bearded Dino Grandi, a former Fascist foreign minister and for seven years Fascist Italy's ambassador to the Court of Saint James, who started the revolt. He rose to his feet to reply to Mussolini. With all his noted diplomacy, Grandi proposed that Il Duce should give up his command of the armed forces, turning it over to King Victor Emmanuel.

"The Italian soldier might show more willingness to fight for his country if the Italian forces were removed from their present political position and made into a national fighting body," Grandi slyly explained.

"This would help the very war effort that is part of Il Duce's policy and program."

General De Bono, perhaps still resenting his recall by Musso as commander-in-chief of the Fascist forces in Ethiopia, quietly arose when Grandi finished speaking amidst cautious applause and seconded the motion, adding a few strong words on how the Duce's war policy had resulted in ever-increasing defeats, with the latest disaster being the landing of Allied forces in Sicily and their inevitable take-over of the entire island.

Ciano spoke next. His wife, Edda Mussolini, had often been credited with having convinced her father to become Hitler's partner in the Rome-Berlin Axis. The usually dapper count minced no phrases in telling his father-in-law that he should resign as commander-in-chief of the Italian armed forces and let the king take over that post while Italy continued fighting.

Dazed but still tough, Musso jutted out his jaw and called for a vote on the Grandi proposal. He announced the results in a faltering voice: "The motion is carried by eleven votes to seven."

Benito's glowering face paled. He turned his back on the meeting and stalked out.

The next afternoon, Mussolini, as was his custom after a Fascist Grand Council session, called on the king to report on the proceedings. The bantam dictator and the diminutive monarch had a real head-on clash with Mussolini, a blacksmith's son, shouting, ranting, and using such Italian invectives as *stronzo, cazzo, merda,* and *figlio di puttana.* The king's always low-timbred voice became a squeak, according to royal aides in the next room, but he stood up to the bellowing strong man, saying that Badoglio, who had been made a field marshal and the duke of Addis Ababa by Mussolini himself, was replacing him as premier. And this should please the Duce.

Mussolini stormed out of the reception room where the meeting was taking place and rushed down the steps two at a time. He reached the inner courtyard of the royal residence. And for weeks nobody knew what happened to him after that. Nobody saw him leave. There were only unconfirmed reports that he had been whisked away to a series of hideouts, a prisoner of Badoglio and the King.

Victor Emmanuel immediately assumed command of all the Italian armed forces and Badoglio, the anti-Fascist hero of the Fascist invasion of Ethiopia, took over the premiership. Italian style, both the king and

Badoglio while plotting to switch over to the Allies formally announced they would continue to fight alongside the Germans.

Many Italians were actually shocked at what they termed the king's lack of noblesse oblige by arresting Mussolini while he was still a guest in the royal residence. One prominent monarchist, who later became a liberal, told me: "Victor Emmanuel should not have arrested Mussolini when he called on the sovereign as a confiding visitor and personal friend. It was a dastardly betrayal even though the dictator deserved it."

# CHAPTER III

Then came the preparations for the landing on the mainland of Italy while the fighting was still going on in Sicily. I was among the volunteers for that mission. Slips of paper, each containing the name of a volunteer, were put into the cap of General Mark Clark's chief press officer, Lt. Col. Ken Clark. He was no relation to the general. I drew, luckily or unluckily, a place with Mark Clark. I was to sail aboard and land from the *Ancron,* known as the brain ship of the invasion.

Like many of the airmen, before taking off on a dangerous bombing mission, I also wanted to be laid. Or for that matter I was like a GI on leave just before returning to the front. He wanted a fuck before risking death: it would be terrible to die without a last piece of tail.

I decided the easiest way was to go to an Algiers brothel the night I boarded the headquarters ship. Now I realized why the two Anglo-American intelligence officers asked me about whorehouses in Rome when I arrived in New York. Only I knew I wasn't going to talk in any way about the little I knew of the forthcoming operation to the inmates of any bordello. The secret was safe with me because I didn't want the ship on which I was a passenger to be torpedoed by a German submarine nor bombed from the air. In the huge Moorish-style house of pleasure, I saw a number of colleagues who also had drawn spots on the invasion. The place was run the French way with a bar in a central display room brilliantly illuminated and full of mirrors on the walls and on the ceiling, reproducing all movement many times over. Many of the girls wore only a scarf around their necks. One blonde, symbolically, wore a small purse over her pussy.

As I was drinking a beer and looking over the inmates, a cry went up: "Here he comes. . . . Give him a hand. . . . Bring out the mattresses."

There was some handclapping, and two of the women hauled out a couple of mattresses from a closet and threw a clean sheet over them. A red-headed captain bowed. He put his crumpled American air corps cap on the floor.

"Here's my contribution to the girls who participate," he said, holding up a ten-dollar bill and then dropping it into his cap. "You spectators must contribute, too. It all goes to the girls."

Almost everybody pulled out dollar bills, from ones to tens, and deposited them in his cap. Then the show started. Two almost naked girls, one Arab and one French, appeared on the scene and helped the red-headed captain to undress. When he was naked, they threw off their few decorative bits of apparel and began to caress him. You could easily tell which girl was which. The Arab had her pubic hair shaved off while the French girl had a luxuriantly hairy triangle.

Their ministrations soon gave the captain an enviable erection. I have noted that most male exhibitionists always have extremely well-developed sex organs.

"It is five past one," a French officer called out, referring to the almost upright angle of the captain's erection. There was general applause. The French girl began sucking his cock, and the Arab girl strapped on a dildo covered with a vaseline-smeared condom and started buggering him.

"Christ," he shouted. "I'm coming." He closed his eyes, groaned as a third girl rushed up to him and kissed him on the mouth.

The U.S. flier then proceeded to make love to six girls one after another amidst melodramatic grunts, groans, and shrieks produced by both himself and his partners. After he had completed his performance with the sixth girl, a British officer rushed forward and helped him to his feet. He held the American's hand up high and yelled: "The Champ!" The redhead grinned happily.

There was more handclapping, and the exhibition came to an end. I went back to the bar and soon found myself talking in French to an Arab girl. She was one of the girls who had been on the mattress with the redhead. I thought to myself she had been pretty good. I ought to try her.

98

I offered her a drink and she accepted. I had an Algerian wine while she sipped some kind of an expensive concoction, that was probably just colored water.

"Let's go up to my room, chéri," she suggested.

"I'd be ashamed to compete with that redhead," I said. "He was so good."

"Don't be silly. You don't need to worry about him. I'll tell you about him upstairs."

I ordered a bottle of Algerian wine to be sent up for me along with two expensive drinks for her and paid in advance for two hours of her time. I didn't want to be hurried. I also liked the idea of a wine and a woman of the foreign country I was in.

As we stretched out naked on the bed, I asked what she meant when she had said I didn't need to worry about the redhead.

"Oh," she replied. "It's just a stunt he pulls off. There's something wrong with him. He can get a beautiful hard-on but he can't come. He just pretends, and the girls pretend, and everybody gets excited and rushes upstairs afterwards. The madame encourages him parce que c'est très bon pour le commerce, but he is frustrated because he can never come. Not even a drop."

She told me her name was Ayesha. She looked more naked without any pubic hair.

"Why do you shave down there?" I asked.

"The Koran says we should."

"Why?"

"Cleanliness. Shaving, I never get crabs. If you stay in Algiers, you had better shave down there, too."

"Even if I screw only girls without hair?"

"Mais oui. You get crabs riding camels, sitting in the cheap sections of cinemas, just mixing with poor people. Assez with such bug talk. Let me make that little prick of yours grow up, make it erect like a soldier, ready to shoot."

She started stroking my cock, she was sucking it, and soon she rolled over on top of me, impaling herself with quick, expert movements. She kept me inside of her while she rotated her body and at the same time pushed herself up and down. She pretended she was in agony, grunting and groaning. I knew she was faking but the sound effect was terrific. It made me come immediately. She let me doze for twenty minutes and then she began all over again. This time the orgasm was longer in arriving and more exquisitely painful when it did.

Finally, exhausted, satisfied, and tingling with prophylaxis, I left her. I walked to the Aletti, picked up my kit, and joined the *Ancron*. I felt ready to face death.

# CHAPTER IV

About the second night out a rumor spread aboard the *Ancron* that German airplanes were searching for the brain ship. If they could smash all the eggs in that one floating basket, there wouldn't be anybody left to direct the invasion. It struck me as a pretty risky operation putting all the big brass in one little defenseless craft. It had high-powered radar equipment that made it stand out in silhouette as the most important communications ship of the attacking force.

"We've broken all radio communication with the other ships and AFHQ so the Germans can't detect us," a ship's officer told me. "It means, of course, we can't call for air cover if we need it."

Then members of the medical corps began placing wire stretchers around the deck, in the lounge, and in the dining salons. They were frightening things to look at. They reminded me of trays in self-service restaurants. The various wire compartments were for blown-off or severed members of the body so they could be placed where they belonged like a sort of physiological jigsaw puzzle. Enemy planes came roaring in overhead, dropping bombs arounds us. Thank our lucky stars, it was a moonless night.

I remember Quentin Reynolds wearing a steel helmet and chain-smoking. He was pale and looked frightened. But I thought to myself, he is not half so scared as I am. I wasn't chain-smoking, but I was drinking White Horse from a hip flask.

This was the occasion that later prompted Westbrook Pegler to denounce Quentin as a scare baby or a coward, but he wasn't any more scared than the rest of us, especially me.

The next day was bright and sunny. I could hear the clangor of the landing craft and the auxiliary ships of Admiral Henry Hewitt's fleet moving ahead. You would think the noise could be heard on the Italian coast.

Clark called Quentin and me to his cabin. He briefed us on topographical maps where the landings would take place in the Bay of Salerno. He said our particular ship would anchor off Paestum, famous for its Greek ruins, and other landing parties would scramble ashore farther north just before the port of Salerno itself. He said he wanted Quentin to explain the tactical maneuvers while I, as co-author with Pibe of *Balcony Empire,* which had become a best seller, was to tell the militaries what kind of people they would meet once they landed on the beaches.

Quentin's voice, confined only to the *Ancron,* was magic over the loudspeaker. Listening to him, I could understand how he became the Voice of Hope when he broadcast in England during the worst of the German air raids.

My voice sounded weak and unconvincing by contrast. I said the American soldiers wouldn't be fighting many Italians because they had already vanished from the military ranks in Sicily. They liked Americans and wouldn't oppose us at Salerno either. "Once we break through the German defenses it will be pleasant going," I said. "Beautiful Italian girls will shower us with flowers, they will kiss us and embrace us." I hinted that a rich sex life was in store for the American soldiers once they got beyond the beaches.

"Already," I continued, "the Italian people have risen up in many parts of Italy against the Germans. The Italian king with his new premier, Pietro Badoglio, have slipped out of Rome and are the rally point in Brindisi, already held by the Allies, in southern Italy. They are the rallying point of anti-Fascist forces who have left the Germans and come over to our side. Mussolini, himself, is a prisoner of the king."

When I had finished speaking, Quentin, who could turn out a book inside of a month with the aid of scissors and paste, asked me for a copy of my speech. I gave it to him, feeling flattered.

"Thanks, Pack," he said. "That'll make a chapter."

That was the night before H hour, D day. I sat in the dining salon where many of the high-ranking officers were going over maps and small models of parts of the shore, studying the terrain. I suddenly started laughing. All these serious colonels and generals were concentrating on landing preparations, but everyone of them had the ringed bottom part of a French letter dangling from one of his shirt pockets. It looked as though they were getting ready to make a pleasure raid on a whorehouse. It reminded me that I should take the same precautions against immersion myself. I put a fountain pen in one rubber, my wristwatch in another, and stuck my war correspondent's identification card and a picture of Pibe in a third condom. I planned to carry ashore a portable Underwood and a Baedeker. In the meantime I typed out notes describing the Bay of Salerno and Paestum from the guidebook. I would send them off as ready-made adds to my landing story.

"Hey, want to go ashore with me at H hour?" a tall slim officer asked me. "General Clark suggested I take you."

"You bet, Bill. That's great."

It was Lt. Col. William Yarborough, a West Pointer from Virginia and the commander of a parachute regiment. He explained that this time he was to go ashore by boat on a special mission for Clark reporting on how each of the various divisional commands had set up headquarters and to bring back his own personal evaluation of the situation. At least I would see some of the fighting if I went with him.

I slept fitfully for several hours, already dressed, and came up on deck to see what was happening. It was still dark, but I could see that the *Ancron* was surrounded by landing craft of all kinds. Apparently everybody was waiting for frogmen to set up colored lights for the various beaches designated by such names as Red Beach and Yellow Beach.

The next thing I knew all hell was exploding. German shells were roaring in, setting fire to some of our naval units, and our naval guns were firing back. Dogfights were going on overhead as German and Allied planes tangled in the air.

Yarborough had a hard time getting sailors to help him lower his boat into the water, there was so much gold braid outranking him. Finally, we were headed for shore. As we neared it, we passed dead bodies, drowned or shot to death but kept afloat by life belts. On the beach we found wounded and more dead. Medics with stretchers were carrying away those who were still alive. Some Messerschmidts came in low over the beach. I dove flat on my face, still clutching my portable typewriter.

Heavy German artillery began finding the beach, tearing up big holes in the sand. I tumbled into one and waited there for nearly half an hour, feeling fairly safe in the erroneous belief that lightning and shells don't hit the same place twice.

There was a lull. I started running, hit or miss, but always inland and toward my right. There was no sign of Yarborough. Finally I came to a tobacco warehouse. I recognized one of the Fifth Army press officers and Tex O'Reilly of the *New York Herald Tribune*. The press officer said a radio station was being set up and soon would be ready to send our copy back to Allied Forces Headquarters in Algiers for relay to New York. The copy was being dispatched in the order filed.

I sat down on the warehouse floor, opened my typewriter, and began belting out a story. It was mostly about my own eyewitness experiences, interspersed with paragraphs from Baedeker describing the Bay of Salerno and the Greek ruins in Paestum. What a waste of time that was!

When the censor finished deleting what he considered military secrets from my dispatch, it came out a very drab message. It read:

11105 DATELINE WITH AMERICAN LANDING FORCE SOMEWHERE IN ITALY STOP US TROOPS HIT ITALIAN COASTLINE TODAY AND SECURED BEACHHEAD AFTER TERRIFIC CLASH WITH GERMAN ARMORED UNITS PARAITALIANS COMMA LOYAL TO KING VICTOR EMMANUEL AND PREMIER BADOGLIO WHO HAVE ARRIVED IN BRINDISI TO COOPERATE WITH THE ALLIES COMMA DIDNT PARTICIPATE IN THE BATTLE PARA GERMAN LOSSES WERE HEAVY STOP LEASTLY ONE DOZEN LUFTWAFFE PLANES WERE DOWNSHOT PARA AMERICAN CASUALTIES WERE SMALL PARA MANY US TANKS COMMA ARMORED CARS AND AMPHIBIOUS DUCKS LANDED AND PROCEEDED INLAND END

PACKARD

It was pretty pathetic mincemeat of all the color and adventure I had written. I protested to the censor, but he explained we could not say the landing was in the Bay of Salerno nor make any mention of Paestum because there had been several diversionary attacks at other points along the Italian coast to fool the Germans, so we couldn't be specific about the Salerno area.

It was all academic anyway because none of our castrated dispatches that day ever reached Algiers. A German station, probably somewhere in Italy, picked up all our messages and gave receipt in the Allied code. They also picked up top secrets sent by Mark Clark and his staff intended for Algiers.

In a few days, the beachhead spread out and included the entire city of Salerno. Communications got better and a new code was established with Algiers. Censors now allowed us to mention Paestum and Salerno by name.

One evening while I was having supper in an officers' mess outside of Salerno, a rumor interrupted the meal. A young officer rushed in and told a full colonel that ten German tanks had broken through the Allied front lines and were headed in our direction. The colonel ordered an ammunition truck to pull up alongside the mess tent. A sergeant started handing out rifles and ammunition to everybody. I hung back. The colonel saw me and noticed my green shoulder insignia indicating I was a war correspondent.

"Hey you, reporter, take this gun," he ordered, handing me a rifle.

"But I'm not supposed to carry a gun," I protested. "It's contrary to the Geneva convention."

"Fuck the Geneva convention. You carry this gun or I'll shoot you dead."

I took the gun gingerly. I had never handled arms in my life except a Baretta in Ethiopia when I escorted Pibe into the bushes to answer nature's demands.

As soon as the scare was over, I returned the weapon to the truck. There hadn't been any breakthrough, but one Kraut tank had gotten lost, and its crew scurrying around on foot to locate their whereabouts were mowed down by the colonel's minutemen before they could surrender.

Clark's Fifth Army was advancing steadily on Naples. Naples had become the next objective, and anything about it was news. I volunteered to fly on any plane reconnoitering above the volcano city. It would make a catchy dateline, I thought: ABOARD A PLANE OVER NAPLES.

By this time I had left the *Ancron* as had all the brains aboard the ship, including Clark. I slept in a slit trench and felt comfortable and snug even during an air raid, figuring the odds of a shell landing exactly inside my gravelike abode were infinitesimal. At least it was consoling logic.

One morning Lt. Col. Clark called me to the press tent to say there was an airplane flying over Naples that morning. If I wanted to make the trip, he said, I'd have to work my weight.

"Okay, I'll go."

I was jeeped to the airport, where besides a crew of two, I met John Whitaker, once of the *New York Herald Tribune* and now in army intelligence. We had met before as correspondents in Ethiopia, Spain, and Rome and didn't like each other.

"What the hell's the mission?" I asked him. "I thought we weren't bombing Naples any more so as not to antagonize the Neapolitans."

"Look at the plane," he said. "It's not a bomber."

As I climbed aboard, Whitaker said, "When we get over Naples, you help me open the floor hatch, and then start tossing out those piles of leaflets. Just be sure you don't go through yourself."

He handed me a parachute and put one on himself.

"I'm too fat to get through with a parachute on," I said. "So forget it."

He laughed and the pilot slammed the door. After we were airborne I read one of the leaflets that were stacked in the middle of the plane. It said: "Citizens of Naples, rise up against the German soldiers occupying your great city by military force. There are only a few of them. Organize yourselves and overpower them. The Allied troops are at your city gates ready to enter and give you liberty. Kill those Germans and you will be freed that much sooner."

It was not signed.

The pilot announced over the loudspeaker, "We are approaching Naples. Start unloading."

Whitaker and I struggled to open the hatch. Then we started pushing, shoving, and throwing stacks of untied leaflets through the hole in the floor of the plane. In my excitement my helmet fell off and went through the hatch with the leaflets.

"That helmet will probably kill somebody," Whitaker said.

His remark upset me, but I kept throwing out the sheets of paper until there weren't any more. I then looked at the streets below. They were empty. It was like a dead city. Nobody came out to look at the leaflets. The mission took less than half an hour.

As soon as I reached the press tent, I started writing out a story about Naples looking like a dead city, there not being signs of Germans, and how the people didn't even come out of their houses to pick up the leaflets. As I was writing Whitaker offered me a drink from a whisky bottle and we made up.

"You're not such a bad son of a bitch after all," he said.

"Same to you," I replied.

The censor of the moment, a paunchy Britisher, came running out to speak to me.

"I say, old boy, we can't possibly pass this dispatch. What you describe is contrary to the Geneva convention which strictly prohibits militaries calling on the civilian population to rise up against its enemy masters."

"How can I get around it?"

"Just delete mention of the bloody leaflets and Whitaker's part in the flight. Describe only what you saw as you did in the message, but don't talk about any leaflets. Then I'll pass your message."

"Okay, I'll do that."

Whitaker started to argue with the censor. The leaflets were his idea, and I had even mentioned him as having personally implemented it by going on the mission himself.

We had just made up but to hell with him. A story was a story. I tore up my original message and began all over again. I just wrote a deadpan eyewitness account which was much better because this psychological warfare stuff almost always fouled up a clear-cut narrative description. At least I had an exclusive bird's-eye account of what Naples looked like on the eve of its fall. I even got congratulations on it from Baillie.

# CHAPTER V

The Fifth Army troops entered Naples, headed by tanks and armored cars, a little after dawn the next day. Three British correspondents were missing. They had been looking down a road near Naples that led to Pompeii. What they were looking at turned out to be a German tank. It opened fire and killed all three of them with a single shell. They were buried beside the road and the advance continued. Most of the newsmen were in jeeps interspersed between the leading tanks. The empty streets of yesterday's dead city were teeming that morning with Neapolitan life. The populace — men, women, and children — crawled all over the vehicles, the artillery and ran up and embraced the foot soldiers, putting flowers in the muzzles of their guns. Italian spontaneity. It was like a bonanza of sex, food, and liquor. Abandon, good fellowship, and the cornucopia of passion spilled out in public. Girls were being fucked on tanks and in trucks. Italian kids were already shouting out: "Caramelle, cigarette, belle donne."

In the midst of this social gala, Mark Clark added to the drama of it all by flying into the center of Naples aboard a tiny two-seater L-5 and landing right on the waterfront not far from the Royal Palace and the San Carlo Opera House.

The correspondents couldn't stay for the saturnalia of victory. They had to rush clear back to file their copy from the press tent still pitched in

Paestum. The boys back in Algiers had already beaten us on the fall of Naples, having flashed from the communiqué issued by Allied Forces Headquarters — still located there — that the Fifth Army had made a bloodless take-over of the great south Italian port. However, we had the kissing and lovemaking and all the excitement of the glorious welcome accorded by the Neapolitans to the Americans and the British. That was a personal story nobody could take away from us. We had our DATELINE NAPLES and the hoisting of the American, British, and French flags over the City Hall and the Royal Palace where once the German colors had been flying. We wrote how the people looked: thin, starving, and haggard; badly dressed, badly nourished, and badly embittered. That was our first impression.

After I had filed my first story from Paestum, I went back to Naples to get a more detailed account of the port city. During the night as I wandered through the blacked-out streets, I found that the most distressing situation involved the thousands of unburied corpses in the city. The smell of death was everywhere. For the past two weeks nobody had been buried. Naples, which generally has a high death rate, had suffered more than usual because of the food shortage and other war conditions. The mortality figures had skyrocketed. Hospitals were piled with decomposing bodies. Private houses also contained corpses.

I reported the situation to a colonel of the medics, who said he knew about the situation, and they would be picking up the bodies and burying them beginning early next morning.

I slept in an abandoned hotel that night on the floor. All the beds and furniture had been removed by retreating Germans or by local pillagers. Twenty minutes after I left the hotel, early in the morning, a time bomb went off in the basement killing four passersby and wounding ten others. From then on, one hotel after another began blowing up from delayed time charges.

Two days later as I was jeeping along with Australian correspondent Noel Monks, whom I had know in Ethiopia and Spain, we passed by the central post office in Naples. There was a terrific blast and the driver, Noel, and I were blown out of the jeep and knocked unconscious. A lethal machine in the basement of the post office, which had been temporarily converted into a barracks for American soldiers, had just gone off. It had been almost a week since the Germans had evacuated the town.

Virtually all the hotels had been wired to explode. Some of the infernal devices were discovered in time and defused, but many hotels were blown up, causing heavy casualties.

The German idea was apparently, aside from killing soldiers, to make it difficult for the Allied Forces Headquarters to set itself up in Naples without confiscating private homes and offices, thus antagonizing the Neapolitans.

Within a few weeks Naples became the crime center of liberated Italy. And the word "liberated" became a dirty joke. It meant to both the Italians and the invaders that an Allied military got something for nothing: such as an Italian's wife or a bottle of brandy which he took from an intimidated bartender without paying for it. Prostitution, black-marketing, racketeering, and confidence games were rampant. Desertions became wholesale: U.S. soldiers would shack up with Italian girls and not bother to return to their regiments. Groups of these deserters banded together and became dangerous outlaws. Scores of amphibious ducks, laden with flour, sugar, and coffee, just disappeared into the underground. Sometimes their drivers would be found unconscious, claiming to have no recollection of what had happended to them.

For many Neapolitans, big business soon became the exploitation of the average GI who came into the city on an occasional day's leave to eat, drink, and get fucked. It was a mixed-up circle. The GIs were selling cigarettes to the Italians, who in turn would sell them back to Americans who had run out of them. But the main trade was trafficking in women. Precocious little boys had the most successful technique. They were constantly offering to arrange for soldiers to go to bed with their sisters or mothers. Not that such statements were necessarily true, but the idea of such depravity seemed to have a Freudian appeal to the fighting man. Or maybe he just thought he was really living it up to buy a sister or a mother from a boy.

Naples became a crucible in which moral values were boiled down to a residue of basic necessities and wild desires.

The urchins soon learned where military buses, bringing GIs into Naples, stopped. They waited there and would chirp their sales slogans as soon as the soldiers got their feet on the ground.

"Want to fuck my sister, only five dollars. . . . Want to fuck my mother. . . . she sucky suck. . . . You can fuck my mother, sister ten dollars. . . ." were some of the sales plugs.

Once he hooked his victim, the kid would suggest going to a bar first for a drink, then to a souvenir shop, and finally to a restaurant. Always there was a commission for the ragazzo from whatever establishment he took a soldier to. And, of course, the girls paid him as the pimp he was.

These juvenile ruffiani had one special brothel for the American Negroes. It was located on a side street just off via Roma.

"You wanna fuck blonde cunt. . . . I getcha girl with blonde cunt. . . . You like blonde pussy. Eatin' blonde pussy?"

One time I followed a boy who was taking a black soldier to the house of blonde snatches. It was true all right. They had blonde pubic hair, but they were wigs which the girls pasted on after shaving their brunette vaginas.

I interviewed one of the high officials of the AMG — Allied Military Government — of Naples. He told me that one of the worst things he had to contend with was GI souvenir hunters.

"The Italian police in Naples have shown themselves almost one hundred per cent nonpolitical in the performance of their duty," he said. "They don't arrest GIs; our own MPs do that. What upsets an Italian cop is when an American soldier grabs him from behind or knocks him unconscious and takes his Beretta pistol away from him as a keepsake. The Italian police have been losing an average of thirty-five Berettas a night."

Some of the AMG official practices also infuriated the Neapolitans. One day I had occasion to call on a count who was a leader of the royalist movement in Naples. After he talked about the party both nationally and locally, he added: "Do you mind if I protest about the indiscriminate way your people put signs on our buildings?"

"Why no," I said. "I'd even be glad to pass it on to Mark Clark himself if it were important enough."

"Did you notice the signs that were officially painted on this apartment building I live in?"

"No, I don't think so."

"Well, when you go out look again. You will see written in very large letters the words: 'Beware. This is a VD area.' I consider such phrases pasted officially on a building in which I live as an insult to both my wife and my three daughters."

"I know, Count, but it merely means that some soldier may have had sex in the courtyard of this building and believed the girl lived here," I said, trying to explain away the offense. "When he was being treated, he had to report where he thought he had picked up the disease."

"Well, all I can say is I consider such signs an indignity to the good families and the respectable neighborhoods of this city."

I felt like saying: Who knows? This whole city is a bordello and your wife and three daughters are probably no exception to the general whoring that goes on in this city that was literally starving to death until the whoring started with the entry of General Mark Clark's Fifth Army. A sign should be put at the entrance of the city, I thought, and clearly marked: This is a VD city.

With all the sins the Neapolitans must have been committing in order to survive World War II, they were still devout Catholics. Many of them were distressed at the delay in the liquefying of the blood of Saint Januarius. It is contained in a small crystal phial usually in a congealed state, but at least once a year in early autumn, it is supposed to become real fluid blood. The transformation was weeks overdue. Then one day the solid blood suddenly liquefied. The priest passed the phial down each row so that everybody in the church could see it.

Then the archbishop himself gave a sermon: "There is no doubt but what the people of this city, afflicted by all the horrors of war — bombings from the air, shelling from the sea, and artillery fire from the ground — have sinned. It has taken many days for the blood of our venerated Saint Januarius to liquefy. We must interpret this delay as a sign that the people of Naples have displeased God but that finally He has shown his understanding. The blood has liquefied, bringing forgiveness and atonement to the people in this hour of their affliction."

I asked some agnostic Neapolitans how they explained the liquefying of Saint Januarius's blood.

"Well," one man told me, "it liquefies quickly when there are a lot of people in the church, but during these war days, people are afraid to gather in crowds, resulting in less body heat, and so it took longer for the miracle to occur this time."

Almost immediately after the fall of Naples, the Allies took over the Royal Palace at Caserta, about twenty-five miles north of Naples as its advance headquarters. Without any furniture, it was converted into a dormitory for officers and a theater was set up to entertain the troops. At first the correspondents had the best rooms in the palace, but we soon were pushed up into the eaves with the pigeons. A good little bar for correspondents was opened, and we probably formed the noisiest, most drunken and obscene group in the entire palazzo.

Ernie Pyle was the best known of the war correspondents, but none of the others wanted to change places with him. Most of us felt the kind of stuff he wrote — GI letters, we arrogantly called it — was beneath the high-powered quality of spot-news reporting. But he was a lovable, whimsical character. Frail, tiny, gray-haired, he used to cry about his fate at the bar, saying that he hated writing about the GIs.

"They are really dull," he said. "Sometimes they are even tough and mean. But my editors won't let me write about anybody except these goddamn GIs. I'm tired of being called the letter writer for the doughfoot."

He bragged one night that he had managed to write a story about a heroic captain, but the only way he got away with it was to describe how the GIs coming up to the blanket that covered the dead captain, shook his exposed hand.

"Goddamn it," he said one night. "I've been ordered to cover the GIs in Japan. I've got a feeling I'm going to get it there."

He was shot to death by a Japanese sniper.

Occasionally, I covered the French sector. It was a real mercenary war area because the French were making use of so many Moroccans, and the Moroccan troops only fought for loot. They used to send great truckloads of furniture and merchandise back to Morocco from the villages and towns they took. They not only raped the women but buggered the young boys as well. The French high command tried to keep the Moroccans' multiple sex desires under control as much as possible by sending motorized caravans of Arab prostitutes right up to the front lines. The censors, however, would never pass such revelations on the usual basis that it would give aid and comfort to the enemy. Besides, the American editors only wanted stories about the American GI even if he was only slogging slowly through mud.

# CHAPTER VI

Allied Forces Headquarters in Algiers finally moved to Naples. Pinkley didn't move with it but was transferred to London. I unexpectedly found myself promoted to Mediterranean bureau manager with Chris Cunningham as my assistant. Other Unipressers on my staff included Don Coe, Dana Adams Schmidt, Pat Conger, Bob Vermillion, Jim Roper, and later Tom Trainer. He was originally with the *San Francisco Examiner*. Trainer was hired by Hugh Baillie because he liked one of his stories about Naples. He said it was much better than anybody else had written. Tom's masterpiece described Neapolitan kids playing at war in the streets of Naples. He had them saying: "Bang, bang, you're dead." I didn't say anything, but I personally hadn't seen any such street scenes. Most of the little urchins were too busy pimping for their alleged mothers and sisters or else were begging for cigarettes, Spam, and chocolate bars.

The Fifth Army really got bogged down before Mount Cassino. I can't recall how many times phony announcements of it having been taken were made by high Allied commands and even contained in eyewitness accounts by reporters. I sent one cockeyed announcement myself. At a special press conference called for at 11 P.M., an air force general announced that the German troops had been annihilated by the Allied pinpoint bombing or driven out of their underground shelters. At that moment, the general said, American tanks were mounting the slopes of

Monte Cassino and taking possession of the natural fortress that had been holding up Clark's advance on Rome. The only trouble was that the Sherman tanks got trapped in the bomb craters, and the Germans had time to retrench themselves like moles back in their comfortable subterranean strongholds.

The main source of news was always the daily communiqué issued at Allied Forces Headquarters in its press room, naming the little towns and villages that had been captured by the Fifth and now the Eighth Armies. All the correspondents used guidebooks to describe the places and gave picturesque histories and descriptions of the towns.

As soon as it became evident that AFHQ would be quartered in Naples, the various bureau managers of the AP, UP, INS, Reuter, and Agence France Presse looked for spacious apartments to liberate. I appointed Pat Conger to find a flat for the United Press and he did. It was located dangerously near the main docks and came under intensive German bombing raids which were aided by the glow of Mount Vesuvius. The volcano was extremely active at that time. It couldn't be blacked out. I gave the landlord a token payment, but actually he didn't want to live in Naples during those grotesque days and was glad to have it occupied by an American organization.

By accident, I found a housekeeper for the apartment. A few days after Naples fell, I was strolling along the via Roma and was attracted by a Rubensesque blonde in dark clothes who was accompanied by another girl. The latter was a slim, dark-eyed brunette, wearing a red coat. They weren't hard to pick up. The one I wasn't interested in was very responsive. I smiled at the blonde and the brunette smiled back. I asked the blonde if I might invite them for an aperitivo in La Galleria, and the brunette accepted immediately.

The Naples Galleria was a sort of war museum in the making. Located not too far from the waterfront, all the glass domes had been broken and were badly patched with strips of wood and cardboard. There were several third-rate cinemas, including one with burlesque acts, a nightclub, and four or five cafés. A daily Italian newspaper was also printed on the premises. There were boardinghouses that had become flophouses since the liberation of Naples. It was a very central spot just between the San Carlo Opera House and the funicular railway which was the basis of the popular song, "Funiculi Funicula," one of the first-ever singing commercials.

Over bootleg brandies we started to talk about ourselves. The blonde appropriately was called Bianca and the other said her name was Flora. We dueled for a while, but Flora soon dropped pretenses and suggested we have lunch at the only waterfront restaurant that was open. She said the place even served white spaghetti and had real red wine, and afterwards the three of us could go to a nearby rooming house and enjoy ourselves . . . the three of us she stressed. She even mentioned the price, which was not too high, but this was just the beginning of the occupation. She said her husband ran a radio shop and that Bianca's husband was a lawyer. She explained their husbands were making no money these days, so the two wives were trying to act as sort of guides to Americans who might give them something in the way of compensation.

I tried hard to shake the brunette, but she explained that this was the first time Bianca had tried to pick up anybody, and she was extremely timid and didn't want to be left alone.

We had lunch at La Bersigliera, situated on a wharf in the Bay of Naples. Our table was next to the railing separating us from the sea. Little boys in scanty tights dived for centesimi in the murky water. After lunch we went to a nearby rooming house, where I paid a small amount at the desk, and we went up to the third floor. Flora drew the heavy curtains over the windows so that it was almost pitch dark in the room. She would not allow me to switch on any electric lights.

"Bianca is modest and timid," she explained. "You are really lucky. This is her first time at this sort of thing, isn't it Bianca?"

"Oh, si. I never thought I would do such a thing."

Finally Flora, who quickly stripped herself to the raw, got Bianca undressed and acting as a self-appointed MC, got the blonde and myself in bed while she pretended that she was half-dyke and tongued both Bianca and me. While Flora was in the bathroom, I whispered to Bianca that I would like to meet her alone — I emphasized the word *alone* — at La Bersigliera on the following Friday at 2 P.M. She promised to come.

We had frequent meetings. She soon lost her initial bashfulness, which must have been an act. She was terrific in bed, going in for cocksucking and buggery as a matter of course. She said she wanted to make enough money to feed her husband, her sister, and her son and at the same time to keep her son in the University of Naples where he was studying law. I offered her a job as housekeeper of the UP apartment. She accepted and soon produced a chambermaid, a waitress, and lined up her husband and son to get us good vintage wines at cheap prices. I encouraged her to be hospitable with all the Unipressers and our guests. I don't know much

116

about the physiology of such things — she was not pregnant — but she was always offering milk from her abundant breasts to those who wanted to be mothered.

Our mess got its supplies like flour, tins of butter, Spam, egg powder, and canned vegetables from the military PX. She used to accompany one of the Unipressers to the warehouse where her flirtations with the supply sergeants produced enough food for her to take much of it home to her family.

She was nicknamed Snow White. I guess the war correspondents were the dwarfs. She shocked a few of them with her sexual exuberance.

# CHAPTER VII

Prominent Italians began pouring into Naples after Victor Emmanuel III and his Premier Badoglio moved there from Brindisi. Benedetto Croce, the philosopher, suddenly appeared in nearby Sorrento. Herbert Matthews, Tom Watson, of the *Baltimore Sun,* and I went to interview him. Croce was a short, paunchy, gray-haired man who never remained still. He darted about as he talked to us. He said he thought better when he was walking. Matthews asked him for a definition of liberty, but we couldn't make head nor tail of his answer. No wonder, I thought, Mussolini had let him write freely against Fascism. Who would understand him? He turned out reams of copy by dictating hours at a time to one after another of his many daughters.

After interviewing Croce, we went to a noted hotel in Sorrento for lunch. The management didn't seem to think much of us and refused to rent us a room with bath in which we could type our stories. We explained we were war correspondents accredited to the Fifth Army, but that didn't seem to make any impression. The manager, whom we finally reached, claimed that the hotel was full of refugee families, and there wasn't any room to spare in the hotel.

"Not even for Americans?" Tom Watson asked.

"That is correct, sir. The place is full up."

We were finally told to use a table in the courtyard for our typing. When we went into the dining room, we had a hard time getting waited on. In fact if we hadn't made a scene and threatened them for the way they were treating Americans, the waiters probably wouldn't have served us. Stuck off in a corner, we noticed that several of the guests exchanged Fascist salutes when they greeted each other. Later Croce, whom we happened to meet in the main square, said practically all the people in the hotel were Fascists. That night Herbert Matthews and I were by chance invited to play bridge with General Clark and his chief of staff, Alfred Gruenther. We told them about our experience.

Clark turned to Gruenther and said, "Remember we were looking for a hotel in Sorrento to take over as a rest hotel for GIs? Let's make it that hotel. Order all the guests evacuated by noon tomorrow."

"That will teach the Fascist bastards," Herbert said.

While the GIs were still held back by the almost invincible Monte Cassino, the correspondents went in for interviewing the anti-Fascist celebrities who were arriving in Naples. Count Carlo Sforza, who had lived abroad, including in the United States during the Mussolini era, was one of the most authoritative talkers. I interviewed him jointly with Noel Monks, of the *London Daily Express*. Noel asked for the names of the three men he thought could save Italy.

"I name them in order of their importance," the distinguished-looking count replied. "First, Sforza; secondly, Benedetto Croce; and thirdly, Badoglio."

He was very much against Victor Emmanuel, accusing him of collaborating with Mussolini and the Germans and then switching over at the opportune moment to anti-Fascism and the Allies.

I managed to arrange an exclusive interview with Badoglio in Naples during this time. He kindly said he remembered me and my wife and asked about her. I told him Pibe was in Turkey, but maybe she would come to Italy to cover the political situation in a few months. The idea that I mentioned on the spur of the moment suddenly struck me as a good one, and I almost forgot to ask the aged Premier my main question. I recalled it just in time.

"What do you think should happen to Mussolini and Hitler, once this war is over? How do you think they should be punished?"

His beady eyes gleamed and his reddish, chubby face wrinkled with a smile. He said: "Both Hitler and Mussolini should be put into a monkey cage at the end of the war and exhibited around the world. The admission charged to see the two biggest monkeys in history would pay for the cost of the war.''

Badoglio had planted a seed in my mind, and it wasn't about a monkey cage. For several days after he had asked about Pibe, I began thinking more and more of her. Despite my sex relations with the now-promiscuous Snow White, I missed Pibe very much. I suddenly wanted her physical and conversational companionship. I wanted her as a fellow staffer to work with me on stories. But most of the war correspondents missed their wives, too, whether or not they were having affairs with Italian girls. So I couldn't very well ask the UP to send Eleanor to Italy on any such personal grounds. I would have to produce a good practical reason.

One day I decided to stay behind in the press room and not go over to the UP apartment by the usual military bus to have lunch. I wanted to write a service message to New York without anybody being around while I composed it. I wrote one trial message after another before finally producing one that I decided was good enough to send, I addressed it to President Baillie. It read:

> 27143 BAILLIE POLITICAL SITUATION IN LIBERATED ITALY CONSTANTLY BECOMING BIGGER STORY STOP EXCEPT FOR MYSELF NO UNIPRESSERS HERE SPEAK ITALIAN STOP SUGGEST ELEANOR WHO SPEAKS WRITES FLUENT ITALIAN HAS POLITICAL BACKGROUND HAVING COVERED MUSSOLINIS REGIME SHOULD TRANSFERRED ITALYWARDS REGARDS

PACKARD

I walked down the hall and handed it to the censor. There was always at least one censor and one radio operator on duty around the clock.

Returning to the press room I found a man in a strange uniform. I couldn't make out his nationality or rank or division.

"May I help you?" I asked him in Italian.

"Well, yes, if you could tell me where I may leave these releases for the press," he replied in English with an Oxford accent.

"What are they about?"

He handed me an engraved card with a marchese's crest on it. It described him as an aide-de-camp to the Italian king.

"They are from his majesty."

"Just give them to me, and I'll see that they are left in the right place for the correspondents who are all out to lunch at the moment. In the meantime you had better give a copy to the censor and explain your position to him. Otherwise he won't pass the release unless he knows it's official. I'll take you to him.''

I introduced him to the censor. The marchese then produced not only the visiting card but also his royal identity card. They satisfied the censor. He gave the censor two sheets: one in Italian and the other in English.

''Fine, Marchese,'' the censor said. ''Just leave the rest of the copies in the press room, and they'll be duly sent. Mr. Packard, the United Press bureau manager will show you where to leave them.''

I sensed I had a scoop here if I didn't mind being a little unscrupulous. I told the ADC to put them on the colonel's desk so that when he came back within the next hour or so, he would distribute them to the world press.

''Thank you for your kindness,'' he said, shook hands and left.

I grabbed the English translation. I read only the first paragraph when I gasped. Jesus Ker-hist! What a story! It really means the pro-Fascist old bastard is really going to do it.

I looked at my watch. It wasn't three o'clock yet. The others wouldn't be back for at least another hour.

I banged out on my typewriter an urgent lead saying that King Victor Emmanuel III had just issued a statement promising to cede his sovereign rights to his only son, Crown Prince Umberto, on the day that Rome was liberated by the Allies. I described the action as virtual abdication.

I then put the English text in the second take. In the following adds I said the king's statement was aimed at strengthening the monarchist cause as many Italians felt that the seventy-four-year-old sovereign had collaborated much too closely with Il Duce. I also recalled that it was Victor Emmanuel himself who invited Mussolini to head the government after the historic March on Rome, unheeding the advice of Badoglio who, standing next to him at the time, said: ''Your Majesty, give the order and I will mow down this Black Shirt rabble.''

I also recalled that at the time of Musso's invasion of Abyssinia, Victor Emmanuel was reputed to have remarked to friends: ''I have nothing to lose. If Il Duce fails, I become really a king and if he succeeds I become emperor of Ethiopia.''

Once I got off my dispatches, I turned over the royal releases so the printed side was down. That way they looked like just another pile of mimeographed handouts. As an added precaution, I put the Italian sheets on top so that the colonel, who didn't know the language, might not realize immediately the importance of the statement.

I then slipped out of the press building after leaving a copy of my story in a sealed envelope for Chris Cunningham, warning him not to call anybody's attention to the release.

Actually, my precautions were wasted. In less than half an hour after I had filed my last take, urgent service messages came pouring in for the AP, INS, Reuter, and French agency correspondents, giving them hell for being scooped and asking them to storify immediately. When I came back to the press room, I was mobbed by furious rival correspondents who claimed I had tricked them. My UP colleagues tried to come to my rescue, but MPs had to be called in to restore order.

# CHAPTER VIII

For some days there had been talk of an amphibious landing near Rome with perhaps a paratroop jump on the Eternal City itself. Then Ken Clark asked for volunteers for a secret mission. Colonel Yarborough offered to take me with him and said he would drop me after the first wave along with his equipment, including headquarters furniture and food supplies.

"We can rig two parachutes for you, so with all your weight you won't come down too fast."

I thanked him but said I doubted if I could arrange it as we had to draw for places.

"Okay, I hope you draw me."

"Same here," I lied, realizing I was too fat for such an undertaking.

I drew an LST that was to hit the beach at H hour, D day. A press officer almost as skinny as I was fat, was assigned to the same boat. He was just about as scared as I was at the prospect.

I think Chris was glad to have me go because it left him as acting Mediterranean bureau manager during my absence. He always seemed to resent my being over him. I guess I was never really meant to be a likable boss. But I decided I had to go on the invasion. After all, New York had been advertising me in full-page spreads in *Editor and Publisher* every time a big city fell to the Fifth Army. The last ad showed a very bloated me typing in front of a bombed-out building. The caption was: Packard

Arrives in Naples En Route to Reopen the Rome Bureau of the United Press. Who could tell at this point how close to Rome the forthcoming invasion would ultimately reach? Perhaps Rome itself.

A couple of days before embarking, one of the generals gave correspondents in the press room a briefing on the operation. Those present included reporters who were remaining behind.

The general scared the hell out of me when he pointed to an enormous large scale map of the Anzio beachhead and explained in detail how the various ships would land and where. On topographical models on a table in front of him, he even put his pointer on the very houses that would be taken by the various regiments. He pointed out that the operation leapfrogged around the German Gustav line at Monte Cassino and brought the Fifth Army to within thirty-three miles of Rome. He said that if the correspondents would like more information, he would give them further details so they could write their dispatches more accurately when the landing actually took place. Would they like more details?

I jumped to my feet before anybody else could answer and said: "Excuse me, General, but I am going on this invasion, and I think the correspondents remaining here don't need any more details than you have already given them. Ker-hist I am scared as hell some of this top secret information will leak out. I'm one of those landing on the beachhead."

"Sit down you sourpuss," a correspondent shouted. Another one yelled: "Are you mad, Packard, trying to suppress news?"

"When I risk my life on a landing I don't see why I should be scooped by desk strategists back in Naples. That's all."

I sat down. There were boos and catcalls.

The general, however, said, "I respect what Mr. Packard has said and will try to give you who are remaining here further information after the landing takes place."

When we left the building, some of the newsmen shoved and pushed me. Later, however, a number of the correspondents who were landing with me said they agreed with me. The thin press officer came over to me, drawing me aside as we reached the street.

"Listen," he said, "what about getting me laid the night we embark for the landing? Maybe that Snow White has a friend for me."

He knew the Snow White, having been a guest at the UP mess.

"Okay," I said. "I'll give her a call."

I did and she said she could get Flora for him, and we could go to Flora's place because her husband wasn't in Naples that week. I invited the press officer to have supper at the UP apartment the night we were to leave and said he could give Snow White and myself a lift in his jeep to Flora's place.

On the night of the embarkation, we called on Flora as planned. It was quite a foursome. The apartment was small but surprisingly well furnished in modern style. All four of us squeezed into one double bed. The press officer particularly liked suckling the Snow White's milk-giving breasts while making love to Flora whose arms and legs were swirling around like the tentacles of an octopus. At two in the morning, he remembered it was about time we thought about boarding our LST. He tried for one more orgasm while I showered in the tiny bathroom with lukewarm water. When I came out he went into the bathroom, and I took my clothes into the living room to get dressed with Snow White obsequiously helping me.

"Here's a little present for you in case something goes wrong," I said and gave her one hundred dollars in American money. She was delighted and kissed me.

"I noticed you brought a bag with you. Where are you going?"

"Just away for a short time. I'll be back soon."

"But where?"

"You shouldn't ask such questions, Biancaneve. It's a military secret."

By this time the press officer was ready to leave, and we hoisted our duffel bags to our shoulders and left the apartment. We were both a bit tight from some bootleg cognac that Flora had produced. He unlocked the jeep which he had carefully chained to a tree, and we drove at a fast clip to the dock area. Just as we arrived at the motor pool where he was to leave the vehicle, he braked quickly. I was thrown forward but not hurt.

"What's wrong?"

"My watch!"

"What about it?"

"It's gone."

"You mean you left it behind?"

"No, I bet one of those bitches robbed me."

"Wait a second," I said. "I know Snow White isn't a crook. Don't say that."

"I think it was Flora."

"What did you pay her?"

"Pay her? She seemed very proper to me. A married woman with two lovely kids, she told me. I couldn't give her money as though she were a common whore.''

"There's a phone booth there on the wharf. I'll give them a ring.''

He waited outside. Flora answered the phone. I asked her for Snow White. She was spending the night there and came to the phone.

"Yes, Packo, what is it? The watch?''

"You bet it's the watch. That press officer is apt to denounce you both as crooks.''

"Caro, you don't understand. He is just a schifoso who wants to go to bed with women without giving them anything for their families. What kind of cheapskate is he? Flora said she made it clear to him she expected to be paid, and he just thanked her kindly for her hospitality, saying he hoped to see her again if he comes back alive.''

"You mean he was talking about what we are going to do?''

"That's right. He said he was going off on some kind of amphibious mission. You said yourself you were going away for a time.''

Jesus Christ, I thought, no wonder women make good spies, and fucking is the best way to get men to divulge top secrets.

"Listen, cara Biancaneve, we men are human. We like to sound big. We are just going back to Salerno to pick up some radio equipment which was left there. We just thought you both would screw better if you thought our lives were in danger.''

"I am glad your life, carissimo, isn't in danger. I love you.''

I ignored the patter.

"I'll pay Flora fifty dollars for the watch when I come back. Tell her to take care of it. I'll explain to my friend that Flora discovered it and is keeping it for him.''

"Okay, amatissimo, but Flora does deserve money for all she did for that cheap friend of yours. Ciao.''

I hung up.

"Flora told me you forgot your watch in the bathroom after you took your shower. She will keep it for you.''

"Well, I don't feel like driving back there now. Besides we're late getting aboard. But I do need a watch. To log dispatches.''

"I'll lend you mine in the meantime.''

"You're a great pal, Pack. I'll help you scoop the world when we hit the beach.''

Jesus, what news-agency men will do for clients and press officers, I thought. We are the real whores in this life.

126

# CHAPTER IX

The LST must have spent three days at sea. I fortunately had brought some books along and nipped from my whisky bottle from time to time. We slept in tiers of bunks like in a dormitory. The thing that impressed me most about my fellow beachheaders was the way most of them slept. They seemed to sleep both day and night. I wanted to stay awake. I wasn't sure how dangerous this operation was going to be. I resented sleeping if I only had a few more days to live.

I landed with the American Third Infantry Division. We hit the beaches just before dawn. It still wasn't light and electric torches were being used here and there. A German military vehicle had been captured on the main street above the beach, but the occupants weren't German or Italian. They were of unknown middle European nationality. Nobody could talk their language. They weren't wearing regulation uniforms. Perhaps they were technicians.

But everything was quiet. For the first several hours an eerie silence reigned. The city seemed empty. There were a few rifle shots. During the first hours there was only one casualty: an American soldier was shot to death accidentally by another American soldier with an itchy trigger finger as they both turned into the same street from different corners.

For several hours we marched slowly and cautiously toward Rome. I always kept near the skinny press officer so I could file a dispatch as soon as I had something to write about. He had been joined by the press office radio unit.

By noon all the positions scheduled to be taken on the first day had been reached without any opposition. Then the order went out to dig in. I dug myself a foxhole among some trees along with the soldiers. There was no sign of any other correspondent. After eating a lunch of Spam, chocolate, and biscuits, I sat down on the edge of my foxhole, my legs dangling into it with my portable open on my lap. I began to write about a peaceful landing without any resistance and stressed the beachhead had been heavily secured with tanks and armored cars. When I was just about to mark it more and sign my name to it, I saw somebody talking to the press officer. He was handing him several sheets of paper. I looked again. It was Don Whitehead of the AP. My real opposition. In accordance with Fifth Army press regulations, during the first few days of an amphibious operation all copy was pooled. It meant that Whitehead's copy could be used by the UP or my copy by the AP. However, the individual competition was still there, and I certainly wanted my dispatch, signed by me, to be the first off the beachhead. I ran like mad toward the press tent. Don saw me coming and couldn't help but chuckle with pleasure, knowing he had already logged his long message of several takes in ahead of mine. His dispatches would go off first.

Crestfallen, I handed in my first take and said, "Where the hell did you come from?"

"I couldn't find the press tent hidden back here in the woods," Don complained, "or I'd have beaten you even worse."

The press officer, who was also acting as censor, logged mine in saying, "Sorry, Pack, but Don gave me his messages first. There's nothing I can do about it."

I sat down inside the tent and started writing a second take. I was going to do the best I could. Then I heard some weird dialogue going on between the two of them. It made me fighting mad.

"What are all these contradictions in this message of yours, Don?" the press officer said. "Here you say 'Units of General Mark Clark landed on a beachhead near Rome meeting terrific slight no opposition. American soldiers ran across the beaches without any shells coming in from the Germans with artillery raining in on the beaches. There were many few no casualties. There was heavy rain drizzle sunshine.' What are you trying to do?"

"I know what the bastard's trying to do," I broke in. "He is trying to get a canned cable logged in before a legitimately written dispatch based on eyewitness facts. That goddamn message of yours, Whitehead, was written in Naples before you even left.''

''I told the press officer when I handed it in that I wanted to make corrections, and I can make them now.''

''No,'' I said. ''You can't make them now. You've already logged the message in, and you cannot touch it again. If you do, it has to be logged behind mine.''

''No, but I have to make the necessary corrections,'' the press officer said. ''I have to make it conform with the truth. It's not raining, there was no immediate resistance, so I have to delete the phrases about heavy resistance and rain and drizzle.''

''That's right,'' Whitehead said. ''I learned that trick from you back in Naples when you used to log in messages saying that certain towns had been captured by the Fifth Army when you didn't know. Just before the communiqué came out. Then the censors would delete the towns in your message that hadn't been captured.''

''That's right,'' the press officer said. ''His message is logged in ahead of yours, and I have to correct it. That's all there is to it. I'm sorry, Pack.''

''Shit,'' was all I could think of to say after getting him laid, promising to get his stolen watch back for which I would have to pay fifty dollars, and lending him my own Omega.

He patted me on the back.

''Cheer up, Pack, there'll be other days and other dispatches. Anyway your message is second on the list.''

And that's how I was stupidly beaten on the Anzio landing.

It didn't take the Germans more than three days to decide that the bridgehead was a threat to Rome itself. Once during the first several days I went out with a six-man night patrol and came to within eighteen miles of Rome. The young lieutenant in charge of the operation insisted on teaching me how to urinate before I left with him.

''Pissing makes a lot of noise at night. So you must scoop out a hole in the ground deep enough to put your cock in, and then the pissing won't be heard. Otherwise the enemy might hear it fifty yards away.''

That was the only instruction he gave me. We came to an Italian farmhouse. One of the soldiers opened the door with a special instrument he carried, and another soldier called out in perfect Italian: ''Silenzio. Siamo americani.''

''Bene, bene,'' came back a reply. ''Benvenuti.''

The soldier interpreting for the lieutenant asked him about the positions of the Germans. He said he wasn't sure but that very afternoon three Krauts had come to his house and asked him if he had seen any americani. He offered to fry us some eggs and give us some salami sandwiches and Frascati wine. The lieutenant accepted.

"I didn't give anything to the Germans," the farmer said. "We don't like Germans. We like Americans. I have a cousin who works in Detroit with the Ford factory."

It was always the same pattern.

Answering questions, he said he was anti-Fascist but admitted that he had belonged to the Fascist party. "If I hadn't belonged," he said, "I would have lost my farm."

I felt nervous all the time we were in the house, eating and drinking by candlelight. The windows were covered with sacks, but an alert German patrol might have spotted us entering and could wipe us out by tossing in a hand grenade. I couldn't see that the lieutenant got any useful information from the questioning of the farmer and his family, which included several sexy daughters whom the father reluctantly presented to us.

The next day, the Germans began moving up armor and centering their artillery on the beachhead. Shells came whistling and crashing in all the time. From the Alban Hills the Germans could look right down on us. The order went out for everybody to dig in deeper. The high command of the beachhead burrowed itself as in a coal mine. The press quarters were set up in a villa that began on the top of a cliff and went down six stories straight to the beach. Once you got below the cliff-top floor you were safe because the parabola of shells coming in couldn't pass through the lower floors. But they were still vulnerable to frequent air raids.

The Germans brought up a railway gun that sent giant shells rumbling overhead. It seemed to be aimed mostly at ships in the harbor or just outside the harbor. One night it caught an ammunition boat which went up in an inferno of flame and explosions, rocking the whole beachhead as though it had been hit by an earthquake.

During the first three days, General Clark paid a personal visit to the beachhead. He let a number of correspondents, including myself, accompany him on his tour of inspection and questioning of local inhabitants. One of them was an aristocrat, a Prince Borghese. In answer to a question by Clark, the prince said, "I returned here the night before you landed."

"Why did you do that?" Clark asked.

130

"Well, everybody in Rome knew you were landing at Anzio the next day, so I came down to look after my villa. I have some valuable paintings and period furniture in it."

Clark was visibly shocked.

"You mean the people of Rome knew in advance that we were landing in Anzio and the exact day?"

"That's right, General. The exact day. It was no secret in Rome, I assure you. That's why I am here."

During this early period I cooperated on stories with Bill Stoneman of the *Chicago Daily News*. He had become friendly with an English major in charge of a photographic unit. The major had a staff which included combat photographers headed by a sergeant. He also had his own personal batman. The major, Bill, and I all liked to eat and drink well. We became a gourmet trio for a time and went hunting for news, chickens, and lambs in the major's jeep. But Bill Stoneman made us pay for everything we liberated, even from evacuated farms. He insisted that we put American dollars or British pounds under rocks to pay for the provender we took. I have often wondered if any of the farmers ever found the money we left for them. The batman did the cooking.

The major was the craziest brave man I had ever seen. Proud of his shock of salt-and-pepper hair, he never wore more than a trench cap, and that generally tucked in his belt. He considered wearing a helmet a form of cowardice. He also liked bridge and had no trouble in inviting women nurses — they all had the rank of officer — to dine and play bridge with us. One of the prettiest nurses would become hysterical every time there was an air raid.

"I know I'm going to be killed during one of them," she said one night.

On her tenth day on the beachhead, she was among the nurses killed by a German bomb that fell — almost everybody believed accidentally — on the hospital tent marked with Red Crosses.

# CHAPTER X

Every day the situation on the beach became worse. It was a half-dime-shaped area protected mostly by the coastline. But the front of it on the Anzio-Rome highway was a barricade of hundreds of Sherman tanks dug in like bulldozers. Their guns were being fired almost constantly. On the right there was the town of Latina, a model city that Mussolini prided himself on building as a monumental tribute to the way he had rid the Pontine marshes of malaria. There was no dug-in armor on that side of the beachhead. Instead the Fifth Army attacked the town and its suburbs almost daily in an effort to prevent the Germans building up an attacking force there.

The Germans used one of the most frightening systems of artillery fire I had ever encountered. It was time-on-target. At a given signal during the day or night, all artillery within range of the beachhead zeroed in on one single spot that measured about one square mile. Everybody in the area was certain to be killed — unless inside a tank or dug in deeply underground. Max Brand, the widely known writer of western stories, arrived at the press villa just as one of the time-on-target blasts occurred. He was killed instantly as he stepped out of the jeep to enter the building.

My worst beachhead experience came during an artillery barrage on the Anzio-Rome highway. I jumped out of my jeep along with the driver. We ran for cover under some tanks. But the firing became so intense that even the tanks decided to move away. The one I was under took off so fast I couldn't do anything but suck in my enormous belly as the vehicle moved over me, tearing my tunic, and then run like hell before being hit by the tank behind it.

The only really good thing I did was when I was jeeping along a road one day and came across an American soldier suffering from battle fatigue. This can mean anything from shell shock to just plain scared shitless. With the aid of my driver, I got him into the jeep. Then I noticed he didn't have a gun. I knew enough about army regulations to know that a soldier in such a condition could be court-martialed, especially if he had lost his gun.

"Where's your gun?" I asked him.

"Fuck it. I threw it away. I've quit fighting this goddamn war."

"Hold him there," I told the driver and went out to look among the bushes. I found a rifle and gave it to him. He threw it away again. I brought it back and held it myself.

"Fuck this war. I'm not fighting any more," he kept saying.

He was a Third Division soldier, so I drove him to a Third Division hospital tent. Just before we got there, I hauled off and hit him, knocking him unconscious.

"What the hell are you doing?" my driver Sergeant Delmar Richardson, asked. "Gone nuts?"

"I don't want to take him into a hospital while he's talking about not fighting this fucking war any more. That's all."

"I got it. Good idea."

Delmar and I carried him into the tent. I explained to the doctor who handled admissions that we had found him unconscious and brought him there in our jeep.

"And here's his gun," I said, producing the rifle I had found.

"Okay. That makes everything in order," the doctor said.

I had one close shave. Bill Stoneman and I volunteered to go on an expedition with the Rangers. They were a highly specialized regiment on the beachhead. We understood that the original aim of the thrust was to see how close to Rome the Rangers could get after breaking through the German ring of steel. Once through they would establish a bridgehead which would be consolidated later by regular doughfoot infantry. The Rangers moved fast and reached the outskirts of Rome, having worked their way through dried-up irrigation canals and ditches. Then the Germans in Mark IV tanks closed in behind them, surrounded them, and mowed down most of them. The rest were taken prisoner.

The night before we were to leave with the Rangers at dawn, the major produced two bottles of White Horse, and we proceeded to kill them. When Bill and I got up with hangovers the next morning, we were half an hour late. We dashed to our jeep, which was waiting for us, but by the time we reached the rendezvous point, the Rangers had gone and we had been left safely behind.

One day I was jeeping with my driver along the main highway to get to a new sector. I heard somebody call out: "Hey, Pack." I looked around. It was a paratrooper who had met me through my associations with Lt. Col. Yarborough.

"Hi-ya, Tim," I said jumping out of the jeep and running over to where he was manning a machine gun. "Where's the colonel?"

"His CP is about one hundred yards ahead on the left of the road."

"I'll give him a visit," I said.

"Well, don't go by jeep. He won't like that. You'd draw artillery fire onto his post."

"Okay," I said, "I'll hoof it and keep out of sight."

I told the driver to wait for me. He pulled over into a clump of trees, and I walked the distance alone. I soon reached the command post. Yarborough seemed glad to see me, but otherwise was very depressed.

"Jesus Christ," he complained. "They called off the parachute jump on Rome. Finally, the casualties got so heavy here on the beachhead, they stationed us in the front lines. After all our special training, here we are doing doughfoot duty."

He swore again as airplanes came in overhead, diving low as they dropped bombs and machine-gunned the trenches. We threw ourselves flat on the ground.

"You recognize those planes?" he asked me.

"Sure, they're American."

"Yes, but they are bombing us, not the enemy. They've been badly briefed. That stupid mistake has probably cost me at least ten men." He cursed again.

He did some phoning to report the mistake. He was also getting in field reports of his casualties. I left him, waving to him as I went away. He was too busy for chitchat or even a farewell handshake.

The original group of correspondents who landed at Anzio on D day started returning to Naples and were replaced by colleagues. I was beginning to feel horny. There was no sex on the beachhead except masturbation or undercover homosexuality. The entire population had been evacuated. There was nobody but soldiers. Not even a milkmaid.

Beachhead-groggy, I enjoyed the early morning air raids by the Germans' "Dawn Patrol" as we once called it in our dispatches; but we were not even writing about the attacks any more, they were such daily occurrences. With army blankets wrapped around me like a cocoon, I heard the bombs like the booming of the surf in a dream. They didn't worry me. I just wanted to lie there, feeling brave and sensuous, feeling the army cot vibrate as the explosions shook the floor. After two months without women, my body was ripe. I could feel myself respond inside to the warmth of the blankets and to the lechery of my dreams, my body naked except for a woolen shirt, being caressed by the nap of the blankets. They were so snug around me that when I got out of them, I left a mold behind me the way a finger does when it's pulled out of a bandage. I seemed to be experimenting with the subconscious and would let it take control as the bombs and the antiaircraft awakened me and then I would doze off again into orgiastic dreams. It was lovely as lovemaking itself, only ethereal and without any of the failures of reality. I would be embracing Pibe and Snow White, and they would be embracing me and each other. And then I was in bed with Pibe only, and she was laughing and crying and I was saying: "It's wonderful, isn't it?" and I would wake up with my thighs, hands, and stomach sticky with sex sap. Sometimes they were wet dreams; sometimes I bashed the bishop.

And then a radio message reached me from New York, relayed by the Fifth Army press office in Naples. It said:

> 28185 PACKARD ELEANOR ARRIVING NAPLES NEXT
> FRIDAY TO COVER POLITICS AS YOU SUGGESTED
> BESTEST

> BAILLIE

It didn't take sex-starved me long to decide what to do. Next Friday was four days off. I would postpone answering Baillie's message by airmail until I got back to Naples, but in the meantime I signaled Chris Cunningham to send Bob Vermillion to the beachhead immediately to replace me. I added I would be in Naples on Friday morning.

Vermillion arrived three days later on a Thursday morning. We barely had time to shake hands. I gave him a file of my latest news messages and recommended Sergeant Delmar Richardson as the best jeep driver.

Bob said, "Oh, Snow White has fixed your room up like a bridal suite. She has produced a clean counterpane and has ordered flowers for your wife. Isn't that sweet of her? I am sure they are going to get along swell."

I caught the sarcasm all right. Boy, oh boy, I thought, that Pibe-Pack goldfish bowl is very apt to crack into smithereens. Pibe and the Snow White and me under the same roof. Ker-hist! The moment of pragmatic truth has arrived.

I hardly noticed the shells that zoomed in around the LST I was boarding. I could only think of meeting Pibe the next day and explaining things to her. Yes, and listening to her explaining things to me. The boat chugged out to sea. There were showers aboard, and I spent a good hour washing the beachhead stench off my body. I used strong green soap; lathered myself thoroughly; washed off the suds and dried myself. Then I showered again. Altogether I took three showers before I really felt clean.

# CHAPTER XI

I rang the door bell of the UP apartment in Naples and waited, wondering who would answer it. I still had the key, but I didn't want to walk in without warning. I think I was just plain scared or nervous. The Snow White opened the door, and I could see Eleanor standing in the living room waiting to make sure who it was. When she saw me she called: "Hi, Pack," and rushed forward.

"Pibe, darling," I replied, dropping my gear on the floor and rushing past the Snow White.

Eleanor and I were in each other's arms, kissing ardently, even passionately, while Biancaneve looked on.

Eleanor must have had her hair done in Ankara the day before she left because it was still beautifully coiffed. She was wearing a war correspondent's uniform, the skirt barely covering the knees of her million-dollar legs. The military garb gave her a masculine touch that I found sexy and arousing.

"You magnificent bastard, you! How I have missed you!"

"I've missed you too. The beachhead seems to have agreed with you. You're as fat as ever. The way I like you, you Falstaffian son of a bitch."

It was our sort of love talk.

Then the Snow White respectfully interrupted to ask if i Signori

Pacciardi would like something to eat or drink? She always Italianized my name. Then I said, "Scusi for not saying hello sooner, but my wife doesn't arrive every day. This is la Biancaneve. My wife, la Signora Pacciardi."

"We have already met," Eleanor said without any show of friendliness, and I realized she intuitively knew that I had been laying the Snow White.

"Have you had breakfast, Pibe?"

"Oh, yes, an hour ago with the rest of the Unipressers. I got here early. At seven-thirty. I'm just waiting for you."

"Great. I had breakfast on the LST such as it was, but I'm not wasting time on eating now that you're here."

Pibe frowned and bit her lower lip. Hell, I was nervous too, I thought.

The Snow White carried my gear into the bedroom that had been mine and was now Pibe's and mine. There were some vases with flowers and on the bureau was a bottle neatly wrapped with a card attached to it. I looked at the card. It read: "For Pack from Pibe."

I ripped off the paper. It was a bottle of White Horse.

"Our favorite brand," Pibe said.

The Snow White was still standing around, not knowing whether to go or stay. She began poking the burning logs in the fireplace.

"You had better leave us, Biancaneve," I said. "If you have any marketing to do, you don't need to stay around. Actually we want to be alone for an hour or so."

I deliberately expressed myself crudely to make an impression on Pibe.

"Si, si, Signor Pacciardi. Io vado fuori per due ore." She left the room.

Pibe and I were alone. Now for the moment of truth. I started to undress. Pibe began taking off her uniform. Soon we were naked on the bed and in each other's arms, kissing and touching each other intimately.

"Shall we talk about our sex lives now or later?"

"Later," Pibe said.

I was very passionate. I couldn't control myself.

"Quick, quick," I cried. "I can't hold it."

I thrust myself into her and came immediately.

"I'm sorry, darling," I said. "I have been two months on that goddamn beachhead, sex starved. My only relief being wet dreams and tossing myself off."

"You poor thing," she said. "Don't worry." She pulled the covers over me and snuggled closer.

"I'll get us a Scotch and water. Then we'll try again," she added. "And you'll have to hold me back."

I almost cried, I was so ashamed of myself, going off like that so suddenly and not satisfying her. That killing, fucking beachhead. We sipped the whisky and talked about the room, the fireplace that warmed it so cozily, the red Neapolitan curtains, the picture of Mount Vesuvius on the wall in front of us. We carefully avoided mentioning anything about the year and a half we had been apart.

Then I started kissing her again, our mouths open with our tongues engaged in a fiery duel. I could feel virility returning.

"It's back again. Surging up big and strong," she said, stroking it with her hand.

I eased it into her. I had control of myself now. It was marvelous. She undulated beneath me, and I rolled her over so she was on top of me. Then she was biting my lips and scratching my back with her fingernails. It was terrific. It was glorious fucking. Even marriage can't spoil it, I thought. Our mutually exhausted bodies separated, but I still had a hand on her breast, and she held one of my thighs. Finally, I kissed her on both eyes, platonically.

"That was really wonderful," I said, "You are a marvelous fuck."

"You're pretty good yourself."

"And how many lovers have you said that to?" I asked, not knowing whether I was joking or not.

"Three."

"Three besides me?"

"That's right. In Turkey."

"Did you love any of them?"

"One of them, yes."

"You still love him?"

"I think so."

"More than me?"

"About the same."

"Is that possible?"

"If you believe in the cornucopia of love. I don't think love is like table salt that can be used up. Love is infinite. Loving you doesn't mean I can't love somebody else. You surely agree to that.''

"Boy. You're throwing my own arguments right back at me. That's the way I used to talk.''

"So you aren't a philosopher any more?''

"Oh, yes. I believe in the cornucopia of sex. But I haven't run into any love since you've been away.''

"This Snow White? I have a feeling she is more than just sex to you.''

"But not real love. I mean I really pay her for her sex. One way or another. In fact, since you and I have been separated, I've only had money sex.''

"Well, I certainly don't object to that.''

I began to feel I had nothing to confess. What were a half-dozen whores: French, Arab, Italian? Only I don't like to call any woman a whore. There was something grand about Pibe. She always embraced life more completely than I did. I hadn't expected our hour of truth to develop into a symposium on life like this. I thought it would have been slightly different. That I would be doing the confessing and making Pibe jealous and trying to argue her out of jealousy as unworthy of her intellect. Here I was beginning to feel twinges of jealousy. Or was it that I was ashamed that I hadn't had sex for free?

"Well, anyway, I'm glad you had a good time while we were separated.''

"That's another thing I want to level with you on. I didn't want to come to Italy and work under you or anybody else. In Turkey I was the bureau manager, and I had at least six tipsters working for me. I didn't want to come to Italy. I was quite happy in Turkey, leading my own life, being my own boss, and having a very good sex life.''

"Who are these three lovers? Friends of mine?''

"You know two of them quite well, and the other you will like if you ever meet him. He's great fun. Tells awfully funny stories.''

"Laughed you into bed, huh?''

"Let's have another whisky. You're becoming jealous. That's contrary to our way of life.''

She got up and poured out two whiskies and water, and brought them to the bed.

"Here's to us,'' she said.

"To us — and to the cornucopia of love. Goddamn it, Pibe. I *am* a philosopher. I love you not in spite of your infidelities but because of them.'' I gave her a real passionate kiss. "You're great. I mean it.''

And I felt great too. I was being understanding and benevolent. The understanding cuckold is greater than the narrow-minded husband who only wants his wife to be sexually faithful to him, I mused, because he is afraid of comparison with her lovers. Sex is grand whether you are good or bad at it. Some women want to be mastered by great cocksmen while others prefer half-impotent males so they can nurse them to orgasmic success. There are so many ways of enjoying sex. It is not just having a tallywacker that's rampant. It's the intimate byplay of it, bringing two people together.

"You want to go to the bathroom first?'' Eleanor asked, interrupting my philosophizing.

"You go first.''

She went and was back in about five minutes. Then I slipped into the bathroom, and as I was using the bidet, the Snow White came in quietly. She started to wash me in the bidet. Then when I stood up, she began drying me with a towel and caressing me.

"Just let me kiss it, I want to feel that it is still partly mine,'' she said.

Before I could stop her she was on her knees sucking my cock, bringing it back to life again. I pulled away, but she held on fiercely to my buttocks and wouldn't let go until I had come in her mouth.

"Get out,'' I said. "I didn't want that to happen today of all days.''

I pushed her through the door and locked it. Then I washed all over again. When I got back to the bedroom, Pibe said: "What was going on out there? Did that blonde sex monster go after you? I heard her come back.''

"Well I guess she felt hurt that I hadn't kissed her when I arrived and went to bed immediately with you and asked her to leave the apartment. Anyway, she only sucked me off.''

"Only sucked you off! That was kind of her.''

"Well, I didn't want her to. She did it out of desperation. You know how Italian women think in terms of sex. She's afraid she'll lose her job if I lose interest in her sexually.''

"Well, explain to her it's just the other way around. There has to be some kind of etiquette even in promiscuity.''

"I agree. I'll try not to let it happen again.''

Jesus, I thought, here I am blaming myself for that kind of cheap sex and my wife had three real affairs.

"Well, let's get cracking. I want to introduce you to the press officers and get you started on your job. You ought to call on Badoglio. He asked me about you the last time I saw him. And there's Pietro Nenni, the Socialist leader, and Togliatti, the number one Commie of Italy who just arrived back from Russia. And you should get acquainted with the AMG officers and the Fifth Army political sector."

I called the motor pool on the phone and ordered a jeep to be sent around to take two Unipressers to the press office.

# CHAPTER XII

It didn't take Pibe long to break in. She always had a political mind and by the next day was sending stories. On the other hand, I was having unexpected trouble with Chris Cunningham. He didn't want to return to being my assistant. He wanted to continue acting as Mediterranean bureau chief.

"You resigned as bureau chief when you went on the Anzio landing," he said. "You went back to being a reporter. I remain as the boss, and I'll assign you to some reporting in the field. Take some days off and rest up. You need a rest."

"I came back yesterday. And I'll start work on Monday. I expect you to give me back my desk in the press room."

The UP had desks grouped around one key desk where there was a service message file for all staffers to read and copies of all the messages sent from Rome. When there was nobody there the files and copies were locked up in the master desk so that the opposition wouldn't be tempted to read them. While I was the only UP staffer in the press office, I sent a wire to New York saying:

04175 BAILLIE THANKS FOR TRANSFERRING
ELEANOR ITALYWARD STOP AM BACK FROM
ANZIO RESTING FEW DAYS BEFORE RESUMING MY

REGULAR HEADQUARTERS POST MONDAY
REGARDS
                    REYNOLDS PACKARD

I had to sign my full name now that Eleanor was in Naples with me. I left a copy of it on the service message file.

On Sunday night, Pibe, Chris, and I were drinking in the living room. It was after midnight. Eleanor was doing most of the talking, telling us about some of her experiences in Turkey where representatives of the Allies and the Germans frequently went to the same cocktail parties but gathered in separate groups in different rooms. Then I looked at my watch.

"Excuse me, Pibe," I said. "I must interrupt you to tell Chris something." She stopped talking and Chris turned toward me. "It's now thirty minutes past midnight. In other words, Monday morning. I just want to inform you, Chris, that I am taking over my old post as Mediterranean bureau manager and you go back to being my assistant."

"Oh, no you don't," Chris said. "I saw that service message you sent behind my back to Baillie."

"It wasn't behind your back. I left a copy of it in the files, for you and every other staffer to see."

"Well, there's been no answer to it. So that shows Baillie likes the way I'm running things."

"Goddamn it, Chris. It didn't require an answer. I just informed New York that I was resuming my post as I am now informing you."

At that moment the sirens began hooting. Most of the household put on overcoats and shoes and made rapidly for the air-raid shelter in the basement of a building four doors away. I told Pibe she had better go, too.

"No," she said. "I'd rather stay here."

So she remained. Chris paid no attention to the warning, nor did I, we were so fighting mad at each other.

"You can inform me all you want. But I am not stepping down to become your goddamn assistant again. Get it?"

I poured myself some more whisky. It was neat. I gulped it down.

"You heard my orders. That's all there is to it."

"No, it's not. Are you man enough to enforce these orders?"

"I don't know but I can try."

"Well, try then."

He jumped up and clipped me hard on the chin. The blow knocked me and the chair backwards. My head hit the floor with a bang. But I somersaulted up onto my feet and lunged for him. He was small and short, stocky and quick. He pounded at my lardy stomach, I tried to wrestle with him, to stop his punches. Then I landed a right uppercut. He went down. I flopped on top of him with all my weight, but he got a stranglehold and began choking me. I tried to get to my feet and throw him off, but he just kept tightening his grip on my neck. I was losing consciousness. The little runt, I thought, how can he be so strong?

Eleanor suddenly moved into action. She picked up the nearly empty whisky bottle and hit him over the head. It knocked him cold. We lifted him up and carried him into his bedroom, where we undressed him down to his underclothes and put him into bed. The next day he didn't go to the press office but had one of the other Unipressers take over a service message for him. In it, he asked for an immediate transfer to another theater of war. New York granted him his request. Oddly enough, he shook hands with Pibe and not with me when he left.

# CHAPTER XIII

Bill Yarborough's paratroopers finally came off the beachhead. They had taken a lot of lead their way and really needed some fun. They were disgusted that after all their special training for surprise attacks from the air, they had to doughfoot it for weeks on end in trenches. Bill decided to do his best to help them get back their old spirit. He billeted the enlisted men in some of the most comfortable quarters in the suburbs of Naples and took over the Club Nautico for his officers. It had been a swank yachting and rowing club of Neapolitan society. The paratroop officers frequently brought Italian girls there for cocktails, supper, and dancing. It was quite gay and cozy and not big and overcrowded like the regular officers' club. Pibe and I used to go to the Nautico several times a week as guests of Colonel Bill.

One evening we were sitting there having cocktails before supper with a group of officers and a number of very male-arousing girls. The conversation, half in English, half in Italian, seldom became political, but that night a well-meaning young lieutenant said he admired the way Italian people had become democratic almost overnight and now were almost all anti-Fascist.

"I don't think I've ever met a Fascist girl in Italy," he said.

"We're all anti-Fascists here," one girl replied.

That sparked one of the sexiest numbers present into an

146

Italian-language tirade. Her name was Lina. Before she started she turned to me and said, "You translate every word I say just as I say it. I wasn't allowed to study English or French in school under Mussolini."

I promised her I would.

"It's a lie. It is the reverse," she burst out, banging her slender, olive-skinned hand on the arm on her chair. "We are all Fascists here, only all of us do not dare to say that this is so because we are occupied by American and British troops. All the girls here are Fascists. They are bound to be Fascisti. They were raised and educated during Fascismo."

"Wait a minute, Lina," I would interrupt her from time to time. She was so steamed up she didn't want to pause even for my translation. She finally stopped talking, but her lips kept moving while I acted as interpreter.

"You Americans," she continued. "What do you do? You go after young girls, twenty, twenty-four. Older than that, you think they are too old for you, right? Well, youth in Italy is Fascist. We were born in Fascismo. We went to Fascist schools, we studied books and history that were Fascist. We read Fascist newspapers, Fascist propaganda. What do you expect? Naturally we are all Fascists."

When I finished translating that she began again.

"Do you think if America loses the war you would suddenly all become Nazis? You believe in democracy because you were educated in it. We were not educated in it. All we ever heard was the goodness of Fascismo from the cradle until the coming of the Americans. Perhaps we change, but not overnight. You talk about liberty. Where? In American-occupied Italy? There is nobody here except me who dares to say that Fascism was not all that wrong nor Mussolini all that bad."

She got up and stalked out. The American lieutenant who had brought her jumped up and started to follow her. Then he halted, apparently changing his mind, and came back and sat down. All he said was: "Let her go." He ordered another drink. Everybody was silent and embarrassed for a few moments. Then a captain remarked that Lina had a point of view, and there was the added remark that she wasn't afraid to express it, and that was the end of the incident. Lina was not invited to return to the Club Nautico. It was not a podium for pro-Fascist ideas.

It left a sour taste in my mouth, too. I had done the translating. I mentioned how I felt about it to Pibe.

"You're supposed to know the enemy," Pibe said. "It's about time the U.S. Army knows that all the turncoat Fascists aren't really anti-Fascists.''

Bill Yarborough got in on the tail end of the conversation, agreeing with Pibe.

''Come on, let's have some food and drink,'' he invited.

We sat down with him. We more or less drank the supper as the colonel produced some very fine Capri wine. It was better than the food. Before we left we had a few glasses of real Scotch. He then bundled us, tight as ticks, into one of his jeeps and a paratrooper drove us home. Pibe and I kissed passionately on the backseat of the jeep. I also was making plans for some sex when we got back to the UP apartment.

There weren't any correspondents around when we got in. They were either still out or already in bed. The Snow White appeared in a bathrobe and asked if we wanted anything special to eat or drink.

''Let's try a threesome,'' I said brusquely to Pibe. ''Snow White's willing to do anything.''

''I know that. She even asked me the other day if I would like to screw her son.''

''What did you say?''

''I told her to have some sense, that I didn't want any young gigolos, including her darling son.''

''Well, what about a threesome with her? That was my original question.''

''I like that. A man's idea of a threesome is himself and two girls. Well, my idea is myself and two men. How about that?''

''Well, we haven't got the third man. I can't wake up any of our bourgeois colleagues and ask one of them to oblige. He would be shocked to death.''

''I agree. And I'm not a deviate. I was just being logical.''

The Snow White could tell we were talking about her and asked: ''Che cosa?''

''I hear you offered your son to my wife.''

''Well, I just thought it would be fair. You had me. She could have my son.''

''Well, Pibe, what about a threesome?''

''If you insist. Let's try it and get it over with. You're going to be disappointed because there's nothing Lesbian about me. I like a good stiff prick.''

''Okay, let's try it just for the hell of it.''

As a cover, I told the Snow White to come into our bedroom in fifteen

148

minutes with a pot of tea and two cups, and we would all three hop into bed.

"That will be fun," Snow White said.

Pibe and I both took showers and were back in bed, naked, when the Snow White arrived with the tea. The room was warm from the glowing fireplace.

I told the Snow White to put down the tea and get undressed immediately. It didn't take her long as she wore only a bra beneath her bathrobe.

"How do we start?" asked Pibe. "Who does what to whom? You'll have to be the professor of the boudoir."

"You and I'll kiss each other, and Snow White will muff you while you fondle my cock, and then I'll screw you and let her suck me off."

"What about her? Doesn't she get an orgasm, too?"

"Well, if you want, you can fondle her and muff her, or I'll do to her whatever you want me to do. So let's get started before we talk ourselves out of it."

I instructed the Snow White how to start. I then began kissing Pibe on the mouth with our tongues licking each other. Then suddenly Pibe's body grew taut.

"What's wrong?" I said.

"She's muffing me. Another woman just repells me. I can't react. It disgusts me."

"Oh shit," I said. "You're provincial."

"I'm just not Lesbian."

There was another air-raid siren, and the Snow White jumped up, put on her bathrobe and slippers, and dashed out of the apartment to the nearby shelter. As the bombs fell, Pibe and I also put on our bathrobes. With the lights out and curtains closed even against the glow of the fireplace, we went out on the balcony and watched the play of colors against the shiny blackness of the night which refracted the sulphur yellows and lambent reds. To the south, Mount Vesusius loomed high like a demon lighthouse, its ruby glow guiding the German pilots in the destructive attacks on Naples.

We watched the spectacle for five minutes. Then, without speaking a word, we left the balcony, shed our bathrobes, and went back to bed. We had two magnificent, mutually satisfying orgasms, as the apartment building shook from the crashing bombs.

"Wasn't that better than a threesome?" Pibe asked, trying to score a point.

All I could answer was: "Well, it lacked the psychological adventure of a threesome. And speaking of three, I figured out who your three lovers in Turkey were, you know."

"How did you do that?"

"By the tone of your voice whenever you mentioned the various correspondents there. Remember, I have often heard you talk about the good times in Ankara?"

"Naturally."

"If I give you the three names will you tell me if they are right?"

"I guess you're entitled to know. Yes."

I gave them slowly, watching her reaction: "Ray Brock, Sam Brewer, and Leo Hochstedder."

"You're right."

"And the one you loved as much as me? That was Sam? Right?"

"Right."

We kissed each other and went to sleep. I was contented. Pibe had been willing to attempt the threesome. And I now knew her three lovers were swell guys.

# CHAPTER XIV

It was the unpublicized Polish troops who took the great natural fortress of Monte Cassino. The victory broke the German's Gustave line and enabled the Fifth Army to join up with the forces on the Anzio beachhead. Now it was only a question of weeks, perhaps days, before Rome fell to General Mark Clark. Baillie began bombarding me with service messages, each one more terrifying than the preceding one. They came chronologically as follows:

> 24163 PACKARD DROP EVERYTHING AND DASH
> ROME FRONT STOP WE COUNTING YOU BE FIRST
> CORRESPONDENT IN ROME SEVENTYTHREES
> BAILLIE

> 28162 PACKARD YOU MUST UTMOST BE FIRST
> REPORTER IN ROME STOP WE BALLYHOOING YOU
> ENROUTE REOPEN UNIPRESS OFFICE CHEERS
> ADVANCELY
> BAILLIE

> 30165 PACKARD THIS IS YOUR BIG CHANCE STOP BE
> FIRST IN ROME STOP YOU ELEANOR TOGETHER
> WOULD BE BELLRINGER REGARDS
> BAILLIE

> 01163 PACKARD UNIPRESS COUNTING YOU

ELEANOR BE FIRST CORRESPONDENTS IN ROME
STOP ITS AAA MUST FOR PRESTIGE
SEVENTYTHREES
                    BAILLIE

As soon as I received the first message I made farewell love to Pibe and assured the worried Snow White that eventually I would return to Naples and reward her financially for all her services when it was time to give up the UP apartment. I instructed Pibe to forget about Italian political stories, which were extremely important for the Latin American service, as soon as she saw Rome was about to fall, and join me immediately at field headquarters.

Each Baillie message gave me the jitters. I hated the responsibility of trying to be first. The trouble was that every other correspondent had the same idea. Dick Tregaskis had been wounded and a number of correspondents, including Bill Stoneman, Clark Lee, and famed photographer Bob Capa, had been transferred to England for an amphibious assault which turned out to be the Normandy invasion. But there was still plenty of competition in the form of Herbert Matthews, Ed Kennedy, Dan de Luce, Homer Bigart, Ed Johnson, Cy Korman, Jim Kilgallen, Mike Chinigo, and a score of others.

Then it was June 4, 1944. Rumors swirled around the advance press camp that General Clark had decided to take Rome that day or, at the latest, the following morning.

I was at the front early on June 4. Each agency had its own jeep and driver. I was saving a place in mine for Eleanor in case she showed up in time. One German tank alone, shelling and machine-gunning the vanguard, held up the whole advance for several hours. Nobody understood why it took so long to blast the Mark IV out of action. It dominated the Appian Way which was designated in prosaic military nomenclature as Highway VI. Finally, the tank was hit and went up in flames. The vanguard moved forward, past the tank that was still smoking and smelling of roasted bodies. It was black as a piece of burnt toast. The front line of the Fifth Army seemed to have dispersed. Nobody knew where anybody else was. I probed lanes and byways but always there were shells and machine-gun bullets that drove me back.

I had returned from the front to the press camp twice that morning to file dispatches about the advance on Rome. There was no sign of Pibe. I jeeped up front again. This time I ran into several jeeploads of other correspondents. Being together seemed to give all of us courage. We

152

raced forward along the Appian Way, passing groups of Italian farmers and members of their families who had lined up along the roadside. They cheered and applauded as we drove by, many of them shouting: "Americani. Bravi, bravi."

We gaily waved back. Then out of a side road appeared a Kraut armored car. Simultaneously, we all took fright and U-turned in panic, our jeeps bumping together in the mad rush to flee to the rear. The Germans, not knowing that we were unarmed newsmen, jumped out and ran in all directions.

We again passed the Italian farm families who had just recently cheered and applauded us. This time they just stared at us in dismay, they didn't make a sound nor a gesture. I guess they thought the Germans were coming back, and they didn't want to be seen being friendly toward Americans.

I slipped away from the other correspondents and tried to find some American troops that were moving ahead. The only ones I saw had taken positions behind houses and hills and seemed to be awaiting orders. I looked at them twice. I couldn't believe my eyes. They resembled Indians with war paint on their faces and their heads bedecked with feathers.

A jeep whizzed by. There were two helmeted people in it. I yelled at my driver, the same Sergeant Delmar Richardson, who had been assigned to me on the Anzio beachhead, to follow them. He speeded up, trying to overtake them. Machine-gun bullets buzzed over our heads. Both jeeps came to a quick halt on the side of the road. As the two people ahead dived into a ditch, I recognized one of them. It was Pibe. She was wearing khaki trousers over her million-dollar legs. Delmar and I also had dived into a ditch.

"Hey, Pibe," I called out. "Where the hell have you been?"

"Hi, Pack. Fancy meeting you here," she yelled back. "I had transport trouble. I finally got a Red Cross plane to fly me from Naples to Anzio, but there were no press jeeps there. They were all up front. I tried hitchhiking and the major here gave me a lift. He's going to Rome."

"That's right," he said. "If this goddamn shooting stops. I'm with the tanks. I was to join them somewhere near here. Only I haven't seen them. Have you?"

"No."

The machine-gunning stopped, but then shells began zeroing in on us.

"Let's find better cover," the major said.

He beckoned to Pibe to follow him. Their jeep did a sharp turn-about.

The sergeant and I followed them. We joined up on the same side road where the major had come from.

It was 5:30 P.M. I was hungry and exhausted. As I talked to the major, I had the impression he was drunk.

"Do you think we can get into Rome this evening?" I asked him.

"I've got to find my goddamn tanks. Then I'll go to Rome."

"You're coming back later?"

"Why should I come back?"

"Hear that, Pibe?" I said, turning to her. "I don't want to spoil your chances of getting into Rome first, but you've got no transport to get back and file your message."

"That's right," Pibe said, reluctantly. "I'd better come with you." She turned to the major, saying: "Thanks for everything. But I think I had better stick with my boss. That way I'll have a jeep to get back to the communications center."

"Okay, sister, have it your way. But you won't be the first into Rome."

Pibe and I decided to go back to the press camp where we could get the latest information and also some chow. She was starving.

"The major expected to lay you in Rome," I whispered to her as we sat in the backseat of the jeep.

"I know it and you were jealous enough to remind me I had no way to file a dispatch if I stayed with him."

"Forget it."

Back at the press camp we had supper at a long table with other correspondents. We sat next to Matthews. The press officers said the dope now was that it was too late in the day for the troops to enter Rome. The entry, they said, had been postponed until first light tomorrow.

Matthews said it made sense for troops not to go into a big city in the dark. He said he didn't believe any infantry or tanks would enter that night. He declined to make one more attempt with us. So Pibe and myself slipped quietly out of the mess tent and ran to the motor pool to get the UP jeep. Delmar had eaten, too. He was in a good mood and fortunately didn't grouse about all the driving he had already done. In twenty minutes we were back at the point where we had flung ourselves into ditches. There was no longer any machine-gunning or shelling.

"Keep on going but slowly," I told Delmar.

We eased along nervously, passing the dead body of a very small woman alongside the road. She had been shot in several places. We drove on but a bit more nervously than before. We saw a Sherman tank in the distance. Delmar speeded up, quickly overtaking it and then passing it. A soldier looking out of the tread-belted vehicle waved to us. The tank moved faster, always remaining about fifty yards behind us. When we slowed down, it slowed down.

Delmar said, "There's something funny about that tank. Watch." He stopped our jeep. The tank stopped too.

"Turn back and I'll talk to them," I said.

When we got beside the tank, I yelled out: "Why the hell are you fellows always hanging behind us?"

One of the tankmen said: "We heard the road is mined. If you guys don't set off a mine then we figure it's safe for us to follow along."

"The hell with that," I said. "Let's play fair. We take turns going first. Now you take the lead for the next mile."

The Sherman moved ahead and we lagged just behind it. Then we took the lead again. A lone shell crunched into the road just ahead of us. Delmar kept on driving.

"Good boy," Pibe said to him.

Then we came to four Sherman tanks. They must have received direct hits. Two of them were black like the Mark IV. The other two were crippled but not burned. Two of the tankmen dashed over to the wrecks and looked inside of them. They reported there were no bodies in them. We resumed our leapfrogging tactics. Soon we could see where an ancient aqueduct disappeared in the blur that was Rome. The dome of Saint Peter's loomed in the haze of the fading light. Houses became closer together. We were in the suburbs of Rome, but the streets were deserted. Then we came upon another Sherman tank. The crewmen were outside studying a map of the city. Our companion tank and our jeep stopped. The second tank crew wanted to know where they were.

"Here," I said, putting a finger on their map. "This is piazza San Giovanni."

The two tank crews began holding a conference. "Look at the infantry ahead of us," Pibe called out. "They're only three blocks away."

"Okay, Delmar. Let's follow the infantry," I said.

We caught up with the foot soldiers. We could see they were frontline troops because the officers had their insignia of rank pinned underneath their collars. We followed them along, past Rome's main station.

"We're not far from the Grand Hotel," Pibe said. "Why don't we go there. We can get drinks at the bar."

155

"Sure thing. Maybe Pietro will still be there mixing a coda di gallo," I said. "Step on it, Delmar."

He drove full speed ahead, stopping at the nearly closed portals of the main entrance. A uniformed doorman looked startled as Pibe and I brushed past him. Delmar remained outside to guard the jeep. As we entered the lobby a group of German officers, including a general, were walking toward us. We kept on going without looking at them and they kept on going without looking at us, leaving through a side door.

The lobby was fairly full of elderly Italians. They stared at the departing Germans and then at us, but remained silent. They seemed baffled. We turned to the right in the lobby and came into the bar. There was good old Pietro, in his white coat, behind it.

"Hey Pietro, don't you recognize us?"

"Ma si, il Signor Packard," he gasped in surprise. "E anche la Signora Packard," he added when Pibe took off her helmet and her hair cascaded over her shoulders. Then he shrieked: "Americani! Americani! Gli americani sono arrivati."

The staid lobby broke into pandemonium. The hotel guests, including two dowagers with canes, flocked into the bar on the heels of the manager who also wrung our hands and seemed almost on the verge of tears in his excitement. Once we had convinced him that we were not trying to take Rome single-handed but had come in with detachments of genuine American infantry, bolstered by tanks, he sped away to have the American and British flags hoisted over the hotel with a spotlight on them. He must have kept them carefully hidden from the Germans. The Grand Hotel was the first building to display the Stars and Stripes and the Union Jack.

Not only Pietro but everybody wanted to ply us with drinks. What did we want? We said we wanted Italian brandy to toast the arrival of the Americans. Everybody was drinking and chattering like mad while embracing us.

The manager came back and said: "Ah Signor and Signora Packard, how sorry I am that those German pigs drank up all my champagne. It seems hardly possible. The last of the Germans left this hotel only twenty minutes ago. This is a great night for the Grand Hotel and for Rome. I want to offer you a luxury suite at a special price." We accepted and said we would be back to occupy it the next day.

"Forget about the champagne," Pibe told him. "We want to drink our return to Rome with Vecchia Romagna, a real Italian brandy."

This being the first correspondents in Rome was proving more of a social success than a newspaper achievement. Nobody could understand why we had to get back to the press camp some thirty miles away. We had a world scoop if we could free ourselves of their enthusiastic grip on us. Finally we succeeded in leaving, with practical Pibe stopping off at the reservations desk to make sure of the suite of rooms promised us by the manager.

It was now really dark outside. Delmar was sipping a bottle of brandy that Pietro had sent him at Pibe's suggestion. He was not being bothered so much now because thousands of American soldiers continued pouring through the streets of Rome and the people were grabbing and hugging them as they went by. As soon as one of the men embraced Pibe and noticed her long hair and bosomy figure, he shouted: "Una donna americana!"

She was besieged with Latin effusiveness. She was kissed and hugged amidst declarations of love for America and Americans. Everybody fought to embrace Pibe, la prima donna americana to enter Rome with the Fifth Army. She put her helmet on to hide her hair. She had never been kissed so much in her whole life.

"Let's rip back fast, Delmar," I ordered. "We've got a great scoop if we can get back quickly."

Pibe and I discussed how we would handle the story as we sped through the night. We would write only one piece but under a joint by-line: By Eleanor and Reynolds Packard. We decided to make our lead:

04220 DATELINE ROME WE TOASTED THE FALL OF
ROME TO THE US FIFTH ARMY TONIGHT AT THE
BAR OF THE CITYS SWANK GRAND HOTEL AMIDST
CHEERS OF ITALIAN GUESTS WHILE OUTSIDE THE
TRIUMPHANT DOUGHBOYS WERE BEING KISSED
AND HUGGED BY THOUSANDS OF ENTHUSIASTIC
ITALIANS PARA WE ENTERED THE GRAND HOTEL
AS HIGH GERMAN OFFICERS INCLUDING ONE
GENERAL WERE LEAVING STOP WE TRIED NOT TO
SEE EACH OTHER PARA

The message went on telling exactly what happened to us as we came into Rome. It was a great story if I do say so myself. When the other correspondents in the press camp saw how excited we were on the typewriter, they didn't hesitate to look over our shoulders and read what we were batting out.

Many of them dashed out to the motor pool and woke up weary sergeants to drive them into Rome. By an odd quirk, a German shell hit the press camp radio as the last take of our story was being sent. So even those who came back later with eyewitness masterpieces weren't able to have them sent all that night, making our story a real world scoop. Baillie sent us congratulations twice.

# CHAPTER XV

The next day Pibe and I returned to Rome to carry out my much publicized mission in Italy: to reopen the United Press bureau in Rome. We jeeped to the Stampa Estera building and went into the bar on the ground floor. Above us, on the mezzanine floor, a fight was going on. I didn't have time to see who the combatants were because some twenty or thirty persons immediately mobbed us, kissing and hugging us and shaking our hands. They were members of the Press Club who knew us back in 1939. They were correspondents from such neutral countries as Spain, Portugal, and Switzerland. I recognized two German correspondents sitting off in a corner and wondered what they were doing there. It was the Grand Hotel treatment all over again. We couldn't buy a drink. There were toasts to America and the liberation of Rome. They hadn't learned yet what a double meaning that word had. Finally things calmed down and somebody leaning over the mezzanine railing called to me: "Signor Packard, per favore, come up here quickly or somebody will be killed."

I dashed up the steps and found six uscieri — Stampa Estera clerks — who were knocking the hell out of a man wearing a partisan's red scarf.

"Che cosa succede qui?" I demanded, trying to give my voice an authoritative tone.

The six aggressive uscieri stopped hitting their victim long enough to chorus: "He is a Fascist. He has killed innocent people."

"Un momento," I said. "I remember him. He is Marcello. But if he is Fascist, why is he wearing a red scarf?"

"Giusto," the battered little man said. "Signor Packard, I am a partigiano, I helped chase the Germans out of Rome. I just came back from shooting at them, driving them toward Civitavecchia. I never killed any Italians."

"Why do you say he killed Italians?" I demanded of the others. "Have you proof?"

"Certainly. He is a Fascist and Fascists kill anti-Fascist Italians when Germans leave a city. And he has not come to work for the past two days."

Suddenly I realized everybody was looking at me for direction and counsel. I was a victorious American, a member of the Press Club, and they expected me to take charge. I suddenly felt I should too. I wanted to make them a little speech. I was thinking of the phrase for bullshit in Italian. It came to me: *merda di toro*. Only it's not used in Italian.

"Basta con la merda di toro," I said. "I remember everybody here since 1939. All you uscieri were Fascists then or you couldn't have held a job in this Press Club. Now you are no longer Fascists but pro-American democrats. I think the six of you are merely angry because Marcello thought of putting on a red scarf before the rest of you thought of it. I don't believe Marcello is a killer. He is a gentle person as I remember him. Just because he missed two days' work while the city was in a turmoil with the Germans pulling out, doesn't mean he killed anybody. If you have any stronger proof than you have given, speak up and I will have him arrested and held for trial. Speak up!"

Nobody said a word.

"Okay. Let us all shake hands," I continued. "This is a great moment for Italy in which the Fascists become anti-Fascists. It's not an easy transition. But if you just forget about people having been Fascists it will simplify your return to normalcy. But if a Fascist has killed an anti-Fascist then he can be tried for murder, but nobody is being arrested just because he was a Fascist once."

I walked over and shook hands with the battered Marcello. The other six ushers then shook hands with Marcello and me. I called down to the barman, who was still Ali, the Ethiopian, of 1939, and told him to bring up plenty of glasses and a bottle of Italian brandy.

"This time the drinks are on me," I said. "I want us all to drink to peace among Italians. The civil war has ended in Rome."

There was enthusiastic applause and glasses clinked merrily. Pibe and I slipped away. We took the elevator down to the ground floor where we had no trouble in convincing the portiere to give us his key to the former UP office.

"Has it been occupied?" I asked him.

"Oh yes. Until yesterday noon. Then they left."

Pibe and I took the elevator up to the fourth floor. There were Japanese characters on the old UP door. I unlocked it and we went in. The same furniture was still there. Only all the heavy typewriters were gone. There were stacks of Japanese newspapers in the big newsroom and some Japanese calendars on the walls.

On my old desk in the office was a piece of white paper with English written on it. An ashtray had been put on top of it as though to keep it from being blown away. I picked it up and read it out loud to Pibe:

> Dear Mr. and Mrs. Packard,
> Remember the night of Pearl Harbor? The night you ordered us out of your office?
> I hope we will be friends again when the war is over.
>
> Maida

"Well, I must say, he left the office in pretty good shape," Pibe said.

"What did you expect him to do, shit on the floor? Shall we set the Jap newspapers on fire so we can put that in my message to New York?"

"No. That's a cheap stunt," Pibe said. "Like witch-burning. Let's just throw them out the window."

We did. Then I phoned the owner of the building and told him I was the United Press chief and wanted to renew our old contract for the office. He agreed with alacrity. I asked him to draw up a contract for signing that same afternoon. He said he would.

Going down in the elevator, I suggested to Pibe that we go back to the bar and find out what those two German correspondents were doing. They were still sitting there, looking very much out of place. The suits they wore were too short and tight for them. We went over and spoke to them.

"Well, we were drafted shortly after you were interned," one of them said, speaking Italian. "Because we knew Italy and its language we were sent to Kesselring's Army. We both became captains on his staff. Yesterday we decided to stay behind. We hid out in my girl friend's home. In fact, we are wearing her brothers' clothes. We are waiting here hoping to find out whom we should give ourselves up to. We don't want to risk wandering around the streets.''

"Are you willing to talk?'' I asked.

"Of course, we'll talk. We were both anti-Nazis. We have valuable information for the Allies.''

"Okay. Stay here and I'll see that the right people contact you.''

"We trust you.''

Pibe and I jeeped over to the Hotel de la Ville located on the via Sistina just before the street reaches the top of the Spanish Steps. It was where the new press setup was being installed. The whole hotel had been taken over by the press office. Correspondents could have private bedrooms in the hotel and eat in its dining room. A newsroom had already been set up with maps and a bulletin board. There were scores of flat tables at which correspondents could write their dispatches. Pibe and I decided, however, to keep our luxury suite, still unseen, at the Grand.

We told the duty officer about the two Germans who had defected, and he said he would immediately call the proper authorities, taking the matter out of our hands. Twenty minutes later, Fifth Army intelligence police nabbed them in the Press Club and took them off for questioning. Set free in two weeks, they soon found newspaper work in Rome.

Pibe and I marked out a section of tables in the newsroom in the Hotel de la Ville for the United Press staffers and put our portables on top of two of them. I sat down and wrote a news story, marked attention Baillie, describing how I had reopened the UP office. Mission completed. The censor deleted the part about the friendly note from Maida on the wartime theory that Japs were bastards and never a friendly people.

# CHAPTER XVI

The first announcement put on the bulletin board at the Hotel de la Ville informed that Pope Pius XII would receive Allied war correspondents in a private audience at four o'clock that same afternoon. Pibe had nothing but the uniform she was wearing, which did not include a skirt. Her wardrobe was back in Naples. She was determined, however, to attend the papal audience despite the strict rules regulating how women should be attired when received by the pope. Vatican protocol, however, provided that uniforms were also suitable garb, only of course it referred to formal uniforms and not battle dress. I lent Pibe my forage cap which I had brought along in my duffel bag, so she could have her head covered but not with a helmet.

When some of the correspondents who had been in Rome before the war saw Pibe in pants in the hallway of the Vatican Palace, they looked at her with astonishment and laughed.

"You never will be received in that masculine rig," Dick Massock of the AP said.

"It'll be a good story if you do get in," Matthews said. "It will be the first time in history that a pope has ever received a woman in trousers. And if you get kicked out, it will be a good story too."

I asked friendly colleagues to surround Pibe so that her trousers wouldn't be easily noticed. In this manner, she sneaked her way into the audience hall. Vatican officials then asked us to line up along the three sides of the room. On the fourth side was the papal throne upon a dais where Pius XII would sit. As the crowd stretched into a single file along the three walls Pibe's pants became immediately visible. I saw an officer of the Noble Guards give her a horrified stare. He was dressed in a Napoleonic-style uniform. He hastily consulted a prelate. The latter turned and looked at Pibe. They both started walking toward her. Pibe darted to another place among the line of correspondents, but they kept following her until they reached her.

At that moment, the pope entered the room, and from then on he was all that mattered. As soon as he stepped onto the dais, a dozen battle-hardened war photographers dashed from their places, converging on him, letting off a barrage of flashbulbs. They came within a few feet of the pontiff. Swiss Guards, wearing colorful Michelangelo-designed costumes and bearing halberds, rushed in and pushed the cameramen back. The Noble Guards, including the officer who had been eyeing Pibe's trousers censoriously, also rushed to widen the space between photogs and the pope. A dozen prelates who were near the pope looked terrified. They had never seen such disrepect shown the head of the Roman Catholic church, not even when the Nazis were in control of Rome. They feared he might even be knocked down. Pius, however, remained serene and smiling. He asked the photographers over a microphone in front of the throne to retire to their places as he wanted to say a few words. He spoke in English. He said after he had finished speaking they could take some more pictures. They quietly retired to their places along the three walls.

In a brief address, also in English, Pius welcomed the correspondents to Rome and stressed their responsibility to give a fair and true account of the happenings of the war. He then raised his hand in the traditional gesture of benediction and blessed the gathering in Latin. At this point the photographers surged forward again to take pictures of the uplifted hand.

One short Jewish photographer was shoved aside in the wild scramble to get the picture.

"Hey Pope!" he called out. "I missed that benediction. Will ya do it again?"

Pius smiled. And did it again.

"Thanks, Pope," the photographer shouted.

The pope descended from the throne and went around the line of correspondents, speaking individually to each one as he gave the person an autographed picture of himself and a rosary which he had blessed. Most of the correspondents, whether they were Catholics or not, kissed the Fisherman's Ring on his right hand.

When he reached Pibe he smiled faintly and looking down at her trousers, said: "I see you are an American."

Pibe told him he was correct. He then asked her for her name and for what newspaper she worked. She explained she was working not for a newspaper but a news agency. The United Press. He held out his hand and she shook it.

"We are happy to have you here," he said as he left her and moved on to the next one in line. When he got to me, I also shook his hand. I wanted to say that I was an atheist but decided that would be more smart aleck than philosophical, so I didn't mention it.

Pibe wrote the story, putting in of course that she was the first woman in slacks ever to be received by a pope. Baillie wired her congratulations adding: "YOUR PANTS MADE THE STORY."

# CHAPTER XVII

The Grand was the quintessence of all hotels in Rome. It was the place where old-world aristocracy, nobility, and even royalty stayed. King Alfonso XIII of Spain died there. Prime ministers, foreign ministers, and diplomats were frequently among the guests as were cardinals, millionaires, literary celebrities, and film stars.

For the first few days after the fall of Rome, Pibe and I were the only Americans in the Grand. All the other correspondents were billeted in the Hotel de la Ville.

The Grand was all Rome in microcosm. Once unbendable in maintaining its austere traditions, the hotel bent before the influence not of the United States so much as under the pressure of Americans fighting abroad. Most of these Americans seemed to hate war, to be lonely and mad about sex; they displayed a frankness and directness in their desires and talk that made Italians think of them as crude, generous, and crazy adolescents in a perpetual state of rut, getting what they wanted with such tender as cigarettes, chocolate bars, C-rations, and dollars.

Most of the guests in the Grand were old. One of the youngest persons we saw there the night we moved in was Diana Vare, the daughter of the brilliant Italian diplomat, historian, and writer. He had been Italy's minister to China for many years, written a modern history of England in Italian and slyly humorous books, such as *The Laughing Diplomat* and

*The Maker of Heavenly Trousers,* in English. When we looked into the almost empty lounge after an evening of drinking at the bar of the Hotel de la Ville with other correspondents, we saw a young girl reclining on a sofa. When she saw us, still in our dusty uniforms, she scrambled to her feet and said, "Aren't you the Americans who came in here last night as the Germans were going out?"

We confirmed that we were. She and Pibe began talking freely, and we went to the bar where Pietro served us a round of nightcaps. During our conversation, Diana confided that she and her father had quarreled and she refused to go home.

"The portiere, who knows me well, said I could sleep on the sofa in the salon."

Pibe immediately invited her to spend the night in our suite as it would be more private although we hadn't even seen it as yet. We took Diana up in the elevator. She kept dropping things from her bag. It seemed to be part of her strange personality.

The suite was enormous. The living room had windows on two sides, a fireplace, an enormous divan, and a chaise lounge. The chairs were all heavy and comfortable. The bedroom was not quite so big, but the double bed was large enough for a foursome to frolic in without anybody falling onto the floor. Just the sight of it incited my imagination. The bathroom had a marble tub that was almost the size of a small swimming pool.

We told Diana to make herself comfortable on the sofa. Exhausted, Pibe and I went straight into the bedroom and, stripping off our clothes, quickly went to sleep. We didn't even bother to bathe.

The next day I ordered Pibe to return to Naples just long enough to close up the UP apartment there and liquidate Snow White, the cook, and the maid. Pibe agreed wholeheartedly that I should give the Snow White a generous cash bonus for her diversified services, including sex. I suspected Pibe liked treating her as a whore. Eleanor groused, however, about making the trip but not too much because she was anxious to get her clothes. Diana, in the meantime, had moved back to her father's home.

When I returned to the Grand, that night, I glanced into the lounge just to see who still might be up and around. There were several people. I noticed a distinguished-looking woman sitting under a lamp, reading a book. She must have been in her early thirties. Ordering a drink at the bar, I asked Pietro who she was. He said she was a duchessa whose Fascist husband was in Northern Italy.

"Is she a guest in the hotel?"

"For the past two months."

"She's a genuine duchessa?"

"Absolutely. She is in the Almanach de Gotha."

Leaving the bar, I passed by the blue-blooded beauty. I smiled and she faintly responded. I turned back and addressed her abruptly in Italian, saying: "Duchessa, may I offer you a drink?"

"Why, of course," she replied in very English-English. "Won't you sit down?"

It was as easy as that. Over the brandy, served by Pietro, we talked about war, the fall of Rome and Italians and Americans. Then, changing tactics, I said in a confidential tone, "You know, Duchessa, I have never been to bed with a titled lady. I have often wondered if they are more passionate than ordinary women."

She didn't say anything.

"Why don't you answer me?"

She blushed. I was thinking it would be nice to confess to Pibe that I had laid a duchessa. Nothing whorish about that.

"Well, really, I just don't know what to say to such a question. I imagine all women are very much alike in lovemaking. It probably depends on the man."

"You're very modest, Duchessa. I see you as something very special. You strike me as extremely sexy. You turn me on, if you know what I mean?"

"Do all Americans have such a direct approach?"

"In wartime, yes."

"You mean the victors must have their spoils."

I laughed. "No, I only meant that the fear of death in wartime makes men — and even women too — more abandoned, more imperative in their desires. Have you ever had a romance with an American?"

"Really, now. Why, of course not."

"Would you like to try?"

"You certainly go right to the point."

"It's getting late. I have a suite upstairs. All to myself tonight. What do you say?"

"I just don't know how to say it."

"Let me help you. What do you want to say? Vaguely, I mean."

"You won't be angry?"

"Of course not. Just say it."

"It's so hard to say, but I must make a condition."

168

"Make it. I don't want to whip you or do anything sadistic. I'm more or less normal."

"I didn't mean that. I mean . . . " She paused for some seconds and then continued. " . . . I mean, you must . . . you must pay me."

I was shaken. It was as though I had been hit in the face with a cold wet towel.

"What? Pay a duchessa?"

"Yes, we need money, too." Then she began talking fast, nervously fast. "My husband is in the north. We cannot get together. I have no money here. He cannot send me any. I must pay my hotel bill and eat. I have sold most of my jewelry. I am desperate, very desperate. That's why."

"Yes, I understand that," I said, trying not to let her see how disappointed I was in her. It would have been wonderful to fuck a duchessa for free. "How much?"

"One hundred dollars. American dollars."

Greenbacks for blue-blooded cunt, I thought.

"I know you're worth it, but that's a lot of money for me."

"For an American?"

"Yes. I am a poor American. Just a correspondent. I work for a living."

"I would feel cheap to do it for less."

"How about fifty dollars."

"No. I refuse to bargain. One hundred dollars or nothing."

"Seventy-five?"

"No. One hundred dollars. It's for all night and as many times as you want."

"Okay. It's a deal."

"What's your room number?"

I told her.

"Right-o. I'll be there in half an hour. You go up now and wait for me."

As I stood up I put my hand in a pocket. "Shall I give it to you in advance?"

"Yes. But not here. Somebody may see you. When I am in your room"

I bowed my most courtly style for the benefit of any onlookers and said in loud Italian beamed on any eavesdroppers: "I hope to see you one of these days, Duchessa. Buona notte."

She was only ten minutes late. As soon as she entered the suite and I had closed the door, she held out her hand. I slipped ten ten-dollar bills into it.

The duchessa was very functional, combining oral and anal skills. I wondered if she had acquired her carnal proficiency from her husband or her clients.

When Pibe returned from Naples, I told her in accordance with our goldfish-bowl philosophy about the duchessa. She gave me an almost maternal kiss on the forehead, saying: "You poor thing. You're still paying for it. And what a price!"

# CHAPTER XVIII

Other correspondents soon began moving into the Grand, but none of them succeeded in getting a suite. They only got single rooms with the result that our private living room became the late-night meeting place of newsmen in the hotel.

One afternoon, after Pibe had come back from Naples, she phoned one of her colleagues who had been writing about the prospects of the monarchy being overthrown in Italy. She had been queried on his story.

"Oh, yes," he said, he would be glad to show her his copy if she would come down to his room right away. He was awaiting a phone call, he explained, and couldn't come up to our suite. She said she would be right down. At that moment she received a call from one of her political informants, who was downstairs in the lobby. He asked her to come right down as he was in a great rush.

"Pack, would you go to Bill's room and make notes on his story about the move to kick out the monarchy. I've got to meet a tipster in the lobby."

"Certainly."

We got into the elevator together. I got off at the next floor, and Pibe continued down to the lobby. I located Bill's room. It was at the very end of a corridor. I knocked. The door swung open and there was our friend who had offered to show Pibe his copy. He was standing there stark naked. The strangest thing about him was his cock. It was painted green.

"Come in," he said nonchalantly.

"Pibe couldn't come," I explained almost apologetically, "because she was called downstairs."

I entered his room, following him to a table where he opened a file. As I started making notes, I said, "Listen, Bill, what are you doing? Trying to cure yourself of the clap?"

"Of course not. I don't go with girls who have clap. I just tinted it green to make it look more interesting. Like a woman dyeing her hair."

"Oh," I said, and continued taking down in my self-invented shorthand the essentials of his dispatch. When I had finished I said, "Thanks, Bill. Pibe will appreciate this."

"Good. Give her my regards."

"I'll tell her she really missed something. A chance to see a green prick."

He laughed and so did I, but mine was a hollow laugh. I never knew what to do about such incidents. He obviously was expecting to show his embellished organ to Pibe. I either had to sock him for his intention or make light of it. I was finding the latter the easier way to cope with such problems.

The Excelsior, on the via Veneto, was taken over by the Fifth Army as a rest camp for officers. Italian girls were allowed into the hotel as long as they were pretty, not too whorish in their appearance, and weren't suspected of having VD. In fact, a special MP medical corps carried out flash inspections of the girls every so often.

One time the American-born wife of an Italian count went to the Excelsior after receiving a phone call from her brother who had been given a brief furlough from his duties on the Florence front. He told her to meet him in the bar on the left as you went into the hotel. If he wasn't there to ring his room. He gave her the number. He wasn't in the bar. She asked the barman in perfect Italian where the phones were located. As he was directing her, two MPs grabbed her and whisked her off to a room in the back of the main lounge. She resisted and demanded to know where they were taking her.

"We haven't seen you here before, baby, and we just want to make sure you're okay."

"What do you mean: okay?"

"Your health."

"I am perfectly sound."

172

"Well, it won't take long to check whether you've got VD or not."

"I'll have you know I am a countess."

"So what?"

She was shoved into a medical office and before she knew what was happening, she was stretched out. A woman nurse lifted up her skirt and took off her panties. A doctor in a white coat examined her vagina. When it was over she was handed a card with the date on it, certifying she had no symptoms of VD.

Her brother, a young captain, met her as she was stalking through the lobby headed for the main doorway. She slapped his face.

"What's wrong?" he said.

"You didn't meet me in the bar. That's what's wrong. Maybe you could have explained that I was your sister and not a whore. I was never so humiliated in all my life. They took off my undies and examined me — intimately for venereal diseases. It's an outrage."

"I'm sorry, sweet. But this is a snafu war. Come on, we'll have a drink at the Grand. They don't examine women there."

Her sense of humor returned. She laughed.

"It's not necessary," she said. "I've got a streetwalker's card, and it says I haven't any signs of VD. We might as well drink here."

# CHAPTER XIX

Randolph Churchill, who was either captain or a major at that time — I've forgotten just when he was demoted — also moved into the Grand.

"Hi, Pibe, Pack," he called to us from a high stool at the bar late one night when we returned from a rugged fight in the Hotel de la Ville. "Have you just come from the front?"

"Hell, yes," Pibe said, "Hotel de la Ville front. We just had a fight with an Australian. He was tough as a kangaroo."

Both Pibe and I had bruises on our faces and I had a black eye. Randolph wanted to know more about the scrap. I told him as best I could.

"There was this correspondent who spoke to me at the bar," I recounted, "saying everybody seemed to be snubbing him because he was an Australian. I told him I didn't think that was the case, and he said, 'Well, cobber, the bloody Limies won't talk to me, and the fucking Americans are just about as bad.' I suggested he might have an inferiority complex and he said: 'Why? Because Australia was once a penal colony?' I said I didn't know why but that I thought even Americans often had inferiority complexes in the presence of the English. He offered to buy Pibe and me drinks. Our glasses were more than half full. We both declined politely, I thought. 'So you won't even drink with me. Because I'm an Aussie, uh?' 'Not because you're an Aussie but maybe because you're so goddamn bellicose.' 'You're a cunt,' he said to me. Pibe socked him right on the chin, saying: 'You can't call my husband a cunt.' He then hauled off and caught me with a roundhouse on the right jaw, saying: 'And your wife can't sock me.' I went down on the floor but got back onto my feet quickly. The three of us mixed it up. Pibe kicked him in the balls, and he didn't even bend over to grab them. I broke a wooden table over his head, and he kept on coming at me, giving me a sledgehammer blow in my stomach. I grunted, the wind knocked out of me, and fell to the ground. He slammed Pibe into an armchair, and she went ass over tin cups onto the floor. Both British and American press officers intervened and made the three of us shake hands. A lot of Americans and British came over and shook hands with all of us. The Australian ended up talking and drinking with everybody. He said everything was dinkum.''

''That's one way of getting acquainted,'' Randolph said. ''How about a drink with me? To console you in defeat.''

We took whisky. There was plenty of it in the Grand now. We were old friends of Randolph having met him in the Spanish Civil War which he was covering for the *Daily Mail* as only second man in the field. The chief correspondent on the Franco side was Harold G. Cardozzo. Randolph was just breaking into journalism and modestly used to show us his copy before sending it. He wanted us to help him make it snappier.

That was the time his father was acting as personal counsel for King Edward VIII during his abdication in December 1936. Once when Randolph had gone off to visit his father on the French Riviera, he came back saying, ''Well, at least my father convinced that Baldwin clique that Eddie must have a proper income. Baldwin wanted just to kick him out without a title. Imagine an ex-king of England wandering around the world with nary a ha'penny and without any social position.''

Randolph had left for France with a bushy beard but came back to Spain without it. All he said was, ''The Old Man didn't like it.'' He obeyed his father almost reverently. He wasn't above using the Churchill name, however, to get small things like a hotel room or a seat at a sold-out theater. Despite his authoritative manner, we found Randolph had a great sense of humor, often poking fun at himself. We specially liked his human defects.

In Spain one of the best stories Randolph told us about his father was the time he was first lord of the admiralty and was trying to push forward at a cabinet meeting some modern reforms for the British navy. He was opposed by most of the government. One minister kept repeating: ''You must not forget the traditions of the British navy.''

''And what are the traditions of the British navy?'' Sir Winston demanded in his stentorian voice. ''I'll tell you: Rum, the lash, and buggery.''

''Got any new stories about your father?'' Pibe asked as Pietro poured a second Scotch for her.

''I've got one about De Gaulle.''

''Let's hear,'' I said.

''It seems that Eisenhower asked my father if it were true that De Gaulle thought he was Joan of Arc. My father replied: 'Yes, but my bloody bishops won't burn him.' ''

Even Randolph couldn't wangle a suite in the Grand. Half of the hotel by that time had been sequestered by the High Command of the Allied Forces and allotted to top-ranking officers stationed in Rome. Randolph was just passing through but managed to get a single room by impressing the hotel manager with the Churchill name. The manager gave him one of the rooms intended for the Italian quota.

''We often have late bull sessions in our living room, and a well-stocked bar of our own up there,'' I told him. ''Come up any time you like.''

''I might do that,'' he said. ''I like to argue with American journalists. In fact, I get along better with Americans than with the British. I should live in the States. Then I'd be almost sure of being elected as senator.''

We left Randolph at the bar and went to our suite. The Pig Misery was dozing on the sofa waiting for us. She was the maid we had hired after we took on the Mackenzie apartment in Rome when Italy went to war against England and France. We both liked her because she continued on with us even after Il Duce declared war on the U.S. I often laughed at the time I caught her posing in the nude for Pomeroy. As soon as Rome fell, she looked us up and when she learned that the Hotel de la Ville had been made into a press center she had no trouble finding Pibe.

''Ah, signora, I always knew the Americans would win this war,'' she said to Pibe in the lobby of the Hotel de la Ville. ''But I am glad the Soviets are giving you help in Eastern Europe. You remember, I was always a Communist.''

''Don't brag about that to me. You can't always choose your allies.''

''I wondered if you could use me as a tuttofare, to look after your laundry, run errands for you, serve at cocktail parties, and be generally helpful. I can cook too. I can press your uniforms.''

"Start to work tomorrow at the Grand Hotel," Pibe said cutting her short. She gave her our suite number. Pibe also arranged for her to eat and sleep in the servants quarters of the hotel. That way there would be no transport problem on getting her to and from work. I only learned that Eleanor had hired her when I came home the next night, and there she was dozing on the sofa.

"Make Signor Packard and myself a couple of whisky sodas," Pibe told her. "And then you can go to bed."

"I didn't know you were working for us . . . Lucia," I said suddenly remembering her right name and shaking her hand. "Welcome back to Casa Packard."

"È piacere mio. La signora hired me yesterday. I am very happy to be back with both of you."

It didn't take Lucia long to give our living room just the right added touch of efficiency it needed. We already had the staid waiters and elderly chambermaids on the floor to do the routine chores, but Lucia was that little bit of extra personal help that speeded up service. A real little guttersnipe, Lucia didn't stand on ceremony and was constantly pouring drinks. She would dash out and get cigarettes or newspapers for our guests or would sew a button on a correspondent's fly or bandage a wound. If correspondents got too familiar and patted her well-rounded buttocks, she laughed and wisecracked: "You jussa like Italians."

Randolph started coming to our late-night sessions in our private living room and soon became a dominant figure. All the Americans thought he was amusing, intellectual, and brilliant while all the British thought he was just stupid and arrogant. Anyway, most of our guests were American.

# CHAPTER XX

Baillie suggested that either Pibe or I cover the fall of Siena, making it into a retrospective sort of piece recalling our internment adventures there. Pibe was involved in Italian politics so I decided to go alone. Delmar Richardson was again my jeep driver. I dozed or looked ahead for signs of the road being mined. Suddenly we got too close to the outskirts of Siena, and German shells came falling in on us. We turned into a lane which led to a small farmhouse. The shells followed us along smashing into the house. Some French officers in there were furious as they were using it as an observation post. They chased us out, so we had to run back to the highway and across it and up another lane, drawing fire wherever we went. Finally we just took cover in a ditch and waited until the shells stopped piling in an hour later.

Eventually we found the advance press camp and spent the night there.

Within about ten miles of Siena, I passed thousands of the notorious Goums — Moroccan mercenaries who had given the French forces in Italy such a bad name with their looting, raping, and buggery. Delmar and I could see they were encamped to stay where they were for a time, and that was the case. Only the real French soldiers marched into the city itself without any fighting. There was only one casualty: one Frenchman accidentally shot another to death. The Germans had all withdrawn during the night. I lunched at the Excelsior Hotel, talked to the management, who seemed delighted to see me again, and recalled the internment days. I called on Count Chigi, visited the zebra-colored cathedral, and said hello to the ticket-seller in the cinema who wouldn't let interned Americans pay admission. It was all anticlimactic after the wild receptions of Naples and Rome. We sped back, arriving in Rome about eight the next morning.

I had written most of my story in the jeep, quickly finished it at the Hotel de la Ville and logged it in with the duty officer. I jeeped over to the Grand.

As I got out of the elevator in the Grand on my floor, I ran into the Pig Misery. She was just entering our suite, carrying a package.

"Che cosa é?" I asked, suddenly worried. "Medicine for la signora?"

"No. Just something she does not want."

"What does that mean?"

"She told me to buy her a sponge. She never uses a sponge."

"Why did she ask you to buy a sponge?"

The Pig Misery began to get red in the face. She was trying to be loyal, both to Pibe and me, but in the case of Italian women, I find they almost always decide in favor of the male.

"I don't want to say why. She will kill me if I tell you."

"Maybe I won't tell her."

"You promise?"

"Word of honor."

"Well, I came in the suite half an hour ago. I have the key. I tiptoed in to see whether you had come back. Whether I should make coffee and toast for two or one. And then I saw there was . . . you promise not to tell her I told you . . ."

"Parola d'onore," I said.

"Okay. . . I see there are two in bed. One is a man. It is not you, not your fat belly. So I slip out into the living room. I think what is the smart thing to do. I go outside and find a waiter. I ask him to knock on the door. I hide down the corridor. La signora answers the bell and tells the waiter she wants nothing. Then I come up quickly and say: 'Buon giorno, signora.' She looks at me, startled and says, 'Wait a minute, I want you to buy me something. It is . . . what do you call it?' She had trouble thinking of what it was. Finally she said: 'Spugna. Si, spugna.' I said I could only get a spugna in a pharmacy and perhaps they weren't open yet. She said to wait until they were open."

"Oh," I gasped. Then I laughed. "La signora doesn't waste time, does she?"

"No. So here is la spugna. The farmacia had just opened so I took a walk around the block just to make sure I give them plenty of time. He must be gone by now."

"What did he look like? Don't bother to answer me," I contradicted myself quickly. I didn't want to check up on my wife's sex life by questioning the maid. "It doesn't matter. I can ask her myself." That was to show the Pig Misery that my wife and I had a very special understanding.

I opened the front door of the suite, the Pig Misery following me, and called, "Hi ya, Pibe. I'm back."

"Hi ya, darling, you got back fast."

I wanted to say, "Yeah, almost too fast," but instead I said, "Well, it wasn't much of a story. Very second rate after Naples and Rome."

Pibe came out of the bedroom in a Turkish bathrobe. I lifted the hem above her knees. "Just to see if those million-dollar legs are still there." I kissed her passionately. Then I whispered into her ear, "Have you been faithful to me?"

"No, not really. But I must explain. It's not too serious. You send the Pig Misery out for something, I just had her buy me a sponge."

She took the package from the maid.

I laughed. "Lucia, I want you to buy me a sponge, too. And don't hurry back. Capisci?"

"Capisco," she grinned and started to leave.

"Have her make coffee and toast first," Pibe said.

As the Pig Misery prepared breakfast, I showered, shaved, and came out wrapped in a bath towel. I sat down in front of a table in the living room where Lucia had placed the coffee and toast. Pibe was already seated and sipping her coffee. The Pig Misery had left to buy another sponge.

"Well, you know how these things happen. We had a late bull session last night, and finally everybody was gone except Randolph and myself," Pibe said, talking very calmly as though she were recounting some ordinary occurrence. "Then he began making passes at me, and the next thing I knew we were both in bed, naked, but he was too drunk to do anything and fell off to sleep. So did I. I didn't know anything else until some stupid waiter banged on the door and I answered it. The Pig Misery arrived at that time, and I sent her out after a sponge. It was the only thing I could think of. As soon as she left, I started trying to wake up Randolph. What a job that was! I only managed to get him on his way just minutes before you came in.''

"She told me you had sent her out for a sponge. How do you feel?''

"What do you mean?''

"Horny?''

"Could be.''

We had a wonderful session. I always like sex more when Pibe had been desired by other men and especially when they hadn't made it. We had a wonderful double-header. We fell off to sleep. The phone rang. Pibe got to it first. I could tell she was talking to Randolph.

"Let me have that phone,'' I said. "I want to tell that son of a bitch a thing or two.''

"Take it easy,'' she said. "You didn't give me a chance to tell Randolph that I told you.''

"I'll tell the son of a bitch all right.'' I paused a second to get into an angry stance with the phone firmly in my right fist. "Listen, Randolph, you lousy son of a bitch. I go away one night and you try to lay my wife. What kind of a low-down dirty trick is that to play on an old friend and comrade-in-arms?''

"You must be crazy to leave your wife alone here in this sex-starved war zone. You're asking for it. You can't expect friends who have been wanting to go to bed with Pibe for years not to go after her when there's a chance. If we hadn't both been drunk, it wouldn't have happened. Besides, I thought you were a philosopher who didn't believe in marriage and advocated free love.''

"That's right. I do believe in free love, and I don't believe in marriage. As you say, you were both tight. Anyway, I just wanted to let you know that Pibe told me you had tried to lay her but passed out while trying.''

"I did have too much to drink, I am afraid. I must apologize to your wife for disappointing her. In fact I was just calling her up to invite her out to lunch. Now I suppose I'll have to invite you, too.''

He laughed to stress that I was really invited.

"Come on up, Randy, and we'll have cocktails here before lunch.''

He had to have the last word. "Don't call me Randy, please.''

The three of us had an amusing lunch together at Alfredo's. The place was slightly changed. Alfredo, once known as the King of Fettucine, sat off in a corner in disgrace. It had been charged he had been too friendly with the Germans. In fact, Pibe and myself had supper there one night during the war when Goering was hosting a dinner party for his Nazi friends at the main table. But one of his sons, a left-wing partisan, wearing a red scarf, was now running everything and personally mixing the pasta with all the professional skill of his father, with what he claimed were the golden spoon and fork given Alfredo by Mary Pickford and Douglas Fairbanks, Sr.

A terrible thought occured to me: perhaps I was being so tolerant with Randolph because he was the British prime minister's son.

# CHAPTER XXI

At first the Allied Commission wanted to close down the Stampa Estera as a Fascist organization, that also was probably full of spies. I intervened on its behalf and told the commission it was my opinion that the Foreign Press Club, like everything else that was foreign in Italy, had become Italianized. I argued that the organization, once sponsored by Mussolini, was no longer Fascist. Just like a lot of Italians, its present members — the Germans, Austrians, and Hungarians were no longer in Rome — were now all anti-Fascist. Very Italianlike, the change of sentiment occurred overnight.

"As for the charge that some of the members are spies, I can only say that having them all under the same roof makes it easier for Allied Intelligence to check on them," I argued. "It might even be a good reason to keep the Club in existence."

The Allied Commission finally decided to permit the Stampa Estera to continue and even allotted it a certain amount of fuel for heating the premises. I undertook to bring the tanks of oil to the Stampa Estera in an old taxi that I had just bought for use in the city of Rome as it was becoming harder and harder to get jeeps from the Army motor pool. The correspondents had to be up front to have that privilege. The taxi, which I dubbed the Green Dragon, was the longest I had ever seen. It was so long and slow moving that somebody had compared it to a freight train, the way it took so much time to pass any given point.

The members of the Press Club were so grateful for my intervention that they called for new elections. I was unanimously voted president and Christopher Lumby, of the *London Times,* was chosen vice-president while Pibe became treasurer.

As president, I frequently was asked to speak at luncheons and was interviewed occasionally. One of these interviews backfired, and I received a query on it from the New York office.

*Il Tempo,* a newly founded liberal daily, was trying to be as democratic as any American newspaper. It creaked with its efforts to exemplify the free press — even though there was still wartime censorship imposed by the Allied Commission. To be on the safe side, the paper went in for a series of interviews with prominent American correspondents in Rome. I duly received the visit from one of its reporters. He ran me down in the Press Club.

"Mr. Packard," he said in flawless English. "You may have seen the series of interviews *Il Tempo* has been running with British, American, and French correspondents. I tried to see you sooner as we had wanted to start off with you, but you were not in Rome at the time."

"Well, thanks," I replied, not believing a word he said, as I had been in Rome ever since the series started. I always like to be interviewed. It forces me to think clearly. "Go ahead and ask me some questions."

The reporter didn't like asking questions. That might compromise him.

"No, I have no special questions to ask. We just want you to say whatever you want to say."

"You mean anything I want to say?"

"Why of course. We have freedom of the press now that the Allies are in Rome."

"Okay," I said, suddenly thinking of the thing that had burned me up most about the Eternal City even long before the war started. I plunged right into the heart of the matter without any preliminaries. "I think it's about time that Italy gives up its monopoly on the papal throne. I think the next pope should be an American. Do you realize the United States, and I consider it a very great country, has never had a pope? I am not being nationalistic about this matter either — it could be a French, English, Russian, or Latin American pontiff for that matter. But something should be done to break the almost uninterrupted continuity of one Italian pope after another."

I was riding one of my favorite hobbyhorses: an American pope. It would really throw a monkey wrench into the calculations of the curia.

"Who would be your choice as the first American pope?"

His question caught me unprepared. I hadn't thought much about the personality. There was only one American cardinal I knew at all and that was the one who once told me that I had not been very Christian in the way I handled his statement on the election of Eugenio Pacelli as pope back in 1939.

"Yes," I said glibly. "My choice would be Dennis Cardinal Dougherty of Philadelphia. He is a very devout Catholic. A great scholar. He has proved himself an able administrator as archbishop of Philadelphia. I am sure he could run the Vatican with the same skill and efficiency."

The reporter frowned as he made shorthand notes on what I was saying. He obviously didn't like it.

"But Mr. Packard," he said in his precise English. "There are so many other things that would interest our readers. What would you say about the future role of Italy in Europe after getting rid of Mussolini and giving up its colonies?"

"Listen," I said. "There's only one thing I want to talk about and that is the need of having a non-Italian pope, preferably an American pope. If you are going to interview me at all, it has to be on that subject. I don't want it buried way down in the bottom of your story."

"But that's a rather unorthodox statement you are making, Mr. Packard."

"I guess you're just not accustomed yet to freedom of speech."

"Oh, no sir. Nothing like that. I will write it just as you have told it to me. I took your words down in shorthand. I am sure the editor will publish it."

"Why the hell shouldn't he publish it after all the drivel I've seen published in those interviews of yours so far? You just tell your editor that if he doesn't publish it, I'll take it around to *Il Messaggero* and tell them I am giving it to them because you are afraid to publish it. Good-bye."

The *Messaggero* was the other big morning newspaper in Rome.

I turned my back on him and ordered another whisky. He left me.

Later that night he ran me down at the bar in the Grand where Pibe and I were having a nightcap with Randolph.

"Mr. Packard," he said, and in an aside politely excused himself to Pibe for interrupting us. "I hope you haven't given that statement to *Il Messaggero*."

"Not yet," I said. "I'm waiting to see whether it's in tomorrow morning's paper."

"It's in all right. A big headline. It reads: 'U.S. Correspondent Urges An American Pope.' Here's a proof for you."

He handed me two smudged galley sheets.

"Great," I said, introducing him to Pibe and Randolph and insisting he have a drink with us.

The next night, while Pibe and I were entertaining in our living room in the Grand, a press officer phoned and read me a query. It ran:

28203 PACKARD NEWYORK TIMES SCOOPS US ON
OUR OWN STORY DASH YOUR INTERVIEW IN
TEMPO URGING NEXT POPE BE AMERICAN STOP
MATTHEWS SAYS ITS FIRST TIME HISTORY ANY
ROMAN NEWSPAPER EVER CARRIED SUCH
RECOMMENDATION STOP PLEASE EXPLAIN WHY
YOU DIDNT STORIFY FOR UNIPRESS AND RUSH IT
NOW

BAILLIE

"Shit," I said. "Scooped by myself. Pibe, you'll have to take the Green Dragon and file that Tempo interview. I can't write a story about myself."

"Okay, slave driver," Pibe said. "Just as I am beginning to enjoy myself. But I agree. You can't send it yourself. Keep things going until I get back."

# CHAPTER XXII

The dead bodies were hanging by their feet, dangling just over the heads of the jeering, screaming crowds that grew ever thicker. There were at first fourteen corpses in all, all of them riddled by bullets. Two of them were tied together: the man had a huge shaven head; the woman had long chestnut hair, matted by congealed blood, that veiled her face. In the beginning her gray, blood-stained skirt had hung down, exposing her silken panties and bare thighs, erotic even in death. But a priest had come along and protested against such immodesty. The two bodies had been lowered; the girl's skirt had been tied above her knees, so that the upper part of her curvaceous legs were covered when the couple was hoisted up again, this time bound together by a cord in a grotesque postmortem embrace.

As newcomers arrived, they could hear the sizzling murmurs of the throng: "That is Mussolini, the shit, and his whore mistress . . . Il fucking Duce and his puttana girl friend . . . Musso and Clara Petacci . . . Look at them . . . the traitors . . . dead at last . . . justice has been done."

A speeding car drove up, braking to a noisy halt. Four men wearing red partisan scarfs burst out, dragging with them a battered and bleeding man. They pushed him just under the bodies of Mussolini and la Petacci.

"Look up at your great master. There you see your great Duce."

The man was Achille Starace, for eight years secretary general of the

Fascist party and one of Benito's most faithful followers. He looked up at the dead man and then pulled together his broken body into an erect posture. He somehow clicked his heels and thrust forward his right arm in Fascist salute. The crowd became silent and his voice, hoarse but powerful, was easy to hear as he shouted as loud as he could: "Viva Il Duce!" Then pistol and machine-gun bullets mowed him down. His body was also jerked up, feet first, by a rope, bringing the number of dead hanging in midair to a total of fifteen.

The bodies were still suspended in front of the gasoline station in the piazzale Loreto, one of the most populous areas of Milan, as the vanguard of Mark Clark's Fifth Army and correspondents entered the city. Milan had already been taken by the partisans. They had carried out quick and bloody justice. In no other part of Italy had the partisans been so unrelenting, so fast and so thorough in their killing of Fascists or suspected Fascists. Partisans told correspondents they acted quickly for fear that if the Americans captured Mussolini, they would give him a military trial and that might result in his life being spared. Besides, they said, they wanted all of the Fascist hierarchy to die for having betrayed Italy.

Perhaps this fierce, bloodthirsty desire for revenge crystallized in northern Italy because there was no longer any doubt who might win the war. The Fascists were finished. There was no need to worry about their coming back into power. When Naples and even Rome fell, there were still some doubts as to what might happen in the future. But with the fall of Milan it was the end of the war in Italy, and Fascists could be killed without any danger of reprisals.

The execution of Mussolini climaxed the story of his ever-waning power after the Fascist Grand Council voted against him just before midnight on July 24, 1943. The following afternoon he called on the king, who informed him that he had already been replaced by Marshal Pietro Badoglio as premier. After a stormy twenty-minute session, Il Duce returned to his car in the royal courtyard but a carabiniere officer informed him that "for security reasons" he must leave in an ambulance that had arrived only a few minutes before.

"It is for your protection, Your Excellency," the officer respectfully said. "The king has insisted that you run no risks of being attacked."

Apparently, Musso believed the officer and, without objecting further, quietly entered the ambulance which took off at full speed, with its siren shrilling. The driver only slowed down after Mussolini objected to such reckless driving in the center of Rome. The ambulance finally stopped at a carabiniere headquarters on the outskirts of the city where, still believing he was being given protection and was not a prisoner, Mussolini spent the night. The next morning he was told he was being taken to his home in Forli, in northern Italy. He entered a curtained limousine along with two police chiefs and was driven off. Pulling back the curtains, he remarked: "We are going south, not in the direction of Forli. What's happening?"

"Orders have been changed," one of the officers said.

At Gaeta, a port between Rome and Naples, Musso was transferred onto a small steamer, *Il Persefone*. He was locked in a cabin. According to letters he wrote to his wife, sailors took up a collection and gave him about two thousand lire. They also gave him some clean underwear, socks, and a shirt. As he had taken practically no money with him when he went to call on the king, Musso was almost penniless. As Il Duce he never needed cash. The boat took him to the island of Ponza where he was kept under guard.

After a few weeks there, he was removed to the island of Maddalena — near Sardinia — from where he was taken after a week or so, to a hideaway near Aquila, in the Abruzzi mountains, known as Il Gran Sasso. Mussolini, now fully aware that he was a prisoner, described the place as the "highest prison in the world." One day while he was strolling around the small hotel reserved for him and his carabiniere guards, a shepherd came up to him. "I hear you are Il Duce," he whispered. "Is it true?"

"Yes," said Mussolini. "It is true."

The shepherd kissed his hand and said, "The Germans are looking for you everywhere. I will tell them."

The shepherd passed the word on to the Germans. They investigated the report and confirmed it. Hitler acted quickly. He sent a rescue force of five hundred paratroopers, headed by Igor Sorensky, plus a detachment of SS. At the time, Hitler put out the story that there had been a pitched battle "and some of the paratroopers were killed." The idea was to convince the Italians that the Führer was willing to spill German blood for a Fascist Italy. But in reality the rescue party carried an Italian hostage — General Soleti — which may have been one of the reasons why the Italian carabinieri didn't shoot. Mussolini watched the arrival of the Germans from his bedroom window, cheering them and wildly waving his arms in welcome.

From the Gran Sasso he was flown by a small plane to the Pratica di

Mare airfield outside of Rome and then transferred to a larger plane which took him to a meeting with Hitler at Rastenberg, Germany. He also met his wife and some of his children who were awaiting him in Germany. It was the first time that Donna Rachele had talked with her husband since she had learned the glamorous Clara Petacci was his mistress. When Mussolini disappeared after calling on the king, Donna Rachele had no idea what had happened to him. Friends trying to be helpful suggested various optimistic possibilities, such as his hiding out with friends. At this point one of the women servants let slip the remark: "Perhaps the Duce is at the home of his mistress."

Signora Mussolini didn't hesitate to ask the name of the mistress. She was reluctantly informed that it was Clara Petacci, an attractive daughter of the physician, Dr. Petacci, who was one of the few doctors accredited to the Vatican. Donna Rachele was not shocked nor surprised. She knew in a general way all about her husband's promiscuity. No woman could take her place, she later told friends.

"I am the mother of his children. I am his wife. I am the woman who has shared all his struggles and successes," she said. "Other women are only of passing sex interest."

Clara, however, had proved to be more than a transient sex adventure, but even so Donna Rachele accepted her as part of the Italian way of life. She reasoned that Benito was a good husband and father, and if he wanted to have a fancy woman on the side, it was his Italian manhood's right. As long as the affair didn't break up the family.

Clara first went to bed with Benito in 1936. It was just after she reportedly staged a fake breakdown of her car on the Rome-Ostia highway over which, she had learned, Il Duce was traveling that day. The randy dictator, seeing a sexy young girl and her chauffeur stranded along the roadside, offered her a lift. She readily accepted and their romance began immediately. She was twenty-four; he was fifty-two.

In accordance with Hitler's designs, Musso returned to Italy as Il Duce in miniature, establishing himself as the head of the Fascist Social Republic on the shores of Lake Garda at Salo. He lived in a luxury villa with Donna Rachele while Clara moved into a nearby cottage. It was from his Nazi-guarded headquarters that he rejected the appeal of his own favorite daughter, Edda, to save the life of her husband Count Ciano. Ciano had been condemned to death by a special Fascist tribunal at Verona with other members of the Fascist Grand Council who had voted against Mussolini at its historic last meeting. Musso was now a sick, disillusioned man. His mind wasn't as alert as before. He seemed to be in a daze, unable to make decisions. He had lost all his fire and energy. He was a complete puppet of the Nazis around him.

When the Fifth Army began advancing quickly through northern Italy, the Germans decided to pull out. Musso was placed in the front seat of an autocar, next to the driver. A dozen armed German soldiers sat in the back. It was part of a small motorized column headed for Switzerland. As the vehicles neared the border, a group of Italian partisans halted the Germans. At first Musso wasn't noticed because he wore a German helmet pulled well down over his face and a German sergeant's overcoat. He also wore black glasses. He had a submachine gun between his knees.

One of the partisans, known as Sergeant Bill, became suspicious. Perhaps it was the black glasses or the way Musso was slouched down in his seat and refused to answer questions in German. The partisan asked the driver: "What's the matter with him?"

"He's drunk," the driver replied.

Sergeant Bill yanked off the glasses and knocked back the helmet. There was the well-known big shaved head of Il Duce. He was pale and trembling.

"It's Mussolini! It's the stronzo Mussolini," Sergeant Bill cried out. The partisans came running.

Sergeant Bill grabbed the submachine gun, which bore the initials B.M., from between Musso's knees and yanked him out of the autocar. Apparently stunned, the onetime dictator didn't attempt to resist. Dozens of partisans, their pistols and rifles pointed at him, surrounded him. They marched him off to the Dongo City Hall where he was taken down into the basement. He took off his overcoat saying, "It is hot." He dropped it indifferently on the floor. Underneath he wore the uniform of a Black Shirt officer. In his belt he carried a Beretta. He was quickly relieved of the revolver. It was 3 P.M. on April 27, 1945.

"I've been betrayed again," he said.

"You betrayed Italy," one of the partisans, identified as Carlo Ortelli, a businessman, rebutted. "You stabbed France in the back and dragged your country into a war on the side of the Germans."

"If I had not gone to war with Germany, the Germans would have killed off all Italians with poison gas."

"That's not true," Ortelli said. "Hitler always said he could win the war without Italy. He didn't even want Italy in the war."

"And the speech you made at Munich, threatening death to all anti-Fascists in Italy, was that spontaneous?''

"Of course not. I was forced to say what I said. I was surrounded by SS troopers.''

"Is there any reason why we should not kill you?'' Ortelli asked.

"Yes. I pardoned many anti-Fascist Italians who had been sentenced to death. I stopped the torture of many Italians by the Germans. I tried to make sure that Italians taken prisoner by the Nazis were treated well . . . I also tried hard to . . .''

But Musso didn't finish the sentence. Somebody shoved him. He asked for something to drink. He was given a glass of water and a cup of coffee. He was then marched off to the carabiniere station where he was told he would await his execution. But before leaving the city hall, he was disguised by the partisans. They bandaged his characteristic head with wads of gauze. A partisan, wearing a white gown walked beside him, pretending to be a male nurse. These subterfuges were aimed at fooling any remnants of die-hard Fascists who might want to rescue their former leader.

The main door of the carabiniere station had hardly closed behind him when a Spanish-make auto was halted by another partisan patrol in the town of Dongo. There were five people in the car. The man, who was driving the car, said he was a Spaniard and, pointing to one of the women, said she was his wife. The two kids were also his, he said, while the other woman, he explained, had merely asked for a ride northward. He showed documents that appeared to verify what he said. The hitchhiker, stylishly garbed in a light blue suit, blue shoes, and a blue scarf around her head, refused to show her documents. The five of them were put up in a Dongo hotel, and two female partisans searched the mystery woman. They found papers identifying her as Clara Petacci. She was immediately taken into custody. The self-styled Spaniard was recognized by other partisans as Marcello Petacci, her brother. He was also locked up.

At three in the morning, Mussolini and Clara Petacci were taken in separate cars in the direction of Milan. At dawn the cars stopped and the two were allowed to speak to each other. Clara immediately hugged Mussolini, asking him: "Aren't you glad to see me? Aren't you glad I'm with you to the very end?''

"Yes, Clara. Thank you,'' he said almost mechanically. She kissed and embraced him and he responded wearily.

Later the convoy stopped again, this time at a farmhouse and the two of them were locked in a kitchen. They were served eggs, bread, and milk.

There was no table, so they ate off a wooden box. They were given a mattress to lie on and they slept — and perhaps made love for the last time — until past noon. Then they were awakened and put in separate cars again. As they neared Milan, the cars stopped at a walled mansion, known as the Villa Belmonte. Here one of the top partisan leaders, Colonel Valery, read their death sentences. The two were stood up against the wall of the villa, their backs to the firing squad. They were separated by only a few feet. Mussolini had lost his helmet and was wearing a worker's cap. Clara had lost her scarf. Submachine guns crackled. Mussolini fell to the ground first, spurting blood from many bullet wounds. Clara jerked up and twisted around as the machine gun slugs ripped into her. She dropped on top of her lover.

In the meantime, twelve ministers of Musso's Fascist Republic were executed in Dongo by a firing squad of partisans. Marcello Petacci, who was to have been executed with them, tried to escape by diving into the lake and was shot to death as he attempted to swim away. His body sank beneath the surface.

During the night the twelve bodies in Dongo were piled into a truck and as it stopped at the Villa Belmonte, the bodies of the late dictator and his girlfriend were dumped unceremoniously on top of the others. The charnel truck was then driven to Milan's Loreto Square where the bodies were strung up by their feet for the populace to see and applaud. It was the end of Fascism; the end of the war in Italy.

# PART III

# THE POPE
# AND
# SOPHIA LOREN

# CHAPTER I

It was Christmas Eve, 1947, when I came back to Rome. Many things had changed. Italy was a republic. Pibe and I were estranged. I had no job and was broke. I had decided I was through with newspaper work after being fired by the United Press in Peking. Now I was determined to be literary. I wanted to write a book about news agencies and what their speed, tension, and a thousand deadlines a day do to a reporter.

Arriving around nine in the evening, I took a single room without bath in the Hotel de la Ville, just out of sentiment I guess. That was where the old Fifth Army press quarters had been located. I could afford it for a few days while I looked for something cheaper, but the Grand, even for a night, was out of the question. I washed up quickly and left the hotel. There was no hurry but I was anxious to see Rome again. I wandered the long way around, including down the Spanish Steps, to the Foreign Press Club. At 11 P.M. on the night before Christmas, it was deserted downstairs except for a barman. I recognized him. It was old Libero who limped. I had hired him while I was president of the club.

"Signor Presidente, benvenuto," he called out to me. "E la signora?"

"Va bene, grazie."

"Is she with you in Rome?"

"Not at the moment."

"But la signora will come?"

"I hope so."

"I admire la signora. Che donna straordinaria!"

I ordered a Vecchia Romagna to get him off the subject of Pibe. I couldn't afford White Horse on my present budget. I asked him to have a drink with me. At first he declined, but when I insisted he accepted, pouring himself a glass of red wine.

"To the signora," he said. We touched glasses. "Are you still with that news agency?" He pronounced it: "Uneeted Press."

"No," I said. "I am trying to write a book."

"With la signora?"

I didn't answer, pretending not to hear him. He caught on then that I didn't want to discuss my present situation and changed the subject.

It wasn't that I didn't want to talk about it, but it was too complicated for me to explain offhand to a nonnewspaperman, Catholic and Italian barman who probably was just trying to make conversation. He would be embarrassed if I told him about Pibe wanting to marry somebody else but not wanting to divorce me although we didn't believe in marriage and about my affair in Peking with the Manchu Monster.

The Manchu Monster was over six feet tall, strong as an ox, and liked to wrestle with me at private parties, ending up with the two of us fucking on the floor or the couch amidst critical boos or cheers. They were terrific days of abandon with nobody seeming to worry about anything: life or pride, VD or crashing airplanes. The Manchu Monster, smoking U.S. cigars, used to lead the correspondents in columns of rickshaws to opium dens and marvelous restaurants with force-fed ducks, looking as though they had been blown up with bicycle pumps. Then I was fired by the UP, and she bedded down with a major in the American secret service.

"You ding hao," she said as she drove off with the major.

I asked the barman where I might find some diversion on Christmas Eve in postwar Rome.

"In somebody's home," he replied, "where there are many children. But as you know, dottore, Christmas is a religious feast day in Italy. It is Epiphany, with La Befana giving pieces of coal to bad children and toys to good ones, that is more festive."

I found his talk depressing, paid up and wished him a Buon Natale. I went out in search of a livelier place. I thought of via Veneto but that was too expensive. I meandered around the side streets sprouting from nearby piazza San Silvestro. On via Belsiana, there was a splotch of light on the sidewalk. I hurried toward it. Looking through a curtained window, I could see the place was crowded. I could hear laughter and arguing going on. I even thought I heard an English phrase or so. Over the door was the single word: Bottiglieria. I went in.

The place was one big L-shaped room. It was ablaze with garish neon lights, only slightly dimmed by the haze of cigarette smoke. Nobody paid any attention to me as I entered, not even the waiters. I found a small empty table and sat down. I looked around. There was no Christmas tree, no holly, no sign of the yule. It was full of all kinds of human oddments that certainly were not family types. There were four street cleaners in their blue-gray uniforms playing scopone, a popular Italian card game, at one table. There were several whores occupying another table. At least, I judged that's what they were from the way they appraised me. There was a big group that occupied three tables strung out in a row. A distinguished-looking gray-haired man in a neatly pressed, tailored suit of expensive cloth sat at the head of it. His attire contrasted with that of the others who, for the most part, were shabbily dressed. There were two women in the group; one also looked like an Italian prostitute, and the other, who was blonde and middle aged, struck me as being a down-and-out intellectual. It was the same old pub ratio of the country: one woman to ten men; and the women were foreigners or Italian prostitutes. As I watched the gray-haired man, he turned his head, saw me, and stared back.

"Isn't your name Packard?" he called out above the hubbub of loud wine-induced talk that echoed and reechoed through the place.

"Yes, it is."

"Come and join us. That's not an invitation to a free drink but to be part of the company. Everybody pays for his own drink here, including the women."

Feeling lonely, I was glad to join the weird collection, which seemed to include at least several queers.

"My name is Alfredo," the gray-haired man said. Then turning to the others he said: "This is Packard, a widely known journalist."

Some nodded, some muttered their names and a few just stared. Alfredo motioned to a waiter who brought me a chair. I found myself sitting between Alfredo and a young American who was filing away on a piece of metal. It took me some time to realize he was fashioning a work of art. I finally discerned that it was the figurine of a man with a gargantuan lingam flung over one shoulder. I also noticed the sculptor wore no socks. A carafe of red wine and a glass suddenly appeared in front of me.

"How did you know my name?" I asked Alfredo.

"I read that article in *Time* about you. In the Press section. It was called 'Odd Man Out' and had a photo of you."

"And you're still speaking to me?"

"It was an amusing article. I remember it quoted you as saying that this was the fifth time the UP had fired you, and that made things even because you had also quit five times, and once it wasn't clear whether you quit or were fired."

"That's right. That was my farewell speech to the American correspondents in Peking. But it also described me as a bit of a bastard."

"Oh, hell, who isn't."

"You mean *Time* ran an article about you!" one of the Americans gasped. He was obviously impressed and didn't care what the magazine had said about me. I was a character. I was accepted at the table.

I found myself attending Alfredo's wine-swilling symposiums almost every evening. The cheap prices fitted my budget and the conversation was at least a distraction. Everybody seemed to be an extrovert and proud of being a failure. They seemed to think that lack of success meant genius. Alfredo, as a self-appointed MC, sat back and adroitly drew out the others around him, not that he was bashful about talking about himself. During his absence the others often referred to him as the Venerable Fag. He knew it and liked the title. In fact, he often talked about his sex adventures with other men and lauded homosexuality at every opportunity.

I asked him one night why he thought so many homosexuals came to Italy. He turned the question over to an unemployed young actor, who had a deep stentorian voice but who nevertheless was as queer as a three-dollar bill. He was an American.

"How would you explain that, Nick?"

"Well, to begin with I think we are welcome here," Nick said in his deep bass voice. "Nobody seems to have any guilt complexes about the subject. And I find most Italian men I've met are half and half anyway. If they aren't really gay, they don't object to a little buggery among friends. Look at all the Italian boys who prostitute themselves on via Veneto and in the Villa Borghese. They aren't really gay; they're rough trade. I even buggered a carabiniere once. He was just being friendly."

"I think you're right," Alfredo intervened. "I'm having an affair with a member of the Lazio football team. He's married, a father of two children, but he's got such a big tool his wife can't take it very often. It hurts her too much."

"But you can take it?" somebody asked.

"Obviously," Alfredo replied smugly. "I said we were having an affair."

One night as the group broke up at 2 A.M. I found myself walking along the via Belsiana with the blonde woman who had attracted my attention on the first night at the Dead Dog. That's what Alfredo had nicknamed the bottiglieria. Nobody seemed to know its real name. Even Italians now called it Il Cane Morto. The blonde was a German woman named Erika who taught in a language school. She was fluent in English, French, Italian, and Hungarian as well as her own tongue. I asked if I could escort her home, and she said yes, it would be nice of me. She told me she lived on the via Gregoriana and that the most direct way was up the Spanish Steps.

At the stone balustrade halfway up the steps, we stopped and looked down into via Condotti. The asphalt shimmered like a frozen river in the winter moonlight. It was very cold for Rome. I put my arm around Erika as we leaned against the balustrade. She didn't object.

"How did you happen to come to Rome?" I asked.

"When Hitler began persecuting the Jews, I slipped into Italy. It was easy during the early days of the Axis if you were German and the Nazi officials didn't know you were Jewish."

"What about the Italians?"

"You know what they are like. You can work things out with them. While Mussolini made anti-Semitic proclamations to please Hitler, many Italians befriended us. I'll always like the Italians because they saved my life."

I squeezed her shoulder to let her know I realized what she must have gone through during the war.

"You're sweet," she said.

I kissed her on the cheek, my tongue moistening her skin. Soon I was kissing her closed lips. She pushed me away, saying: "I thought you were a queer."

"Me? How could you think that?"

"Well, for one thing you seem to get along with queers."

"I haven't anything against them, but I'm certainly not one of them."

"And another thing, you seem to like talking about homosexuality."

"Well, it's an interesting subject. I'd like to learn more about it."

"Maybe Alfredo's right."

"What do you mean."

"He says you are a latent homo. He thinks if you tried it once, you would be converted."

"You mean I'd turn queer?"

"That's right."

"Nonsense."

"He also asked me to tell you he would be glad to try to convert you."

"Why that Venerable Shit. Convert me! I'll show you how queer I am."

I grabbed her and kissed her hard on the mouth. She finally opened it and my tongue darted in between her lips. It was arousing, succulent kissing, made wonderful by just being on the historic Spanish Steps. I had fantasies of erotic Rome-by-night tours with fucking in the Colosseum, the Forum, the Pantheon, in the Catacombs, and on the steps of Saint Peter's Basilica. I opened our overcoats so that our bodies came closer together without interrupting our ardent tongue-and-mouth play. I rubbed her crotch through the outside of her skirt, and her hand fumbled with my fly. She finally opened it.

"Oh, the poor little thing," she said fondling it with her bare hand.

"Your hand is like ice."

"You want me to stop?"

"No. Americans like ice."

"If you want I'll kiss it."

"Please, please do. That warm mouth of yours will bring it right up."

She bent down on her knees.

"Che succede qui?" a rough voice demanded.

I looked up as I pulled Erika to her feet and closed my overcoat. It was a policeman glaring at me.

"What do you mean what's happening here?" I said, suddenly recalling that Alfredo had told me that the best way you could cope with a bad situation in those days was to accuse an Italian of being a Fascist.

"We are sweethearts embracing each other in the moonlight on the beautiful Spanish Steps. What's wrong with that?"

"You have committed an obscene act in public," he said.

"That was an old Fascist law. I am an American journalist, and I will report to the American press that Italy is still applying Fascist laws to Americans who helped to make Italy a democratic country. I will denounce you as a Fascist."

I felt like a soapbox orator as I made my little speech, but I could see

202

that I was impressing him. He became uncertain. Before he had time to ask me for my documents, I pulled out my American passport and a dozen press cards from a dozen countries which I always carried with me. He only glanced at them.

"No, dottore, I am not being Fascist. I merely asked you what you were doing. I did not realize you were two romantic sweethearts just embracing in the moonlight. It could have been illegal prostitution. Robbery. Rape. I don't know what. I had to investigate." His tone was apologetic.

"Well, let's forget it," I said, trying to sound benevolent, "for the sake of Italo-American relations." I pulled out a pack of Chesterfields. "Would you like a cigarette?"

"No, grazie. I don't smoke while on duty."

"Then take the pack and smoke later."

He hesitated but finally took it. I held out my hand and he shook it. Then Erika held out her hand and he shook that. We were all friends together. After a few more pleasantries he left, wishing us a buona notte.

"Christ, that was a close call," I said to Erika. "My cock is hanging out under my overcoat."

Stepping behind her so the policeman couldn't see me if he were looking, I pushed it back into my trousers and buttoned them.

"You were wonderful," Erika said.

"Not really. Alfredo deserves the credit. He told me that was the way to act with tough Italians. Accuse them of being Fascists."

We were silent for a moment and then, without saying a word, we resumed walking up the steps. The incident had killed any sex desire in both of us.

When I left her at the front door of her pensione she said, "I'm sorry I can't ask you up." She unlocked the door and started to go in. Then she hesitated. "What shall I tell Alfredo? You know, about wanting to convert you."

I surprised myself with my answer. "Tell him I'll think it over."

# CHAPTER II

After I had been in Rome a couple of months, I decided I was having too good a time and not getting enough work done on my book. I had to do something about it. I was already in my third pensione, but my tiny dark bedroom was not an inspiring place to work and the management objected if I typed after 10 P.M. For a time I tried working in the press room of the Stampa Estera, but not being a correspondent any longer, I didn't feel at home in the place, and also everybody kept asking me where and how was Pibe.

At the Press Club, I inquired about small Italian towns where I might concentrate on my book but most of the suggestions didn't click with me. I decided to sound out the habitués of the Dead Dog. There they were unanimous. According to them, there was only one place I should go to. The sculptor of junk miniatures described it as the sex capital of Europe. Even Alfredo recommended it.

"It's full of Moorish history," Alfredo said. "It was discovered by some of the gay clan. Now it has become a colony of writers and artists. And the locals, mostly fishermen, are friendly. There's a wayward bus from Rome that takes you right to the place."

The place was Positano on the Amalfi Drive, midway between Sorrento and Amalfi. I looked it up in reference books at the Press Club. What I read convinced me it was what I was looking for. So I announced one night at the Dead Dog that I was leaving for Positano in a few days.

A cub reporter of the *Rome Daily American,* who dropped in at the bottiglieria almost nightly, said, "You'll miss the Rome whorehouses."

I had become friendly with the young reporter after he had taught me that the one way to keep warm in Rome in wintertime was to go to a brothel, stay until the madam kicked you out, and then go to another one. We used to spend entire afternoons talking in one bordello after another. He said he was so busy collecting material for a book that he didn't have time to write. While cafés, tearooms, and bars were cold, the Italian brothels had central heating, the result of an old Fascist law still in effect.

Whenever we went upstairs, we always took the same girl, one after another, of course. There was no fancy sex, like a threesome, in an Italian brothel. Later the reporter and I compared notes on the prostitute's reactions. He described it as psychoanalytical fucking.

"I'm sorry to hear you're leaving," Alfredo said. Later when nobody was listening, he whispered, "You must walk home with me tonight. We must have a talk."

After the Dead Dog closed, Alfredo and I slipped away from the others who were still lingering outside the bottiglieria.

"Listen," he said, "you told Erika you would think it over. But of course, leaving suddenly like this is your decision I suppose."

"Not really. I thought you wanted to talk it over."

"Fine. Come up to my place for a nightcap."

"But only for a nightcap."

He chuckled, getting what I meant.

We walked about a dozen blocks until we came to a tall office building. He took out a big key, opened the huge portone, and led me to an elevator. We went up to the top floor, then walked another flight to his penthouse. It overlooked the piazza Minerva where there is an obelisk balanced on the back of a white elephant.

By the time we reached the living room, a shapely young maid appeared and asked Signor Alfredo what we would like to drink.

"La bottiglia di Scotch, Pina." As she left the room, he turned to me, saying, "It's a special occasion. We need something better than wine."

I looked around the brightly lighted room. Alfredo and I were seated in two old-fashioned Morris chairs, facing each other across a narrow low table. Off in one corner was a green-baize card table reminding me that Alfredo had said he played bridge. In another corner was an oversized divan, covered with black velvety material and wide enough to hold all four cardplayers if they became interested in a more intimate kind of game. There was a big writing desk, some more comfortable chairs. The walls were hung with paintings of the American scene, including two by Grandma Moses. The room made me think I was back in Pennsylvania or New Jersey.

"I like the American decor," I said.

"I have a reason for it. It impresses my Italian boyfriends."

The maid returned with a tray containing a bottle of Ballantine's, a pitcher of water, and a bowl of ice. She set it on the low table. After serving us, she immediately withdrew.

When I had nearly emptied my glass, Alfredo said: "Now what about your decision? Am I going to have a chance to convert you?"

"You'll have to work fast because I am leaving next Monday on that wayward bus you mentioned. Tonight is Thursday." Alfredo started to interrupt me, but I kept on talking. "I would like to have a homo experience with you because I think you really are understanding; it's a mental thing with me. A mental adventure. I don't want to replace your Lazio footballer. I just want to sample it a bit. I like to think of myself as a sort of Marco Polo of sex. If you are willing to be that understanding, we will give it a try. Just once before I leave. Also I will only do the things I want to do. Would you agree to that?"

He thought a moment. Then he said, "Yes, that's better than nothing. It would be an adventure for me, too."

"Fine. There's one other condition."

"What's that?"

"I'd like to have Erika participate. Without a woman present, I don't think I could bring myself to have sexual contact with a man."

"I can understand that, but Erika would create a problem. You saw that tuttofare of mine?"

"You mean the one who served us the whisky?"

I held up my empty glass. He got the hint. He poured Scotch into my glass and passed the ice bowl.

"Well, Pina would object. You see she is like most Italian maids in a man's apartment. They get tangled up with him sexually and become very jealous. This case is more complicated because I'm gay. She doesn't care how many men I have, but I musn't bring women in here for sex or she will make a god-awful scene."

"Is she Sicilian?"

"No. From Parma, North Italy. But all Italians, men or women, are possessive as hell.''

"So, what do we do?"

"We can use my maid instead of Erika."

"Poor Erika! I'll never get to screw her."

We kicked ideas around for a while. Then we finally agreed that I would come to his place on Saturday afternoon at five; Giuseppina, or Pina as he called the tuttofare, would be the girl and not Erika, and he would not insist on anything I didn't want to do.

We shook hands on the agreement. I left immediately, looking over Pina as she escorted me to the door. She was about thirty-two. I tried to imagine how she would look without her clothes on, and suddenly I wondered whether Alfredo had a big or little cock.

# CHAPTER III

Nervous and full of misgivings, I arrived ten minutes late. It was
Alfredo himself who answered the bell. He was wearing a short blue
woolen bathrobe and soft leather slippers. He helped me take off my coat
and escorted me into the living room which, to my surprise, was really
warm. Two gas stoves were burning and sending out a surprising amount
of heat. The lights were on because the windows were all tightly
curtained.

"Where's Pina?" I asked, feeling uneasy at being alone with the
Venerable Fag in a bathrobe. He was a very tidy homo. I noticed a huge
white bath towel had been spread over the black divan, I imagined, to
catch any stains of the sex orgy we were about to have.

"Pina is making herself pretty for you. She'll be in any minute. Why
don't you start undressing. It's nice and warm in here, isn't it?"

"I'll wait till Pina gets here."

"Pina," he called. Then to me he said, "I've described you to her only
as Signor Renato."

The Italian woman, obviously ready, came walking in through a
doorway. She was wearing a knee-length, canary-yellow bathrobe made
out of toweling. She carried another bathrobe; it was red. Well, we
couldn't get mixed up no matter how we became entangled, I thought.
Pina, who on my previous visit had struck me as obsequious, almost

slavelike, suddenly became authoritative, a sort of MC. She led me over to the divan, pushed me gently down on it, and started tactfully undressing me. By tactfully, I mean she didn't irritate me by the way she did it with her nimble fingers. First she took off my shoes, then my necktie. After removing my jacket, she had my torso bare in a few seconds, then slipped off my trousers and socks. While I still had on my swim tights which I always wore as drawers, she helped me put on the red bathrobe. It was the first time anybody laughed. Alfredo was convulsed as well as Pina. The bathrobe didn't even meet over my big whalelike belly. It turned me into a caricature of a fat man.

"Put it on backwards," I told Pina.

She did as I said, then took off my trunks. She slipped out of her bathrobe and carefully hung it over a chair. She had a willowy figure, a bit too thin for me, but I understand that's the way fags think women should look — like boys. Her furry triangle and brown-ringed nipples emphasized her nakedess. Her black hair fell below her shoulders; and I noticed her armpits were unshaven; that was fine with me. I chuckled, recalling the old joke: How do you tell an Italian airplane? By the hair under its wings.

"The lights. Can't we turn off the lights first?" I asked timidly.

"I will dim them, Signor Renato," Pina said. "We must see what we are doing."

She pressed a number of buttons. The room became half-dark but we were more than just silhouettes. I could still see Pina's luxuriant triangle. Alfredo carefully took off his bathrobe and draped it over a chair. When he turned around I could see that he had a good physique for an elderly man. Only his upper arms were flabby. Even in the semidarkness I could see the size of his cock. It was big, much bigger than mine, but I noted with satisfaction that his balls were smaller. I took off my red bathrobe and threw it on a chair.

When I glanced at the divan, I saw Alfredo already stretched out on one side of the divan, stroking himself with his right hand. Pina maneuvered me so that I had to get next to him and then she lay down beside me. Like the lucky Alphonse, I was in the middle. She reached over me and put my right hand on Alfredo's cock and his left hand on mine. Pina then began kissing me on the mouth so that I was having my wish of a bit of normalcy along with the homosexuality. It was a strange feeling touching another man's dong and feeling it grow and harden in my hand. I soon had an erection under Alfredo's expert manual manipulation. Pina, who was as active as an octopus, managed to take my free hand and put it on her snatch. We messed around like this for some time, then Pina suggested I suck Alfredo. I said I didn't think I could do that and she said, "Bene, let him show you how." This took some acrobatic moving around, ending up with me at the end of the divan, my legs dangling over the side. Alfredo, who by this time was kneeling on the floor, pushed his head between my legs; my cock disappeared in his mouth as though he were a sword-swallower. In the meantime, Pina had straddled my head and lowered her raven-pelted crotch onto my face.

"Lick it, caro," she said. "I've put wine on it."

My tongue found the nub of her clitoris. It was like a baby's penis. I lapped it. Alfredo reached up with one of his hands and pinched a nipple of mine. Pina squeezed my other nipple. Meanwhile, Alfredo never stopped lowering and raising his mouth like a suction pump. The stubble on his jaws scratched my thighs.

"Christ, I'm going to shoot," I gurgled into the vulva clamped over my mouth. "I can't hold it any longer."

There was an immediate reaction. Pina raised her bottom high in the air so that my lips were free of her clit, and Alfredo removed his mouth from my nearly exploding shaft.

"God, don't come yet," Alfredo said. "We are just beginning."

Pina suggested that if I tried sucking Alfredo, I wouldn't be in danger of shooting so soon. "Would you?" she asked.

I didn't answer her but thought this was the moment of truth. Mr. Marco Polo, are you going to show any philosophical courage or not? I asked myself. Are you afraid of life? Not sucking a cock is like not eating snails in Paris or bulls' testicles in Madrid or raw fish in Tokyo. You haven't really lived sexually if you haven't sucked a cock.

"Bene," I said to Pina. "I'll try my best." I cautioned Alfredo, "But don't shoot in my mouth."

"I'll pull it out in time," he promised.

Pina as MC shifted us around, and Alfredo and I were facing each other on our sides on the divan in what was an all-male version of soixante-neuf. Our feet were extended beyond each other's head. His genitals were right in front of my face and mine were in front of his. By this time we were both limp down there.

He started sucking me off again. Pina came over to me.

"Coraggio," she said, lightly pushing my head toward Alfredo's phallus. "Put it in your mouth."

"Do something to me, Pina, and then I will."

She started tonguing an ear and running her hand up and down my spinal column. At the end of each run, she pushed a finger into my anus. I looked at Alfredo's lingam. It was gray and pulpy, like the thick stem of a giant mushroom. One ball seemed smaller than the other in the wrinkled brownish pouch of his scrotum which had long white hairs on it. If it hadn't been for Pina's ministrations, I would have abandoned my determination to go through with it.

"Coraggio," I heard Pina say again. "Close your eyes and put it in your mouth." She pushed her finger deeper into my asshole.     Here goes, I thought.

I put the flaccid thing in my mouth. It tasted like asparagus. I tried to imitate Alfredo's technique of shuttling my head back and forth on it. Several times Alfredo let out a yelp: "Ouch! Your teeth!" Then it began to swell up, and I couldn't keep much more than the purple knob in my mouth. There was no way I could get it past the palate the way he seemed to do,swallow it the way beer-drinking champions open the whole gullet and swill down the entire contents of the big stein.

"Deeper, deeper," he called out.

I tried, but it was useless. I either choked or felt nauseated. Finally, I drew my mouth off his cock.

"I'm afraid I can't do any more of it," I said. "I tried hard."

"You did all right for the first time. Let's have a break," Alfredo said. "Pina turn on more lights."

The room immediately became brighter. Pina knew the routine. She passed me a glass of gargle and another to my host. She held out a blue and orange beach bucket for us to spew the mouthwash into. She also handed me a bottle of alcohol and a towel. We put on our bathrobes — mine backwards again. Pina filled our glasses with Ballantine's, ice, and water.

As the three of us sipped the whisky, I told Alfredo that I was sorry, but I wanted to call off the rest of the lesson or whatever it was I was receiving.

"Oh, no," he protested. "We haven't even come yet. We at least have to come. All three of us."

"Christ, Alfredo, I'm not going to do any more than I've done."

Looking like a Roman senator in the days of the Caesars, in his togalike bathrobe, Alfredo settled back to talk. He wet his lips with the Ballantine's and said: "Pack, you may think you have just dabbled in homosexuality, but let me tell you that cocksucking is not really a homo act. If you're oral, you like to suck things. You've lapped cunts, in fact you just lapped Pina's. There's no difference when it comes to putting a sex organ in the mouth whether it's a pussy or a pecker. Both of those are oral objects. Fellatio and cunnilingus are the same. The real act of homosexuality involves the anus. Homosexuality is anal not oral. The prostate of a man is like the clitoris of a woman. You bring pressure to bear on the prostate just right, and it's like titillating the clit. In fact, the prostate is the clitoris of the male asshole. So you really have not had much of a homosexual experience so far today.''

''I certainly am not going to be buggered. If that's what you mean.''

''You've buggered a woman, haven't you?''

''Yes.''

''Well, then you can bugger me. That'll fix me up. But first you should fuck Pina, that'll fix her up. She deserves it.''

Alfredo apparently made some kind of sign to Pina because suddenly she came over, purring in my ear: ''I really need it, caro. I'm going crazy for a cazzo duro. I need a real normal man, like you.'' Kissing me on the mouth, she drew me to my feet, pulled off my bathrobe, and tickled my behind. Her tongue probed the inside of my mouth. I became excited and erect again. She dropped back on the divan pulling me with her and into her. Her buttocks moved up and down and rotated at the same time. She was like a supine bellydancer.

We climaxed together.

As Pina and I lay on the divan breathing hard, and holding onto each other, Alfredo did the honors. He brought us each a fresh basin of warm water and before we dried ourselves, he poured out more drinks for the two of us. He also refilled his own glass and then sat on the side of the bed, giving me a chance to recuperate. He was a sly old fox.

''Here's to a good time in Positano,'' he said, clicking his glass against mine.

''To Positano, '' I echoed, knowing he was just waiting impatiently for me to recover my virility. I was in no hurry. Now that Pina had satisfied me, I would rather forego what was in store for me, but I couldn't be that mean to the old queen.

We finished our drinks, then Pina said: ''I think you two had better begin.''

Stripping off his bathrobe, Alfredo placed himself on the edge of the divan, lying on his back, with his bare feet on the carpet. Pina stripped off my robe and took off her own. Suddenly, like a magician, she produced

212

out of nowhere a bottle of olive oil. She rubbed it over my tallywacker which soon became stiff and vibrant; then she pushed an anointed finger up Alfredo's rectum to lubricate that, too. Immediately, Alfredo lifted his feet off the floor so that his thighs splayed above his belly. Pina guided my greased dick between his uplifted legs and into his bunghole. She kissed me on the mouth as a heterosexual gesture. Next she placed my right hand on his cock, whispering in my ear, "Milk him." At the same time I penetrated deep into the rear of him.

"That's it. Just there," Alfredo muttered, his eyes closed. As I moved back and forth inside of him, his truncheon grew in size and rigidity in my hand. "Faster, faster," he cried.

I obliged in both ways. His face became flushed and distorted as though with agony. He moaned and then shrieked, "I'm coming, I'm coming. Don't stop."

Cream spurted from his pego, splattering over both of our chests. He scooped up the translucent semen with avid fingers, licking them like a child who had been eating sticky candy. His eyes remained closed. He lay without moving, breathing hard. I flopped down beside him on the divan, but was careful not to come in contact with his body. After my orgasm inside of him, he revolted me; everything revolted me. I noticed the two Grandma Moses pictures on the wall. For a moment their folksy quality made me feel like a sinner, only I didn't believe in sin; I didn't believe in god. Pina cleaned the mess off my peter with a washcloth and warm water. I didn't look down at what she was doing. I didn't want to see the streaks of brown excrement being removed. Suddenly, I jumped up and rushed to the bathroom and vomited.

# CHAPTER IV

The bus proved to be wayward all right. It stopped ten minutes at Terracina so passengers could have drinks and go to the toilet; an hour at Naples for lunch; half an hour at a cameo atelier; and two hours at Pompeii simply because some tourists aboard wanted to see the excavations; it halted again at Sorrento, then retraced itself over ten miles in order to get back on the highway to Positano. I noticed the driver drank without paying at the cafe in Terracina; ate for free in the restaurant in Naples in front of which he had halted his bus; received tips from the English travelers who wanted to visit Pompeii; and I imagined he got a commission on what his passengers bought in the cameo workshop we visited. I also observed that he was a chain smoker.

"Would you like a Chesterfield?" I asked him after moving up into the seat behind him as we left Sorrento. I was the only remaining passenger by that time. It was about 7 P.M. but dark, the sun having disappeared behind the mountains.

"Si, grazie," he said.

"Take the whole pack."

He did, thanking me profusely. That was a big tip in those days.

"You know Positano?"

"No. This is my first trip. Do you know a good cheap place to stay?"

"Sure. I am a Positanese."

"Look out," I cried, as the bus swerved around a hairpin bend with its headlights revealing a great void of nothing between the precipitous side of the highway and the sea a thousand feet below. I thought for a moment we were going over the edge.

"Niente. I know these curves by heart. A bus did go over recently and everybody was killed. But I'm a good driver."

I was afraid to talk any more for fear he would turn around to answer me, but he kept turning around just the same, asking me questions.

"Where do you want to stay? Up high or lower down?"

"On the beach, if possible."

"Try the Buca di Bacco."

I held my breath as we skidded around another sharp turn. It sounded as though he had said the "Hole of Bacchus" in Italian.

"What is it?"

"A tavern on the beach."

He concentrated as he put on speed entering the upper, mountainous part of Positano. Then we corkscrewed down to the piazza Mulino in the center of the town, but still high up. The driver got my suitcase and portable typewriter out of the baggage compartment. He called to somebody.

"Hey, Toscanini, show this signore to the Buca."

I looked up. There was a dirty, gnomelike-looking man near the bus stop. The light of a tabaccaio shone on him. He was conducting an imaginary orchestra. And from time to time he would change roles with a violinist, a pianist, or drummer in his make-believe combo, pretending to play their various instruments and humming all the while. The driver had to call him several times before the old man interrupted his antics and came over to us.

"You-a Amuricun?" he asked. "Me like Amuricuns. Best-a peeple in whole world. Sure-a ting. Take-ya to Buca. Jussa follow me." He picked up the suitcase and took the Remington from my hand. I followed after him.

We went down some spiral steps, along a curved, walled path, and past a church with a green and yellow dome. Then we came to a piazza made impressive with two bronze lions at the top of a row of five steps leading down to the beach itself. We passed a few fisher types on the way. They all greeted us with "Ciao, Toscanini. Buona sera, signore." We turned left at the end of the steps. Toscanini opened a door and I followed him into a brightly lighted room. It was huge. Some tables were set for dinner but they were unoccupied. Off in one corner were several bare tables where more fisher types were playing cards or watching the games.

"Joe," my guide called out. "Come-a quick. I gotta Americun wit me. He wanna room a gudda a room. Hey, Joe, where the hell ya hiding?"

The group around the card tables also called out cheerily to us.

"Buona sera," I called back, liking the way everybody seemed friendly. A husky young man wearing corduroy trousers, a blue sweater over an open-neck shirt with a flowing collar appeared from behind the bar which I hadn't noticed at first. It was behind an arch.

"Dissa man is Joe," Toscanini said to me. "He getcha room. So long."

I called Toscanini back and gave him a tip. He then disappeared quickly as though knowing he wasn't permitted to stay long inside the Buca.

Joe turned out to be Giuseppe Rispoli, one of the sons of the Rispoli family which owned the Buca. His particular function was that of barman. He led me upstairs. A maid in a blue uniform had taken over my baggage, and on the first floor I was introduced to Giuseppe's brother, Giulio, and Giulio's wife, Doya, a German Jewess who also had found refuge in Fascist Italy during Nazism. I told them I had come to Positano to write a book.

In no time, they installed me in a large comfortable room overlooking the beach. It was furnished simply with a double bed, a table, three wooden chairs, and a washstand complete with pitcher and basin. Snake-shaped coils of cloth filled with sand were placed on windowsills to keep out the cold wind from the sea. There were electric lights but the bulbs were small, offering only a dim illumination. There was a toilet and bathtub down the hallway for general use.

I looked out the window. I felt thrilled and cleansed by the sight of the sea. It reminded me of my birthplace — Atlantic City — only the Mediterranean was so mild compared to the wave-laced Atlantic.

# CHAPTER V

I tidied up a bit, poured myself a drink from the White Horse bottle I had extravagantly brought with me as a traveling companion, and went downstairs for supper. It must have been about 9:30 P.M. I went over to the bar and ordered an Italian beer thinking of my budget. Giuseppe interrupted a game of poker dice with an Englishman and a French girl to serve me. I watched them play while I sipped my drink. As they finished a game, which was won by Giuseppe, the Englishman turned to me, saying, "I say, wouldn't you like to play for a round of drinks?"

"Thanks, very much, but not right now," I said. It sounded rather unfriendly. I always wanted to explain myself, so I blurted out, "I'm on a budget."

"All the more reason to play. Maybe you won't have to pay anything."

"I always lose."

"You're an American?" the girl asked, tactfully changing the subject.

"Yes. And you?"

"Française. De Nice." She spoke the words in trilling French. "Je m'appelle Odette. Et vous?"

"Packard."

"I'm Ronnie," the Englishman said. We shook hands all around. They stopped playing and we talked about Positano and tried to find out something about each other. The tables in the dining section of the room began filling up. After a time, Giuseppe looked at his watch and said to me, "Scusi, Signor Packard, you have pensione, so you must eat now as it is after twenty-two o'clock."

I excused myself and left the bar. A waiter led me to a vacant table. It was next to a gray-haired man in an orange sweater and a light blue scarf around his wrinkled neck. On the other side of me was a young blindman wearing black glasses. A seeing-eye dog was stretched out on the floor beside his chair. In front of him was a buxom girl in a white sweater that seductively molded her high-perched breasts. She was cutting some meat for him as I sat down.

At another table was an Italian dressed in a formal business suit, wearing a silk tie. He adroitly tucked a monocle into the folds around his right eye from time to time to look at the menu or at some person. He had a sad-faced but beautiful middle-aged Italian woman with him. At still another table there were two American women also dining. The older one wore a costly pearl necklace and her fingers glittered with diamond-and-emerald-studded rings. Her companion, by contrast, was shabby and seemed very subdued. I couldn't make head nor tail out of all these strange characters and what they were doing in a small Italian fishing village.

The blindman broke the ice. While I was asking the waiter about local wines, he called out, saying: "The best local wine, which really isn't local, is the vino rosé from Ravello. That's close by. I recommend it."

"Thanks," I said, "I'll try it then."

"Is this your first visit to Positano?"

"Yes."

"Are you a painter, writer, beachcomber, or fag?"

"I was a newspaperman. Now I'm trying to be a writer. And what are you?"

"I'm trying to be a sculptor. Maureen here is resting between husbands." His dinner companion smiled complacently. "Do you play bridge?" he continued.

"Yes."

"Then maybe we can get up a game later with that sparkling nymphomaniac over there and her sad companion. They like to play as a team. Maureen doesn't play bridge."

"Okay with me if the stakes aren't too high."

"Don't worry. I don't play for big stakes."

During the conversation, I learned that Maureen, who must have been about thirty, was Irish and the blindman, slightly younger, was a Canadian. He said he was doing a nude statue of Maureen. I didn't say anything, but I just wondered how a sightless person could sculpt and play cards.

Apparently feeling left out of it, the gray-haired man in the orange sweater broke into one of the silences to say to me, "I'm Jack Emerson, an opera singer." He held out his hand and I shook it. I volunteered a few unimportant particulars about myself.

"Schiaffo, schiaffo," the cry went up. Then Giuseppe, the Englishman at the bar and his French girlfriend, and a number of young Italian men in black turtleneck sweaters moved out into the center of the room. The jewel-bedecked American woman joined the group.

"This is an amusing game," the opera singer told me. "It's too strenuous for me, but why don't you play it?"

"I'll wait and see."

There was a bustle at the door. A man sitting in a rocking chair was hoisted in by four young stalwarts, almost papal style.

"Salve, maestro," several people called to him.

"Salve," he replied, waving back. He was lowered to a spot where he could see the entire room and the bar.

By this time Giuseppe had covered his eyes with one hand and put his other hand behind his back between his two hips. A great pantomime went on behind Giuseppe's back. Suddenly, the bejeweled American woman ran up behind Giuseppe and swung her hand down in a powerful slap against the target of his palm. Then several of the young Italian men, waving their right forefingers in the air, danced in front of Giuseppe as he uncovered his eyes and studied the people around him. He looked at his hand. It was red from the impact of the blow, but there was also a tiny drop of blood on it.

"Era Lei," Giuseppe said, pointing to the American woman.

The opera singer explained to me: "He could tell immediately it was the millionairess who hit him because one of her rings scratched his hand."

The American woman, in accordance with the rules of the game, then took Giuseppe's place, covering her eyes with one hand and offering the other behind her back to be hit. She didn't guess right until the fourth time her hand was slapped. Then it was a handsome young man, who looked very distinguished. He tapped her hand lightly, then let it slip down to give her rounded buttocks a quick feel. On being identified, he took her place.

"That's Count Vittorio. He's a real Casanova," the opera singer informed me. "He's after the millionairess."

By the time I finished my supper, the game had broken up. Giuseppe, acting as disc jockey, began playing music. Soon couples were dancing. The blindman and Maureen were among them and so were the young Englishman and the French girl and the count and the millionairess. When the American woman came close to the Canadian, she paused and spoke to him. The millionairess then looked at me and nodded her head, apparently in assent.

When the dance was over, Maureen guided the blindman to my table. Bending over, he said to me in a whisper: "Lady Rich Bitch wants you and me to play bridge with her. Now. Okay?"

"Sure," I said.

Bridge was one way of getting acquainted. I was anxious to learn more about the blind boy, as I thought of him, rather than as a blind man. Perhaps it was because he looked very young behind his black glasses. Also, I thought, I haven't anything against meeting a woman who is described as both a nymphomaniac and a millionairess.

I shook hands with the opera singer as I got up to follow Maureen and the Canadian over to another section of the rambling room where there was a table spread with a green baize cloth. The seeing-eye dog followed after us. I was introduced to the millionairess and her companion. We agreed on fifty lire a hundred as stakes. Maureen produced the cards and we drew for deal. I was high. As I dealt I could feel a roughness on a corner of each of the cards. Every one was identified in abbreviated Braille in the right-hand corner: ace of spades, king of hearts, four of diamonds, etc. When it was the blind boy's turn to deal he asked Maureen to do it for him.

"I don't want to be accused of knowing where the cards are when I make a successful finesse," he explained.

While she was dummy during the first game, the millionairess signaled to one of the waiters. He brought over a bottle of Black and White and five glasses.

"I am the hostess," she said, addressing all of us at the table. "Help yourselves to all the whisky you want."

I protested but she overruled me saying, "Don't be silly. I live in this hotel and you are my guests tonight. Let's not hear any more about it."

"But I do, too."

"But I'm the hostess."

I decided to forget it and enjoy myself.

During the third rubber, Giuseppe turned on an old-fashioned Argentine tango. It was just between deals.

"Does anybody tango here?" she asked.

"Not me," said the blind boy.

"And you, Mr. Packard?"

"I learned it in Buenos Aires years ago, but I'm rusty now."

"Let's try it. I just love to tango."

She rose and waited for me to join her on the floor. We fitted into each other's arms. I waited a second to catch the rhythm. Then I whirled off, she followed me perfectly. When I made a mistake, she followed along and it didn't look like a mistake. I became bolder and began dancing cheek to cheek. Sometimes I would fling her away from me while still holding onto her hand, then abruptly pull her back to me. We glided harmoniously together, dipping down, touching the floor with one knee each, then springing up and plunging forward always at terrific speed. Soon the floor was empty except for the two of us. People were wildly applauding us and laughing. They thought it was funny to see a fat man so light on his feet. I made a parody of my fatness. It became a comic performance. Some people yelled: "Bravo Jumbo!" When the music stopped there were cries of "Bis . . . ancora." The clapping continued.

Giuseppe quickly turned on another Argentine tango. We started dancing again amidst cheers. My partner was loving it.

"Who would have thought a potbellied guy like you could dance so well," she whispered in my ear. "Can you do other things as well?"

"I'm willing to try."

"My room number is One. Number One. Come up after it's closed down here."

# CHAPTER VI

As soon as Giuseppe called out: "Time please," in mock imitation of a London barman, I paid up my small bridge losses and slipped out along with the others. As I went up to my room, I snooped around in the corridors for room number One. I located it. It was on the floor below mine. I continued up the staircase to my door, entered, and waited for things to quiet down. On the moonlit beach I could see Maureen and the blind boy walking along with the seeing-eye dog. Every so often she would stop and give the Canadian a long kiss on the mouth. It was already after two. Soon silence prevailed in the Buca. I stripped, put on my wool bathrobe, with nothing underneath it, and tiptoed downstairs to room number One. I tried the door. It was not locked. I went in without knocking as I didn't want to disturb other guests. Burning logs in a fireplace gave out a glow and warmth.

"Here I am," I called, sotto voce.

The lights suddenly were turned on. There she was entirely naked untangling herself from a maze of sheets and blankets. She threw them back of her in a pile.

"You're late," she said, coming toward me. Her pubic hair was blonde and curly. "I'd given you up."

"I waited for everybody in the hotel to go to bed."

I walked toward her. As we met I shook off my bathrobe and hugged her. She switched off the lights. Both naked, we tumbled onto the bed and started kissing sensuously. She rolled on top of me. Her lips roved over my body, nibbling at my nipples, tonguing my navel and suddenly her mouth found my genitals. She then sucked my scrotum, one ball after the other into her mouth. Next her tongue slithered up the base of my phallus and her lips closed over the swollen knob of it. I could feel her left arm pushing at something alongside me and under the pile of covers. I wondered what she was doing. Trying to find out, I groped cautiously for her arm with my right hand and found her wrist. It was acting like a fulcrum for her hand that was bobbing up and down. I grabbed for it. She drew it away quickly, but I clutched something else. It was a shaft of flesh. I moved my hand up and down on it.

"Christ," I yelled. "Turn on the lights."

"Shush," she said. "You'll wake everybody up. What's the trouble?"

"I've got somebody's prick in my hand. Turn on the light."

"Si, si. Accendi le luci," a male voice called out. It sounded familiar. The cock dwindled and eased away from my grasp. Somebody jumped out of bed. Then the lights went on again.

The millionairess maintained her poise while both the other man, who also was stark naked, and I were embarrassed. This was probably because of the way fright had caused our erections to collapse into dangling flabbiness.

"Have you two met?"

"Not formally," growled the man.

I recognized him. It was Count Vittorio, whom the opera singer had described as a Casanova. Houdini would have been a better description, I thought, thinking of the way he had disappeared beneath the bedclothes when I came in.

"I saw you playing schiaffo," I said. "Somebody told me you were Count Vittorio. My name is Packard."

We shook hands coldly.

"Now that we are all friends," the nympho said, "shall we continue?"

"No threesome for me, thanks," the count quickly replied.

"I'm not much inclined that way myself, especially with you. But I was invited here."

"You're the intruder. I've been coming here almost every night."

"Don't argue about it," our hostess said. "If we can't have a threesome, I'll take you one at a time."

"Never mind," I said. "I'll retire. I only have to go upstairs." The count seemed relieved.

"My villa is at the top of the mountain," he said, subtly trying to score a point. "I had planned to spend the night here."

"You're the one I invited, Packard," the woman said.

"I'll give you a good time before you go. In the meantime let's have some whisky and try to become friends."

She found three glasses and opened a bottle of Dewar's. The three of us sat naked around the fireplace and drank solemnly. We talked very little. I wasn't getting along with the count. He didn't like me and I certainly didn't like him. I didn't know why. I couldn't believe it was jealousy. Or maybe I attributed mercenary motives to him in his going after the millionairess. Perhaps it was premonition. As it turned out he proved to be my bête noire in Positano.

"Well, it's getting late," I said, starting to put on my bathrobe. "I'll see you all tomorrow."

"No, no," the woman said. "I won't have a guest of mine leaving without being satisfied."

Taking my hand, she led me to the bed. I didn't resist. The count remained in his chair by the fireplace. But when we started making love, he got up and turned off the lights.

"He's a prude," she whispered in my ear. "He hates seeing someone else screw me. Jealous like all Italians. He's a bore. He doesn't like group sex. Forget him."

"I'm trying to."

Despite the adverse conditions, the performance was smooth, without any inhibitions: you name it; she would do it. She was a real nymphomaniac. She didn't need to be in love to enjoy coition. It was like a meal. She didn't have to love the cook to appreciate his cuisine. She was rich enough not to care what anybody thought of her. She was really economically independent. She sincerely believed in the pleasures of sex and was not ashamed of herself. When I slid off her lean, firm belly, she held on to me, saying in a low voice: "I adore fat men. It's a father complex. I always wanted to screw my father, but he would have belted hell out of me if ever I had hinted at it. He was fat like you."

I got up, groped for the switch in the flickering dim light from the fireplace, found it, and put on my bathrobe that was still on the floor beside my slippers. The count, glowering into the flames in front of him, didn't speak.

I gave my hostess a theatrically noisy, succulent-sounding kiss just to annoy the count before I slipped quietly up to my room.

# CHAPTER VII

Little by little I got to know most of the people in Positano, including the local inhabitants, who were just about as crazy as the members of the foreign colony. Almost everybody was an oddball. The young man who was carried into the Buca much the way the pope is paraded around Saint Peter's in his gestatorial chair turned out to be a crippled German painter who had been afflicted with polio as a child and never recovered the use of his legs. He had developed a following of artistically inclined Positanese youths. Like student disciples they mixed his paints, posed for him in the nude, ran his errands, and helped him move about. They also tried to paint like him and according to gossip served as his buggerboys.

In any event his work was of the phallic school of art, portraying naked boys with robust penises, also symbolic snakes and eels as well as suggestive still-life canvases of bananas and apples, sausages and onions. He was very friendly with a wealthy American who owned a villa on a nearby point that could only be reached by boat. He was known as the Fairy Queen. The painter screened visitors to Positano to determine whether some of them were interesting enough and potentially homosexual enough to be received by the big queer himself. Apparently the artist recommended me, but after being invited to lunch at the villa twice, I never was asked again. I think I failed the homo test.

The opera singer was always to be seen on the beach. Nicknamed the

Pied Piper, he would walk along the water's edge, singing in his trained tenor voice, followed by a crowd of children trailing behind him in Indian file, laughing, singing, and pushing each other. They seemed to love him.

One time I saw some of the local kids throwing sand on the village idiot, a powerfully built young man with curly hair, who would snarl, yell, and run after the boys. They always got away, came back, and threw more sand on him. I complained to one of the fishermen, saying: "Why do you allow those ragazzi to tease that poor idiot?"

"Why? Because he likes it. At least he is getting attention."

The fisherman was right. I watched more closely. I was convinced the moron was enjoying himself.

I stayed one week in the Buca and then moved into a sparsely furnished appartamentino on the beach. It was really a loft over a wintertime storehouse for rowboats. The loft had been partitioned by beaver board into two compartments. As you entered, you came into the dining room and kitchen, combined, containing a round table and four wooden chairs; next you went into a mixture of living room and bedroom that was remarkable for a primitive double bed made of tin. It gave forth a terrible din when used for lovemaking. There was a toilet, with a raffia seat, located outside on a small balcony and hidden from view in a wooden shack. The rent for all this was only seventeen dollars a month. I began to feel wealthy myself. The owner of the place was Pasquale, a bald-headed old man who ran the gasoline station in the piazza Mulino. He had lived in America for twenty years and returned to Positano to die among his children and grandchildren.

He was a screwball too. One time he really startled me. I was drinking at the Buca bar. He came in, stood next to me and ordered a small beer.

"Signor Packard," he said in a serious tone, "I have decided to cut off my balls."

"But Pasquale, why?"

"I'm tired of carrying them around. They aren't any good any more."

He laughed. Until then I had thought he was being serious.

I let my beard grow long, even flowing. It came out red with flecks of gray, adding a certain venerability to my belly, which bulged out below it.

I was working on my book every day. In fact my life seemed almost too pleasant to be true. I worked at the typewriter four hours daily — bridge with the foreigners and scopone with the locals — and managed to get in a certain amount of sex. The millionairess, who was a widow, invited me to tea with crumpet almost every afternoon.

"You know," she said apologetically one time, "I had to take on that count as a steady lover just to protect myself against other Italians. I was raped one night right on the beach in sight of four or five people who just watched in silence. What could I do? I lay back and enjoyed being raped, that's what I did. But after that I decided it was smart to make the count my official lover. Now I'm protected. I am told that if he can't beat somebody with his fists, he will use a knife. But he has become too possessive. I'll probably have to leave Positano to get rid of him."

"Is he jealous of me?"

"He was. You don't know how close you came to being beaten up that night we made love in front of him."

"I'm not that easy to beat up. What about our tea parties?"

"A calculated risk. I have told him I don't see you anymore. He doesn't have any idea that you slip in to visit me. Besides, I hear he spends most of his afternoons visiting the blind boy. He's after that Irish girl."

Mrs. Greenbacks had one very peculiar idea about how to improve her complexion. One afternoon as she was sucking my cock, she suddenly popped it out as I was about to spend and, holding onto it as though it were a nozzle, squirted the semen all over her face. She kept her eyes and mouth closed as she rubbed the creamy fluid into her cheeks and over her forehead.

"It's so good for the skin," she said.

She insisted on this treatment at least two times a week. She called it a seminal facial.

Holidays were great times for picking up girls in Positano. During the Easter vacation there were crowds of young people from Rome dancing and drinking in the Buca. One night I got mixed up with a group of them. When the Buca closed at 2 A.M., they were trying to find a place to continue. I suggested my loft. All the men bought bottles of whisky, wine, and beer, and we transferred to my place. I hardly remember anything about the party. It was noon when I woke up. There was a naked girl in bed beside me. She was still asleep. Everybody else had gone. I kissed her. She opened her lips, responding passionately. I felt impotent from having had too much to drink, but as we continued with our sex play — I wasn't sure whether she was fully awake — Junior began stiffening. I suddenly moved my head between her thighs and started lapping her cunt. She became delirious.

"That's good, oh, so good. Rub your beard over it," she groaned, opening her legs wider and lifting her vagina up high so I could get into it deeper with my tongue. Her groans and movements aroused me. The bed protested with tinny clangors. My cock was on the verge of erupting. I drew my head away, but she tried to hold it where it was. She wanted me to continue licking her honeypot. I managed to heave up and push my dick into her. I squeezed one of her nipples as I kissed her mouth. She drew back her head.

"Don't," she snapped. "Your mouth tastes of cunt."

"It's your cunt."

"I still don't like it."

Her remarks slowed me up, but I recovered in time and began pumping her slowly, then more swiftly. It was gorgeous. It was going to be a marathon grind. All the liquor, plus her nasty remarks, had slowed me down, but that was good because it prevented ejaculatio praecox. Then she was moaning as before and her teeth were biting her lower lip.

"I'm coming, I'm coming," she cried and locked her legs around my waist. The bed sounded like a tin shack being blown over in a windstorm.

"I am too," I cried.

We lay exhausted. I wondered if the revelers had left any whisky. I could see bottles on the floor, but I couldn't make out whether they were completely empty.

She disengaged herself from me. She jumped up in bed. Her movements made metallic tintinnabulations. She looked down at me.

"Who the hell are you?" she demanded, anger shrilling her voice. "I've just fucked you and I don't even know who you are." I tried to explain but she kept on ranting. "Why you fat, bearded bastard, you are old enough to be my father. You took advantage of me while I slept."

"Calm down. There's a bidet under the kitchen sink in the next room. There's a bottle of gargle there, too, and soap. You'd better wash. You're so young you're probably fertile as a rabbit."

"I don't care if I have a baby. It will serve you right."

"Well then I'll use it."

I washed myself in the kitchen, straddling the portable bidet. I also gargled and brushed my teeth, recalling that she had said my mouth tasted of cunt. I also applied a prophylactic.

When I went into the bedroom, she was already dressed. Despite her youth, about twenty-four, I'd say, she looked bedraggled and troubled. She flounced out in a rage, saying: "You've robbed me of sixty thousand lire." That was about one hundred dollars in those days.

"Let's look around. On the floor, under the bed," I called after her.

She kept on going. I searched the room. There was no sign of money, bag, nor purse. I drained a bare slug from one almost-empty whisky bottle. I slipped into my corduroy trousers, blue sweater, and moccasins and went out, headed for the Buca and more of the hair of the dog that had bitten me. Giuseppe, as always, knew who all the girls were. She was English, a schoolteacher from Rome, who had come with a girlfriend, also a teacher, to Positano for the holidays. While we were talking my recent bed companion came into the Buca, accompanied by two carabinieri.

"There he is," she said, pointing to me. "He's the thief."

Politely but firmly, they took me into custody, explaining that the girl had filed charges of theft against me.

"You must come with us."

I followed them out, calling back to Giuseppe, begging him to do something for me.

I must have been sitting in the carabiniere headquarters answering questions for more than an hour when Giuseppe came in with an Anglo-Saxon-looking girl. It turned out to be my accuser's traveling companion.

She produced documents, showing that she also worked as a teacher in the same school as the plaintiff. She then explained that her friend was under psychiatric treatment and that every time she went to bed with a man she accused him of robbing her of sixty thousand lire. Always the same amount, she said. She also added that the two of them arrived in Positano two days ago with only a total of twenty thousand lire between them and that she still had most of that intact.

"I carry the money for both of us," she explained, "just in case of such an incident."

Giuseppe then vouched for my character. The maresciallo of carabinieri was very understanding. He shook hands with all of us and assured us that there would be nothing on the records against me or the girls.

"Just a misunderstanding," he explained, making me realize why people like to live in Italy.

# CHAPTER VIII

Late one afternoon a yacht flying an American flag anchored off the beach just in front of the Buca. A dinghy brought a sailor ashore. He delivered a letter to Giuseppe addressed to Mrs. Greenbacks. Giuseppe let it be leaked out that the owner of the yacht was a brother of the millionairess, and he had invited her and her companion aboard for supper. Later, the two women, in evening gowns, were accompanied to the dinghy by Giuseppe. The sailor lifted the two women into the cockleshell of a craft, one after the other, getting himself wet up to his waist. He then vaulted aboard. Five minutes later a big man in yachting garb helped the two women up the gangway. They disappeared immediately below deck.

Many of the habitués of the Buca were on the beach to watch the proceedings, including the count, the opera singer, the English playboy, and his French girlfriend, the Irish girl with the blind boy and myself.

Mrs. Greenbacks waved to all of us impersonally, saying:

"We're having dinner aboard."

It seemed like a dumb remark but at least made us all think she was coming back that night.

Several hours later while I was dancing with the Irish girl, I heard people saying, "The yacht is gone." We all rushed out on the beach. There was no sign of the trim craft. Some days later, Giuseppe admitted that Mrs. Greenbacks had left a letter instructing the Buca to send all the belongings of her companion and herself that had been left behind to the freight department of the American Express in Naples for forwarding to her. She enclosed a generous check to cover all expenses.

That's one way to slip out of the clutches of a possessive Latin lover, I thought.

As far as I was concerned the doldrums had hit Positano. The young women on Easter vacation had all left, and the summer tourist invasion hadn't yet begun. It was still May, the weather was beautiful but I missed my afternoon tea and crumpet with Mrs. Greenbacks. I didn't wake up anymore with a strange girl in my tin bed. I would have to do something about my sex life.

Suddenly it occurred to me. Why hadn't I thought of her before? The Snow White! She lived in Naples, not very far from Positano. Just the thought of her buxom white body with its milk-flowing bosoms and her carnal techniques got me all excited. I decided to get in touch with her immediately. Yes, by Jesus, I even remembered her phone number.

In those days, long-distance calls weren't easy to make from Positano, even to a nearby city. I put the call in through the Buca hotel desk and waited impatiently in the bar sipping beer, waiting to hear the sensuous voice of the Snow White. I even wondered if she were still alive.

Finally the bar phone rang, and Giuseppe told me Naples was on the line upstairs. I careened up the steps two at a time to get there quickly.

"Allo. Allo. Biancaneve?"

"Chi?" came the astonished reply.

"Biancaneve. You know, Snow White."

"Ma chi parla?"

"Who's speaking? Me, Packard. Don't you recognize my voice . . . I'm Packard."

"Ah, si, si, now I remember. Il Signor Pacciardi. The war correspondent."

"Is that you, Biancaneve? You sound different."

"Yes, I am the one you called Biancaneve. Yes. And I called you Pack-o."

"That's right. Listen I am living here in Positano. Not far from Naples. You know where it is?"

"Certamente. It's a lovely place on the Amalfi Drive. What are you doing there ? There is no war."

"No, there is no war and I am no longer a war correspondent. I'm just here trying to write a book. I have a cozy little apartment right on the beach. I want you to come and visit me for a couple of days. A week, a month, as long as you like. What do you say?''

''Signor Pacciardi, there is only one thing I have to say to you. Thank you for all your kindness, but the war is over. Thank God. I am once more a respectable wife.''

''But all the passion and ardor you had? You did such wonderful sexy things. I can hardly wait to have you suck me off.''

''Sh . . . Attenzione! These phones have ears. We must never see each other again. The war is over.''

She hung up on me. A few days later I received a call.

''New York calling Signor Pack on the phone.''

Giuseppe's clear, deep voice cut through the canned dance music and the shuffle of feet in the Buca. I was drinking and talking with the blind boy and Maureen. As soon as I heard my name coupled with New York, I jumped to my feet, panic-stricken, stepping on the tail of the seeing-eye dog, which leaped up, knocking over drinks on the next table. I thought something terrible must have happened to Pibe. She is the only one, I thought, who knows that I would be at the Buca at this hour. It was nearly midnight. Despite our estrangement, I had kept in touch with her occasionally by mail. In one letter I wrote her about Positano and all the oddballs who were there; about the loft and the Buca and my sex adventures. Then I remembered that Mrs. Greenbacks was crazy enough to phone me from New York just on whim, but she was last heard of in Rapallo. Giuseppe told me to take the call upstairs in the phone booth. It must have been a good ten minutes before I established contact. First I had Naples, next Rome, then New York and at that moment I was cut off and it began all over again. Finally I was asked in English if it was Mr. Packard on the phone. Then the voice said one minute please and eventually another woman said: ''This is the *New York Daily News*. We want to speak to Mr. Packard.''

''It's me,'' I said. Then I heard another voice saying, ''Hello, darling I finally got through to you. How are you, you old fat son of a bitch you? As terrible as ever?''

It was Pibe all right, being sentimental and trying not to show it.

''What's wrong?''

''Nothing. I'm fine. I called to tell you I'm coming to Rome for the *New York Daily News,* but I'm coming by slow boat, a Polish freighter, that leaves tomorrow. The foreign news editor, Bill Sunde, wants you to file for me until I get there. Will you do that? It'll only be about a fortnight.''

"But I haven't finished my book yet.''

"You'll just have to forget your goddamn brainchild for a couple of weeks. You'll do this for me?''

You might have thought that we were as much in love as ever; that we hadn't decided to separate.

"You always dominate me, you wonderful bastard,'' I said. "I'll do it.''

I felt as though we were in love again, only we didn't believe in love.

"Thanks. I'll pass you the editor. He wants to tell you how to file. They've gone mad in America about the Italian elections. They think the Reds will take over the country, Vatican and all.''

I knew Sunde. He was almost as fat as me. We had met in Paris at the end of the war in the Hotel Scribe, where all the war correspondents were staying. I was there en route to China from Italy, and he was there covering an animal story. A GI had picked up a wounded German police dog on a battlefield, tended it, and was trying to take it back to the States with him. Army brass had blocked his efforts. Bill wrote a series of sob stories and as a result, the GI was granted special permission to take the dog home with him.

On the phone he said: "It's the Italian elections. What we want from you, Pack, is hot top spot news and features about it. By cable. Brevity is our slogan. We're a tabloid and not ashamed of it. Eleanor tells me you can get to Rome by early tomorrow afternoon. I want you to start filing tomorrow evening. You're on expenses while filling in for Eleanor, so stay in a good hotel. All the best. Good-bye.''

He hung up. Here I was back in newspaper work again. I was secretly glad. I liked the excitement of reporting under pressure.

# CHAPTER IX

I had a hard time understanding what Sunde really wanted me to send. I had never before been a correspondent for a tabloid. My first message described an incident that had happened to me in Positano two nights before I arrived in Rome. A group of ten Italian sailors, headed by a boatswain, came into the Buca and took over. At the end of one of the dance records, the boatswain told Giuseppe his group would perform the next number. A violin and an accordion were suddenly produced by two of the sailors. With the boatswain conducting, they played the forbidden Fascist anthem of "Giovinezza" ["Youth."] The sailors hummed and soon most of the Italians began humming too.

"Don't be afraid to hum," the boatswain told his captive audience. "You can only be arrested if you sing the words. But you can hum 'Giovinezza' without any fear of trouble from the police."

The humming immediately increased, and even some of the foreigners joined in just because it was a catchy tune. With the instincts of the reporter still alive in me, I went over to the bar and mingled with the sailors. As soon as the humming performance stopped, Giuseppe quickly switched on more dance music, tactfully ending the political demonstration.

"What party are you fellows?" I asked the sailors.

"Ex-Fascists and now MSI or Monarchists," answered the boatswain as self-appointed spokesman. "From Naples south the Monarchists are powerful. And don't forget that the 1946 referendum ousting Umberto II just barely passed and many of us don't believe it was a fair vote. Some of us are MSI, a cautious postwar form of Mussolini's Fascism. But one thing is sure, the bloody Communists and left-wing Socialists aren't going to win this election. And if they do the MSI will do something about it later. Fascism may be badly wounded but it isn't dead yet."

Sunde wired me:

> 22183 PACK HOLDING YOUR GIOVINEZZA FOR
> SUNDAYS EDITION AS FEATURE STOP WE WANT
> YOU TO SEND HOT TOP SPOT NEWS REGARDS

The next three days I tried to write interpretive stories as though I were a *New York Times* correspondent except my dispatches were much briefer. Sunde bluntly wired me after receiving each one that it was unusable. He kept repeating that what the *News* wanted from me daily was "Hot top spot news." It took me until the fifth day to realize what those cryptic words meant. Then it struck me. That's what I had been doing all my journalistic life for the UP: Bang! Bang! Bang! So many dead and wounded, so many bridges blown up, so many arrested, so much damage, all in the first sentence. Then I went into descriptions of the destruction, mayhem, and gore that had been wreaked that day, stressing somewhere near the lead that all this was taking place in a postwar struggle between pro-Soviet Marxist parties on the one side and pro-American democratic parties on the other for control of predominantly Catholic Italy, including Rome, the capital of Catholicism. Sunde wired:

> 27183 PACK TODAYS DISPATCH IN GROOVE STOP
> KEEP IT UP CONGRATULATIONS

From then on I had no trouble. I just filed as though I were still working for the UP.

I put up at the Hotel Inghilterra on the Mouth of the Lion — via Bocca di Leone — which was near both the Foreign Press Club and the Dead Dog. Now that I was working for the *News* I was given every facility and reinstated to full membership in the Stampa Estera. I had Pibe made a regular member at the same time in anticipation of her arrival.

When I sent off my last take between 11 P.M. and midnight I would go to the Dead Dog and sup on a plate of spaghetti and a carafe of red wine. The talk of the Venerable Fag's symposium was relaxing. I usually sat next to the German Jewess.

236

The secret weapon from America was flour. Boatloads of it came in every day. U.S. Ambassador James C. Dunne had lost weight dashing from one port to another to greet the ships bringing tons of white flour from donors in America. He scrambled aboard the ships and would make a speech stressing that the flour was from the bounty of the American people who hoped Italy would remain a democratic republic just like the United States. He had hard competition from Catholic priests who also went up the gangplank right behind him and from Communist mayors who managed to get aboard the ship from municipal motorboats while the vessel was still being towed toward the docks. The voters had a difficult time trying to determine whether the cargo of goodwill came from Uncle Sam, the pope, or Stalin.

The usually drab, gray and white walls of Rome, darkened by the patina of centuries, were plastered with multi-colored posters, that gave the Eternal City a carnival atmosphere. Some of them showed America as a benevolent Uncle Sam handing out bundles of wheat to Italians; others depicted Uncle Sam as a fat, thick-jowled slob gobbling up little Italians. It was a gigantic struggle between communism and capitalism, between Russia and America.

After a few days of silence, Sunde started masterminding me again. He wired:

> 30131 PACK LETS HUMANIZE THESE ELECTIONS
> STOP DESCRIBE PARTY LEADERS PHYSICALLY
> MENTALLY SARTORIALLY STOP SOMETHING
> ABOUT THEIR SEX LIFE IF ANY REGARDS

From then on I began making the electoral struggle not only between Moscow and Washington but also between Italian leaders. One was Washington's man in Rome. He was Alcide De Gasperi. Moscow also had a man on the spot. He was Palmiro Togliatti.

I had met Togliatti in Naples during the war when he always wore a black or red turtleneck sweater. He didn't strike me as particularly impressive in those days. But now he had power behind him — two and a quarter million Italian Reds. He now looked taller than his five foot seven inches and was an impressive figure despite his unpressed suits, rumpled shirt collars, and sagging tie. At fifty-four, he was secretary-general of Italy's Communist party, the biggest in Western Europe. He was known as the Red Fox of Italian politics and was by far the best orator in the country. He could outtalk, outharangue, and outvilify any Christian Democrat speaker. He had been trained by the Kremlin in political strategy during the nineteen years of exile that began when he had to flee the castor-oil wrath and worse of Mussolini. With his horn-rimmed glasses and flowing black hair, he looked like a down-and-out professor of philosophy.

His great twist of fact and phrase was: "That whatever economic aid that comes to Italy from America never reaches the poor Italians because the distributors of such largesse are the Christian Democrat party, the Church and their henchmen." He had personality which exuded from him like ectoplasm when he spoke. He could jam any square in Italy with his oratory, including the enormous piazza del Popolo, which could hold more than two hundred thousand people. The Communists and left-wing Socialists in Italy were not only workers, but included many tens of thousands in the professions such as law, medicine, and education. Down to earth, Togliatti promised "more bread and higher wages."

Togliatti had the all-out support of Pietro Nenni, a onetime friend of Mussolini. Nenni and the young Benito were pals when they were Socialists together in Milan and worked on the same left-wing newspaper. When Mussolini suddenly became the leader of the Fascist party, Nenni broke off their friendship. Nenni was editor of the Socialist newspaper *Avanti,* and after Musso took over Italy as dictator, he fled to France where he became the secretary general of the underground Italian Socialist party. Later Nenni became a political commissariat on the Loyalist side during the Spanish Civil War.

In the election campaign, Nenni, who was again secretary general of the Italian Socialist party, threw his lot in with Togliatti. Their parties were united in a bloc known as the Popular Democratic Front. Its symbol was the head of Italy's outstanding hero of all time — Garibaldi.

The leader of the powerful Christian Democrats was a drab figure, Alcide De Gasperi, aged sixty-seven. He was hardly Italian. He was born in Austrian Trento while it was part of the Austro-Hungarian Empire and had been a member of the Vienna Parliament. German was his first language, Italian his second, and when he spoke French, it was with a German accent. He became Italian only after the annexation of Trento by Italy at the end of World War I. During World War II he sought refuge from the Germans in the Vatican, where he was employed as a librarian. With the fall of Rome, he became active in the formation of the Christian Democrat party. He had already been premier for two and a half years and the undisputed head of the movement against Communism when the electoral campaign started. He was the archetype of the Catholic layman.

He attended mass every morning. He made no political decision before praying to God for enlightenment. Of his four daughters, one was a nun. Long-nosed with irregular features, he was always neatly and conservatively garbed in tailor-made tweed suits. His hobby was mountain climbing.

His assistant in the electoral campaign was a man even more powerful than himself although he had to remain somewhat hidden in the wings. This man was Pope Pius XII, then aged seventy-two, who regarded the Communists as a threat to the very existence of the Roman Catholic church. Although never mentioning the elections or Communism by name, the pontiff made it clear that he expected Italian Catholics to vote against atheism, materialism, and violence.

Italian cardinals, however, came out with pastoral letters and proclamations threatening religious sanctions, such as denial of the sacraments, against any one who voted for or collaborated with the Communists or other Marxist parties.

Each priest also worked in his own parish against the Communist candidates running for Italy's first postwar parliament. They were aided by the powerful lay organization of Catholic Action. Many of the priests declared that it would be a mortal sin not to vote as God wishes when the fate of the faith was at stake. God could hardly wish for anyone to vote for godless Togliatti.

When I came to Rome to start covering for The *News,* the violence of the electoral campaign had already taken a toll of fourteen dead, more than two hundred seriously injured. Most of the casualties had occurred in open gunfights, ambushes, stabbings in the back, and street demonstrations.

The ghost of Mussolini was also a factor in the elections. Less than eight months old, the neo-Fascist party of MSI — Italian Social Movement — was actively campaigning. Never mentioning the word Fascism or the name of Il Duce, the small party was trying to bring together enough right-wing voters to snag some 20 to 30 seats in the 574-seat Parliament. Its secretary general was Giorgio Almirante, aged thirty-two, who despite his wispy physique had a strong oratorical voice. He had once been undersecretary of propaganda for Musso's last-stand government at Salò. He articulated a program, shunning both the United States and Soviet Russia and advocating an international neutrality similar to Switzerland's. His main appeal was a nostalgia that still existed in some part of the country for what they called ''the good old days of

Mussolini,'' but most of the members were youths too young to have been Fascists themselves.

One morning at ten o'clock, I received a phone call from Genoa. It was Pibe, who had just disembarked from her Polish freighter.

"Pack, darling," she said, "I was hoping to see you tonight. I missed you so. But Bill Sunde radioed me telling me to stay in the north of Italy until after the elections and that you are to keep on covering the overall picture. I'm to interview the man in the street in Milan, Turin, and in the red belt of Bologna. Eyewitness crap and so forth.''

"Oh shit, Pibe. That's awful. Awful for me. I've got such a rail-on just listening to you that I'm resting the phone on it. If we're disconnected, it means I've gone off.''

"I'm pretty horny myself," she laughed. "Try to save it for me.''

"Let's see. We've only got six more days before election day. April eighteenth? Right? I'll try. But it's going to be difficult. You should be in Rome about the twenty-fourth.''

"I'll make it without fail. Naturally Sunde wants me to get the reaction of the man in the street to the results.''

We hung up. I was infatuated with Pibe again. Oh, how I longed to fuck her again, just straightforward fucking, which she liked so much.

One day I was having lunch with Jean d'Hôspital, a French correspondent whom I had known in the Spanish Civil War. He was *Le Monde* correspondent and no competition for me. He nudged me and nodded toward a table by an open window that gave on to via Belsiana. Two starved-looking beggars were in the street looking enviously at a priest and two laymen eating at a table next to the window. One of the beggars put his hand in through the window for some kind of charity. The priest handed him two rosetta rolls. The flour was really white now that election day was approaching.

"Here's a roll for you and one for your friend," the priest said. "This white flour comes from the Christian Democrats. Be sure to vote for them next Sunday.''

The two beggars went off, munching away. When the waiter made out the bill, he charged the priest for the two rolls he had given away.

"You charged me for the bread I gave to those beggars," the priest protested.

"That's right," said the waiter. "You also told them the flour was from the Christian Democrat party and that they should vote for the Christian Democrats.''

"Well, isn't that right?"

"No, the flour is from Moscow."

"What party are you?"

"I'm a Communist, and I know the flour comes from Russia through the Communist party."

Secretary of State James S. Byrnes announced a program of two and a half billion dollars aid to Italy as a climax to the torrid campaigning. Togliatti also had a hard time trying to explain away Russia's support of Yugoslavia's claims on Trieste.

The day before the election was Saturday. It was a day of cooling off; all electoral machines clanked to a halt at midnight Friday. There was no more blaring of loudspeakers in automobiles advocating the various candidates. Leaflets were no longer dumped into the breeze from autos and small airplanes overhead. Political speeches ended in all the squares throughout Italy just before the stroke of Friday midnight.

Then Sunday came. It was a day of prohibition. Decrees were posted forbidding the sale of liquor, wines, and beer in bars and restaurants. In the trattoria where Jean and I ate lunch, it looked as though the management was throwing a tea party. Everybody had a teapot and a teacup in front of him. It was just more Italian-style lawbreaking. Every teapot contained liquor, wine, or beer. It was like the bootlegging days in America.

There was an enormous turnout at the polls. In Italy that didn't mean anything. Everybody voted because if you didn't it was a black mark against you and could cause you trouble in getting a passport, a pension, or a civil servant's job. About the only people not voting were the officially registered prostitutes in brothels and card-carrying streetwalkers. As social lepers they were barred from voting by Italian law.

I remember the lead of the story I wrote that day. It ran like this: "Italian voters went to the polls today to choose between two uncles — Uncle Sam and Uncle Joe."

There was also voting until 2 P.M. Monday. Then the counting began. Italian bureaucracy entered into this. Any ballot that was smudged by lipstick invalidated the sealed vote. By Tuesday morning the final results were known. They were an overwhelming victory for the Christian Democrats, who polled a total of 12,712,562 votes as compared to 8,137,047 votes gained by the Popular Democratic Front, combining the Communists and left-wing Socialists.

It was a victory for Alcide De Gasperi, the Christian Democrats, Pope Pius XII, and Uncle Sam. Most important of all, it meant Pibe would be joining me soon in Rome.

# CHAPTER X

One morning a few days later, Pibe burst into my double room in the Hotel Inghilterra. I had told the management that my wife was joining me. I was still in bed, asleep. A facchino, bending beneath a load of four suitcases, followed her into the room. Pibe told him to put the luggage down in a corner and tipped him.

"Darling, Pack, wake up and kiss me," she cried out as soon as he left. "I love you so. I filed my last dispatch and took the next train for Rome. And here I am. I like your beard."

I had downed too much red wine at the Dead Dog the night before. My reflexes were slow. I looked at my watch. It was after eleven. I had on a blue T-shirt and an old red-and-white Tahitian pareo (a Polynesian loincloth), my idea of comfortable bedwear. Pibe pulled back the curtains, letting in the fierce Roman sun. I closed my eyes. I opened them and zigzagged to the washstand. I doused my face with cold water, reached for a bottle of Binaca, swished some of it around in my mouth, and gargled, trying to get rid of the birdcage taste. Then I lunged at Pibe and kissed her passionately. She had on a tailored suit, a jaunty cloche hat. Her eyes were bright and her lips felt sensuous against mine. Oh, I was glad to see her! I poured White Horse into two tumblers and splashed in some water.

"Here's to us," I said.

"To us."

We clicked glasses.

"Shall we talk first or fuck first?" I asked. By talk I meant mutual sex confessions.

"Talk later."

Pibe tossed her cloche hat on the chaise lounge and soon was peeled down to her skin. In the meantime I closed the curtains a bit and slipped out of my T-shirt and pareo. We fell onto the bed, clutching each other. Our mouths conjoined in a long tonguey kiss. Her hand reached for my peter. I knew she only wanted to find out whether it was already hard. She would never tease it to erection.

"It's not stiff," she used to say when she found it limp. "You aren't really interested in sex." She would jump up and walk away.

This time it was like granite. She guided it into the narrow well of her loins which was already moist and slippery. Even at that moment I realized that her character was superimposing itself upon mine. This was our first reunion after a long separation, and she already had manipulated me into her favorite position of what I thought of as the conventional way to make love: man on woman, man pumps woman, they both climax. No embroidery work: no muffing, no cocksucking, no assholing. As I moved back and forth, in and out of her vagina, Pibe suddenly grabbed my hips and held them firmly, stopping their movements. I could do no more depth-bombing.

"That's it," she said. "Right there. That's the little man in the boat. You've got the little man in the boat. Don't lose him."

I twisted and turned my body, but I didn't release the pressure on the small bubble of supersensitive membrane. The head of my cock continued titillating the clit. I could feel the tiny lump hardening and the juice of passion oozing from it. Then Pibe was making strange whinnying sounds with her mouth; soon we both shuddered in ecstatic spasms of a mutual orgasm. Depleted, I rolled off her belly and lay silent beside her in postcoital bliss. Finally, I made the first move and, getting up, refilled the two tumblers with whisky and water. I handed one glass to her and kept the other, sipping from it as I sat down next to her on the edge of the bed.

"You're the best straightforward screw in the world," I said.

"Is that a compliment?"

"In a way. But I still like to do what you think of as my perversions."

"I'll try to please you occasionally as long as you continue to give me plenty of the kind of lovemaking we just had."

"Fair enough."

I laughed it off. I didn't want to discuss the point. Hell, we were trying to get together again. So why argue?

"That was so good, let's not risk an anticlimax. Let's talk now and get it over with. You begin, Pack."

"I haven't much to say. I've written you about all my experiences from the Venerable Fag to the nympho millionairess and the schoolteacher who accused me of robbing her. Oh, I guess I should mention that last night I went to a whorehouse for your sake. You know I suffer from premature ejaculation. So I went there just to calm myself down so I wouldn't go off too soon with you. Don't worry, I used a rubber and afterwards a pro. It was like going to a comfort station."

"Well, it's easier for me if I begin backwards. Last Tuesday when the partial returns indicated the Christian Democrats had won, I started my own Gallup poll of the man in the street in Bologna. I found that in interviewing people on the sidewalk, I drew such a crowd that the situation got out of hand. So I started going inside stores and offices and asking managers or employees what they thought of the result. That worked better. Just before lunchtime on Wednesday I went into a small furniture shop. It turned out to be empty except for a man who said he was the owner and a Christian Democrat. He was a zero type. Short, swarthy and had a big black mustache. As I made notes, he looked at his watch and said he would have to pull down the iron shutters in front of the shop or he would be fined. I waited inside while he lowered them. Then I asked him more questions. He suddenly undid his belt, opened up his fly, and let his trousers drop to the ground. He pushed down his blue drawers. I remember they were blue. His thing was stiff as an iron bar. 'You're disgusting,' I told him. 'Put your hand on it and feel how hard it is.' To my amazement I put my hand on it. The top of it was already damp and glistening. The sight of it set me on fire.

"See what you do to me, you beautiful signora,' he said. And with that he lifted up my skirts and I found myself helping him push down my panties. We fell back on a table that was for sale, and I tried to put his thing inside of me. Talking about shooting too soon. He came before he even got into me. That made me furious and ashamed of myself. Letting a little Wop with a stiff prick, whom I didn't even know, rape me. Only it wasn't rape. I helped him and I didn't even come. The egoist.

"I was fighting mad. Getting up, my hand touched a heavy ashtray. I grabbed it and smashed him on the side of the face with it. He fell to the floor unconscious.I adjusted my clothes and ran out back. There was an apartment behind the shop. In the kitchen I could see a woman cooking and tiny tots playing on the floor. I saw a door leading into an alley and walked out. I left Bologna half an hour later on a train for Milan. I never saw anything in the papers about it, so I guess he didn't dare report it to the police. If he had died, there would have been a story about his death. Can you forgive me for such a sordid act?''

''Forget it, darling. I love you for your spirit of adventure, for becoming honestly horny at the sight of a rigid dong. I am not a phony philosopher. I really admire a woman like you. Even as a boy I disliked virgins. I thought of them as stupid prudes, dumb conformists, or mean, calculating girls.''

I drew her to me and kissed her, platonically. I sipped some whisky. ''I think you're great.'' She squeezed my hand affectionately.

''Now, as for the big thing with Sam Brewer, I think that's over. I'm afraid he doesn't have your tolerance of my promiscuity. I don't think he's in love anymore with his wife, but we have stopped talking about marriage or a future together. We're still good friends. And I get along with his wife, too. They're in Beirut right now.''

Later, I met both Sam and his wife, whose name was also Eleanor, in Rome while they were still married and had their daughter with them, then again in Lebanon after they had been divorced and she was married to Kim Philby, the superspy and double agent, for both Britain and Russia. One day Kim slipped off to Moscow just as the British Secret Service were about to nab him. When I last saw Philby at a cocktail party in Beirut he struck me as being much too much of a drunk to be a spy. He seemed a terrible lush, but probably that was just a cover. I also knew him during the Spanish Civil War when we were both correspondents on the Franco side. Then he talked like a Fascist. Again probably that was a cover. You never know what can happen. Now Pibe and I were back together in Rome, and Rome was the bond uniting us.

# CHAPTER XI

After an Italian lunch that included spaghetti alle vongole, capretto arrosto, and a liter of Chianti, topped off with Strega, courtesy of the house — il Re degli Amici — we sauntered over to the Foreign Press Club and had coffee and more Strega. Pibe asked me how much of my book I had finished. I told her I had written about two hundred and seventy-five pages, but the book was to be four hundred pages long when completed. The telephone operator upstairs leaned over the mezzanine railing and called out that New York wanted to speak to either Signor or Signora Packard. I told Pibe to answer it as it was undoubtedly Sunde, and I had now finished my assignment with her arrival in Rome. She rushed upstairs. The male correspondents followed her up with their eyes, admiring her million dollar legs. A minute later she called down to me to come up quickly because Sunde wanted to talk to me.

When I got off the phone I had been wheedled into writing my book on the side and working full time for the *News*. The way Sunde had put the offer, no newspaperman in his right mind could refuse it. He said he liked the way Eleanor and I had covered the Italian elections so much that he wanted us to continue on as a husband-and-wife team with one of us always available to fly off as a troubleshooter to Greece, the Middle East, Yugoslavia, North Africa, Spain, and Portugal, and if necessary to backstop on the French Riviera, including Monte Carlo. The pay was

247

good. Expense accounts were liberal, and we were authorized to have an office. I remembered how Pibe was always resentful that I had gotten her transferred from Turkey where she was bureau chief to just a member of the staff under me in Italy during the war. So I asked, "By the way, Bill, just as a matter of administration, who is the bureau chief? Eleanor or me?"

There was silence. He had to stop to think a bit. Then he answered me.

"Well, Eleanor originally asked for the job and got it. You've been hired next. So I think in all fairness to her, she should be the boss."

"I just wanted to make sure. That was why I asked. It's swell with me. And thanks again, Bill. So long."

We hung up. I came out of the soundproof phone booth, sweating. It had been so hot in there.

"Did you take the job?" Pibe asked. She had been standing there waiting for me. I kissed and hugged her first in front of gawking correspondents and uscieri.

"You bet I did. We're that goddamn awful man-and-wife team again. Only this time you're the boss."

Most of our colleagues, especially the Europeans, resented the fact that Pibe was my boss. They didn't approve in principle of a wife being over her husband or for that matter any female being over a male. I actually got a kick out of it. It made me feel that I had eliminated all jealousy from my character. If I wasn't jealous of Pibe being my superior on the *News,* why should I be jealous of her extra-marital adventures. It all fitted into the pragmatic makeup of an original thinker free of all bias. Yes, I admired myself for it: I was not like the millions of male squares in the world, I thought.

We rented an office on the top floor of the Stampa Estera building. It was just two flights above the old UP office where we had worked during the war. Our new place was smaller, but contained a large newsroom, complete with an ANSA (Agenzia Nazionale Stampa Associata) teletype, three desks: one for Pibe, another for myself, and a third one for the use of any colleague who might be passing through Rome. There was a tiny room in the back with a couch on which one of us could sleep if we had an all-night deathwatch on the pope; and it was convenient for sex. There was also a bathroom.

The *News* boasted that it carried all the news that the *New York Times* published. The only difference was in the treatment. Our paper reduced Italian politics to small paragraphs among the truss ads and smashed sex and scandal stories about Dolce Vita folk and movie people on the main pages while the *Times* did just the reverse, often not covering the juicier items.

But when Roberto Rossellini got Ingrid Bergman pregnant before they were married, that was even fit to print in the *Times*.

# CHAPTER XII

When Miss Bergman belatedly saw the film, *Open City,* which Rossellini made in Rome in 1945 while the war was still continuing in northern Italy, she wrote the Italian director that she would like to star in one of his neorealistic pictures. He wrote back saying he accepted her offer. A few months later they were on the volcanic island of Stromboli working together and falling in love. The name of the film was *Stromboli.* It was in the spring of 1949. Reports first circulated in Hollywood that Ingrid, then thirty-four and still the wife of Swedish-born neurosurgeon Dr. Peter Lindstrom, was with child fathered by the Italian Lothario, Rossellini, then forty-eight. He was still the husband of Marcella de Marchis. Ingrid and Roberto refused to comment on the report. When Ingrid came to Rome it was evident, however, that she was several months gone.

Anna Magnani, who starred in *Open City,* had hoped to be cast in *Stromboli.* But Ingrid got her role. Engaging in a jealous feud, Anna grabbed the leading part in a rival film, entitled *Volcano,* and worked overtime on location so that it would have its world premiere in Rome ahead of Rossellini's *Stromboli.*

La Magnani won the race, but Ingrid stole the show by giving birth to her first child by Rossellini — Robertino — the same night as the premiere of Anna's film. Hearing of the birth during the screening of the film, movie critics and reporters deserted the cinema in the middle of the picture to rush to the hospital to get the bigger news of Ingrid's newly born love child.

Rossellini got a Vienna divorce in December 1949, but Lindstrom held out against the joint pleas of Ingrid and her Latin lover. Five days after the birth of Robertino on February 2, 1950, Ingrid was granted a proxy divorce decree in Juarez, Mexico. And on February 12, her illegitimate son was officially registered in Rome as Renato Roberto Giusto Giuseppe, "Son of Roberto Rossellini," now known to the world as Robertino — little Roberto. But it was not until the following May 24 that little Roberto's position was fully legalized. That was the day his mother and father were married by proxy, also in Juarez. Two years later she bore Rossellini two girls — Isabella and Isotta.

It was one of the great newspaper romances of modern times and used by the *News* to up its circulation. For fifteen years, this love affair in one form or another ricocheted through the press, picking up particular momentum when reports began to circulate that ever-amorous Rossi had fallen in love with a glamorous doe-eyed Indian beauty named Sonali and had abandoned his Swedish wife. Sonali Das Gupta was married to Hari Das Gupta, a hefty Indian film director. He was furious with the Italian seducer, who finally began living openly with Sonali in Bombay's plush Taj Mahal Hotel. And it was Hari himself who had helped make most of the arrangements for the shooting of Rossi's documentary on India. The one mistake he made was to introduce Roberto to Sonali.

During this time, Rossi, Ingrid, and Sonali were big headline news, and the foreign desk in New York couldn't get enough copy about them. One of the most human stories I got was an exclusive interview with Aldo Tonti, Italy's leading camerman, who broke off a twenty-year association with Roberto because "he is love mad over Sonali and it's impossible to work with him when he is amorous."

Tonti, then forty-seven, short and bespectacled, told me he had just written to Rossellini that he would not return to India with him.

"Roberto knows that after what he's done to Sonali, it's even dangerous for him to go back to India," Tonti told me. "He might even be killed. I refuse to work for him anymore after the indignities he made me suffer in India. No self-respecting cameraman would work for such a director."

Tonti who shot most of Rossellini's films that starred Ingrid Bergman, went on, "I just couldn't understand how Roberto fell for Sonali. She's not only dumb, she's not even beautiful. She just sat cross-legged all day in her Bombay hotel suite trying to be a lady. Her Asiatic personal habits certainly aren't ladylike.''

Asked if Sonali was pregnant, Tonti said, ''I understand so.''

Rossellini's film work in India was a slow, slow business, Tonti said. In a year, Roberto had only completed three of nine projected subjects.

''Indians,'' Tonti continued, ''are slow in the first place, but when Roberto's in love he is even slower. He used to spend day after day in his hotel room with Sonali, and when I asked him what he had been doing, he would say he had been working on the script. But when I asked to see the script, he replied it was written in English which I wouldn't understand. He can't write English at all. He can speak only a few words.''

But a few years later, I managed to catch Rossellini coming out of a Rome tribunal where he and Ingrid were finally granted a legal separation, paving the way for Rossi to get a Mexican divorce so he could marry Sonali. By this time, she was hiding out somewhere in Europe.

Just before Rossi came scurrying out, Ingrid slipped through a thin opening of the heavy courtroom door and darted away, crying. She looked furious but wouldn't stop for any reporters.

I waited and then Rossi appeared.

''Signor Rossellini,'' I said, ''would you say a few words about the outcome of your meeting this morning with Miss Bergman? She just left in tears.''

He replied in very fluent and incisive English: ''I hate and despise the American press. It is only interested in sex. It doesn't care about art or Hindu philosophy at all. Just sex. It's the lowest press in the world. You should be ashamed of yourself for working for it.''

Court officials and lawyers of the director closed in around him and ended the abortive interview.

He finally married Sonali, who opened an Indian curio and boutique shop on Rome's via della Vite not far from the Foreign Press Club. In the meantime Ingrid married Lars Schmidt, the Swedish millionaire producer. Later there were reports that the two were talking about a separation.

# CHAPTER XIII

As soon as it was confirmed that Don Giovani Rossellini had gotten Ingrid pregnant during their movie making on Stromboli, the newspaper world went mad for the story. The charm of Rossellini as a Latin lover fascinated Anglo-Saxon editors. Along with our American and British colleagues in Rome, Pibe and I were bombarded by requests from the home office for explanations of Rossellini's sex appeal in particular and that of Latin lovers in general. Finally we were asked by Sunde to do a special Sunday piece in depth, running some ten thousand words, on what makes Italian males click as cocksmen. Pibe insisted that I should write it mainly because despite her free-and-easy amours she was very much of an introvert when it came to putting her by-line over sex-charged articles. As a result she developed into the Vatican expert and I became the office sexpert. I've never been reticent about signing my name to anything I write. As an extrovert, I don't believe in noms de plume.

It took some thinking and preliminary work to get started on this particular story. It was a real controversial issue, and I don't suppose it will ever be settled. The question still remains: are Italian men lousy or wonderful lovers? But I tried to answer it as best I could in a sort of one-man Kinsey report. Besides mulling over all the clichés I had heard on the subject and rereading many of Italy's scandal stories, I also interviewed women I knew who had had affairs with both Italians and non-Italians. One of the best analyses came from a Swedish woman correspondent. She talked freely to me over drinks, lunches, and late-night suppers about her experiences. Sometimes Pibe was present and helped to draw her out by recounting erotic adventures of her own.

Known familiarly as Sugar, because of her Nordic complexion, flaxen hair, and sweet disposition, the reporter, who had worked in Italy before, during, and after the war, stressed that she found no difference between Fascist and non-Fascist lovers in bed.

"They all think they are God's gift to women," she said. "Perhaps the only difference is that Italian men in wartime, particularly while Italy was losing the war, were slightly subdued. But not undaunted. They still thought they were scoring victories on the mattress if not on the battlefield.

"Perhaps that very vanity of theirs is what makes them good lovers to many women," Sugar continued. "Their self-assurance is infectious. There was this lover I had off and on for nearly ten years both during and after Fascism. I found him very amusing. Perhaps because he had one sex eccentricity. He would take off all his clothes, get into bed, snuggle up to me, and then say: 'Oh, where's my hat?' He would then scramble out of bed, get his hat, and then put it on. It intrigued me but I found that most Italian men use some cute trick or other to make them seem interesting. Anyway, he disappeared from Rome toward the end of the war and didn't return for several years. He had a wife of course and about six children by this time. He phoned me at the Stampa Estera one day, saying he was back and wouldn't I like to come around and see him in his new apartment? I did. His family was still in the North. He pulled his hat trick again, was very ardent but reached his climax very quickly, leaving me unsatisfied. Nevertheless he said, 'That was a wonderful orgasm you had, wasn't it?'

" 'Well, I'm not sure,' I said, not wanting to hurt his ego.

" 'But of course you had a wonderful orgasm, I could feel your fig fluttering like a butterfly and exuding love juice. That was what made me come. It was really magnifico, wasn't it?'

"I agreed. In fact, he convinced me that I had come. He was always convincing like that."

"What do you think of Americans?" Pibe asked her.

"I've only had two American lovers. They were both like the Swedes I know. Not sure of themselves. They admit they might not be good in bed but with my help they might be. This makes me nervous and both affairs ended badly. That 'I'm good' technique of the Italians is reassuring.''

An American girl named Marge who wanted to be a foreign correspondent and hung around the Press Club just to be with newsmen used to have lunch with Pibe and me sometimes. She talked freely to us about her sex adventures in Rome.

''The Italian men don't waste any time,'' Marge told us. ''Just yesterday I went out to Cinecitta to interview a director there. I wasn't looking for a job. Just a story, but even so he went right after me. As I sat in his office making notes he suddenly stood up.

'' 'Look,' he said.

''I looked up. His cock was dangling out of his fly onto the top of his desk. It was soft.

'' 'Touch it,' he said, 'and see how big and hard it will get.' I was hypnotized, I guess, because I just reached forward and touched it, saying it didn't look like much. 'Jerk it, jerk it,' he cried. I did and it got big all right. The next thing I knew he had my skirt up and my panties down and rammed it into me. He came right away but I didn't come at all. I was disappointed because he didn't try to satisfy me.''

''Something like that happened to me in Bologna,'' Pibe said, but she didn't elaborate.

''I find Italy is one big dose of aphrodisiac,'' Marge continued. ''Ever since I've been here, I feel as though I am being given Spanish fly. The whole atmosphere is sex arousing. The art in the churches is full of sex. Cherubs with their tiny peckers, shapely madonnas, and naked saints like Sebastian, his powerful body pierced with arrows. Even Christ on the cross has a sexy torso and virile thighs. In the buses, the men pat your bottom and somehow manage to brush your breasts as you go by. In the cinema or even at the opera, a girl has to contend with la mano morta . . . ''

I must bring that into the story, I thought. The dead hand. It is one of the slyest of lewd tricks performed by the Italian male. If he is sitting beside you, he just lets his hand touch your thigh. He doesn't move it for a long time. If you object to it, he protests indignantly or politely says: ''Scusi.'' And if you don't object the hand eventually becomes alive and begins to tickle and explore the legs or buttocks. I couldn't help but think of the reverse of this ancient Italian practice. Pickpockets and petty thieves take advantage of it.

One evening an elderly English woman in the Hotel Inghilterra bar sorrowfully told me of an incident that had just happened to her in a Rome bus.

"I suddenly felt a hand on my thigh," she said. "Oh, I thought, this is the famous dead hand. It made me feel young again. Somebody found my body appealing. But when the hand became too aggressive, I slapped at it. I looked around to see which man was doing it, but all the male faces near me bore innocent expressions. I slapped some more, as the touching continued. I even turned to try to identify the bloke who was molesting me. The bus stopped and people got out. There was suddenly less of a crush and I noticed my bag was missing. It had been neatly snipped off its strap which was still draped over my right arm. So you see what a silly old fool I was. I was so ashamed of myself, I didn't even have the courage to cry out 'Thief, thief.' Now I must return to England tomorrow, I'm so short of cash."

I also talked to tourists sitting next to me at the Cafe de Paris on via Veneto. It was the original Dolce Vita cafe of Fellini's movie named after the sweet life. Some of these American girls admitted they came over to Italy with the preconceived idea of having an affair with an Italian. What was the purpose of flying all the way across the Atlantic if you were just going to go to bed with another American from back home? Their idea seemed to be: try the wine and the cock of the country you're visiting; otherwise don't bother to go abroad. They were ripe for the first Latin lovers they met, as they didn't usually have time to be discriminating.

"Thank God for the pill," a Philadelphia schoolteacher told me at the cafe. "These Italian men seem to like to make a woman pregnant. It appeals to their virility. I've been vacationing in Italy for the past ten years. At first they complained about the diaphragm as spoiling the romance of lovemaking, and some even claimed it hurt their sturdy but sensitive member. Most of them made me remove it. If they get you pregnant, they don't even help you out. It's your fault for going with a man. Not his responsibility at all."

A Pittsburgh girl chatting over a glass of Strega one night told me that her Italian boyfriend, whom she forced to use condoms when he made love to her, confessed he had been piercing the tip of them with a pin so they would tear open inside of her.

"He just wanted to make me pregnant," she said. "He didn't intend to marry me."

256

In fact, I was convinced that most of the Italo-American marriages, in peacetime at least, generally involved wealthy American girls whose fortunes were the primary appeal.

After all this preliminary work, I wrote an article that left it to the reader to decide whether the Italian made a good or bad lover and ended with the old saw that still goes around in Rome: Italians are good lovers, but Americans make better husbands.

Poor Sunde died of a heart attack before I finished the feature. Hugh Schuck, who replaced him as foreign news editor, wrote me a brief comment on it: "Congratulations. Your feature was well balanced and impartially analytical, showing many of the defects of Italian lovers while also making them seem romantic and interesting. It didn't offend the sensibilities of our Italian readership."

# CHAPTER XIV

Clare Boothe Luce came to Rome amidst a cheesecake splash in the Italian newspapers and magazines. Attractive photos of her vied with the sexy pictures of Italian actresses like Sophia Loren and Gina Lollobrigida. She was the first woman ambassador from America to traditionalist Italy where women weren't supposed to be diplomats but wives of diplomats. That put Henry Luce in a strange position and he was soon nicknamed the Little Ambassador. The *Time-Life-Fortune* office in Rome was enlarged so as to enable him to run his magazine empire from the center of the Eternal City. He also made trips around the country, talking to industrialists, statesmen, and diplomats. Some people believed he frequently was interviewing people for his wife.

Shortly after the blonde envoy arrived, she gave a big luncheon party for the American press in Rome. I remember her sitting at one end of the table and Henry at the other. They both carried on simultaneous conversations almost as though competing with each other. Clare won out because she was news and got most of the correspondents' attention. He rambled on like a scholarly lecturer before a university audience explaining that synthesis was the idea behind *Time*. It was a complicated idea. I listened to him because he was attempting to explain the meaning of a news magazine. It had always baffled me because it contained mostly a rehash of events which already had been written about in the dailies. He stressed that *Time's* approach was from every angle — not just the latest spot news development — but especially the background, entailing profound research into the subject. He described newspaper datelines as old-fashioned, limiting the reporting geographically. He also claimed that the unhurried treatment of current events by his weekly resulted in a wealth of details, human interest, and valuable interpretation as well as greater accuracy. While he was talking I thought of the fact that I had collected eleven thousand dollars damages from his pet publication, *Time,* because of its inaccuracy in reporting why the UP had fired me in China.

Clare was a spontaneous, outgoing person. Once an anti-American demonstration was staged in front of the embassy. She boldly stalked out and spoke to the demonstrators, trying to put them right about what they thought they were against. When she got through talking to them in a mixture of Italian and English, they broke into applause and dispersed quietly. She also got credit, and I believe she deserved it, for the settlement of the dispute between Italy and Yugoslavia over Trieste. She gave good press conferences. I liked the way she was so natural in her answers to loaded questions. Informal, she often referred to Yugoslav statesmen as Jugs and adroitly dodged being drawn into committing herself on a delicate issue by saying with a laugh: "That's a very iffy question. I don't think I'll answer that one."

Clare got very angry with me when I reported that the then president of the Republic, Giovanni Gronchi, who tended to be somewhat auuthoritative in his post, which was primarily decorative, regarded her as a persona non grata and was trying to get her removed as U.S. ambassador to Italy. She called me to her office to reprimand me for the story. While she was doing this, I asked her why she didn't seem to like me although I was a great admirer of hers. She replied that while coming over to Italy by boat, she had been warned by other newsmen that she had better look out for Mike Stern and Reynolds Packard when she started her duties in Rome. In those days Mike was a star reporter for *True* magazine.

"They said you and Mike had announced that you were both out to get me," she said.

I answered that I certainly wasn't, and Eleanor and I were the only reporters in Rome who really esteemed her and yet she was constantly playing ball with other correspondents who definitely didn't approve of a U.S. woman ambassador to Italy. Our voices became so tense that her aides in the next room closed the door so as not to overhear our argument.

I didn't tell her, because I had to protect my source, but I got the Gronchi story from a member of her husband's Rome staff. I often wondered if Henry himself had ordered it to be leaked because he undoubtedly was against her holding such an important post. My own private opinion was that he was jealous of her talents. I was convinced of this more than ever when *Time* magazine broke the story that she was being poisoned by arsenic falling into her morning coffee from the ceiling of her bedroom in Rome. Some of the newspapers around the world, including London dailies, spoofed the poison angle by headlining it: "ARSENIC AND OLD LUCE"

In any event, she resigned the post shortly afterwards, in February 1956, giving her state of health as the official reason. It seemed to me an unnecessary and anticlimactic end to what had promised to be a brilliant diplomatic career. I chalked up her resignation on my personal scoreboard as a victory for Henry.

# CHAPTER XV

Most correspondents based in Rome acted as troubleshooters for the Middle East. Being one of them, I was sometimes sent to Lebanon, Jordan, Syria, or Egypt whenever there was war or revolution. Almost always I would get a case of crabs, especially in Cairo. Once when I hadn't even been near an Egyptian bellydancer — they were mostly Armenians I discovered — or any Arab girl, I still was plagued with the tiny insects that had taken residence in my pubic hair. Having forgotten what the Arab prostitute told me during the war, I told the doctor I hadn't had intercourse with a woman. He replied in all seriousness, "Maybe it was a camel."

When I emphatically denied any relations with the humped beast, he said: "I meant riding one. No. Well, then, do you go to the movies?"

"Yes," I said. "Often. I go to Arab films to study the language."

"Where do you sit?"

"Near the screen. Downstairs. My eyes aren't too good."

"That's where you got them," he said. "The poorer Arabs sit down there. It's cheaper. You pick them up from the seats."

As always, the doctor told me to shave off all hair on my body and use blue ointment. But one time I came back to Rome with something more complicated than crabs. It was a girl whom I had nicknamed the Elf. I had wired Pibe that I would be flying to Rome the following Saturday

261

with a friend, not specifying whether it was male or female. Pibe figured out the time of arrival and was at Fiumicino to meet us.

"This is Pibe, my wife and this is my good friend, the Elf," I said making the introductions.

They shook hands, looking appraisingly at each other. The Elf knew all about Pibe or at least I thought she did as I had told her everything, but then Pibe was always more complicated than me. She was all for promiscuity but being an introvert, she didn't like group sex very much.

As Pibe drove us to the Press Club in the secondhand Fiat she had bought, I explained that the Elf was leaving her husband because he had found out she was having an affair with a Greek correspondent and me.

"Both at once?" Pibe asked.

"That's right," the Elf replied, half laughing. "It was your husband who started me off with all that wonderful sex talk of his."

"I can believe that," Pibe said, nodding in assent. "Pack loves to talk about it."

"Well, he certainly did a good job this time," the girl said.

She was a tall, slender blonde with surprisingly rounded breasts and buttocks for one so slim. Her eyes were porcelain blue. Her mouth was a mixture of determination and voluptuousness with her upper lip being thin and the lower one full and sensual. She wore her hair fairly short, so that it just reached her shoulders. Her legs were long stemmed. She was only twenty-eight, years younger than Pibe and me.

"Are you a correspondent?" Pibe asked.

"No. I'm not really anything. I was supposed to be a housewife, I guess, but now I am running away from my husband."

"Where do you expect to go?" Pibe asked. There was anxiety in her voice. I think she suspected I was trying to force the Elf into our menage.

"I plan to go to Positano," the Elf said. "I want to write a book. Pack says it's a wonderful place. He calls it the sex capital of Italy."

"Every city is a sex capital for him," Pibe said, laughingly but nevertheless disparagingly.

"He thinks I should fall in love with a blind boy there. He says this fellow is terrifically sensitive and that I could help him. I would like to do that. Help him, I mean."

Then suddenly changing her tone, she continued: "Please don't think I'm trying to take your husband away from you, Mrs. Packard. He has told me how much he loves you and all about the cornucopia of love you both believe in. That he can love me and still love you as much as before.

I believe that too. I love so many people and want to make love to so many people. Sex is such a glorious thing. No, don't worry about me being a bother. I only want to stop off in Rome for a night on my way to Positano."

"I told the Elf I would take her to Positano and introduce her to the blind boy, Giuseppe, the opera singer, and all the other interesting people there."

"And don't forget the Englishman," Pibe said. Pibe had made several vacation visits to the fishing village on my recommendation. Once she had an affair with the Englishman, she told me, while the French girl was away.

Pibe parked the car not far from the Press Club with the luggage of the Elf and myself still locked in the trunk. We then deposited the Elf at the Club bar with a beer and a sandwich while we went up to our office. I knew that Pibe just wanted to get me off alone to question me about the girl. I had filed a last story from Cairo just before I left, so I had nothing to write. I waited while Pibe banged out two dispatches and sent them off by messenger to Radiostampa, the Italian Western Union.

"Now come clean, Casanova, and tell me what this is all about," she said.

"Okay. It's the old story about a wife whose husband suddenly loses interest in her, and she becomes full of passion and desire and just has to do something about it. She was intrigued by my accounts of my Paris days, including when I met you. I even recounted how as the youngest member of the UP staff in Paris, I was expected to take VIPs to brothels for an exhibition if they wanted to see one and how sometimes the husband or the wife would enter into the sex circus with all kinds of bizarre results. Well, one night I was talking about the good old Hemingway and James Joyce days of Paris to a group of correspondents and their wives in my Cairo apartment when the Elf interrupted me. As usual her husband wasn't with her.

" 'Pack,' she called out, 'You're always talking about sex. Why don't you do something about it?'

" 'Like what?'

" 'Like fucking me.'

" 'Okay,' I said. 'Let's go into my bedroom, get undressed, and we'll fuck each other and anybody else who wants to join in. Come on everybody.'

"I started taking my clothes off as I led the way into the bedroom. It was small with a double bed taking up most of the space. The Elf and I were soon undressed and on the bed. The overhead light shone down on our nakedness. I was afraid I wasn't going to produce a hard-on, but the Elf kissed my cock and it leaped up like a magic wand. I plunged it into her immediately for fear it might lose its bone. We kissed and humped away. The rest of the guests just stood there gaping at our two entwined bodies. We both groaned and mewled as we writhed in orgasm. There were about eight people watching us. When we became still and silent, they broke into applause.

" 'Who's next?' I asked, not knowing exactly what I meant.

" 'You'd better get dressed quickly,' somebody said. 'Her husband may come along any minute.'

"It was just an excuse to cover up the fact that nobody dared to screw in front of the others. It made me feel pretty big. A real person. Not just a bullshitter.

"We all went out to supper and afterwards, a Greek correspondent who had watched the Elf and me make love, took her home. About five in the morning the phone rang. It was the Greek talking.

" 'Listen, Pack,' he said. 'The Elf wants to speak to you.'

" 'Hi, Pack. Is that you? Good. Listen, as a disciple of yours, I'm in bed here with Aristotle trying out your cornucopia of love. It's wonderful. He is great in bed. If you were here I'd take you on again!'

"Well, that was the beginning of a very pleasant threesome," I told Pibe. "The next night the three of us made love in the Greek's apartment, and afterwards we went to a café in the old quarter of Cairo and smoked hubble-bubbles. There was no jealousy. While she sucked him, I muffed her, and occasionally he and I would touch each other's cocks, but he wasn't enthusiastic about that. He said he didn't want to become a queer.

"The Greek wrote her love letters and I wrote poems to her. Anyway, the husband found these letters and poems. He was furious. He threatened to kill both the Greek and me either separately or together. He made her life hell. So she decided to sneak off with me when Schuck ordered me back to Rome."

"As you know I am the bureau manager as well as your wife," Pibe said with a tone of authority. "I'll let you go down to Positano tomorrow morning and introduce her around. But you must be back here within the next three days."

"Okay, captain," I said giving her a mock salute.

"And furthermore tonight you're sleeping with me. I haven't had time for sex since you've been in Egypt the past two months and I'm really horny. You've had your Egyptian threesome, and you probably will have some orgies in Positano. So I am being more than fair. You can have the car if you want."

"Thanks, but we can go by the wayward bus."

Having put me straight on how I was to behave, Pibe became a very amiable hostess to the Elf. The three of us had a pleasant dinner at the Re degli Amici, and then we went home to the studio apartment that Pibe and I now occupied in the via Margutta. There was a spacious courtyard with a fountain and a pet goose that strutted around as though it owned the place. Our bedroom was a balcony at the end of one big room which was both living and dining room. There was a huge sofa in front of a fireplace and a divan off in a corner where the Elf was to sleep.

The three of us sat on the sofa in front of the fire before going to bed. I asked Pibe if she would mind if the Elf came up to our balcony bedroom while we made love.

"I don't feel in a lesbian mood tonight," Pibe said. "I just want to feel your prick, good and stiff, inside of me. I haven't had it for a long time."

"Oh, never mind," said the Elf. "I am really tired after that flight. I'll just go to sleep."

But she couldn't sleep. I could hear her moving on the divan, rustling the bedclothes. I imagined she was turned on by the squeaking of our bed as Pibe and I made love two times. Bedsprings can make a very arousing noise to say nothing of the whispering of two people coupled in sex.

"I think she's masturbating down there by herself," I told Pibe.

"I don't feel sorry for her. What do you think I've been doing while you were away? It's not all that bad."

The alarm went off at 6:30 A.M. Pibe forced herself out of bed and made coffee for the Elf and myself. She wished the Elf good luck and went back to bed. By five that afternoon the Elf and I were drinking wine with the blind boy in his cottage on the beach. Maureen had gone to Paris to be married for the third time. Her new husband was a Frenchman.

# CHAPTER XVI

Polly Adler called me up at the office and asked me to take her to a Rome brothel. She was the literary madam of one of the best-known houses of prostitution in America; her book, *A House Is Not a Home,* was a best seller. She was staying at the Excelsior on the via Veneto. She suggested I meet her in the bar of the hotel to discuss it. We had never met.

Feeling she might make a good news story, I accepted her invitation. She was sitting alone in the bar waiting for me. Smartly dressed in a tailored way, she looked very much like the prosperous businesswoman which of course she was. I told her I had read her book and liked it immensely. She asked me what I wanted to drink. I told her: White Horse.

"I hear Italy is closing down its brothels," she said, after I had been served. "Is that right?"

"Yes. The law abolishing legal prostitution goes into effect in another two months."

"Well, I would like to see the inside of an Italian brothel before it's too late."

"It may not be that easy. Italian whorehouses are very proper. They don't stage exhibitions like the French bordellos used to. They don't even serve drinks in them. Women who are not licensed as official prostitutes aren't even allowed in them. Not even for a quick look-see. Even a dressmaker can't go in to give one of the girls a fitting."

266

"I hear you are an expert on prostitution in this country. If anybody can get me in, I'm told you can. That's why I called you."

"I'll try my best. How long will you be here?"

"Another week or so."

"I'll look into the possibilities and give you a ring tomorrow night."

The next evening, I phoned her. I reported that I had talked with ten different madams, and they all had turned her down. She asked me to come to the Excelsior bar anyway and discuss the situation over more drinks. She had an idea.

As soon as the waiter disappeared after bringing me a White Horse and Polly a Campari soda, she told me about her idea. It struck me as crazy, especially because of her figure.

"I can dress up as a man and go in with you," she said enthusiastically.

"But your breasts and bottom are too rounded for that. You'd be arrested for impersonating a man."

"It might be worth it."

"If you want to try it, I'm game. It would make a wonderful headline in the *Daily News*." I could visualize it:

U.S. Madam Dressed as Man,
Arrested in Roman Brothel

She laughed. "So you don't think I could get away with it?"

"No, I don't. But if you want, I could introduce you to one of the madams. You'd have to meet her here or in a café."

"I don't want to meet another madam. I just wanted to see how these houses operate. But I can't understand what the objection is."

"There's the Italian bureaucracy to begin with. And then, as one madam said, the government is already closing down brothels wherever possible to get Italian men used to going without them before the final shock comes on the last day of official prostitution. Of the six hundred brothels throughout the country, employing some forty thousand girls, about one hundred have already been shut down because of one provocation or another. These madams are afraid they might be closed prematurely if any kind of incident happened as a result of your visiting one of the houses."

Polly shrugged her shoulders in disgust. "What nonsense. And what a mistake Italy is making. Venereal disease is going to increase. There will also be an increase in rape. It doesn't fit the moral thinking of Latins."

"I agree, but morality is not the reason it's being abolished. Almost everybody in Italy secretly approves of legal prostitution, including the pope. The average Italian believes that whorehouses are the backbone of the Italian family. When the wife is pregnant or menstrual, the husband can go to a whorehouse as if it were a comfort station and ease his sex urge without getting involved in a love affair that might break up the home. Many cardinals in the curia fear a divorce law will follow the abolition of official prostitution.''

"Then why is Italy abolishing it?''

"Because it can't be a member of the United Nations if it continues with prostitution sanctioned by the government. It makes the government a pimp.''

We ping-ponged the subject back and forth. I finally suggested that she might like to have a talk with Senator Angelina Merlin, the woman parliamentarian who authored the antiprostitution bill, but Polly wasn't interested.

"I know all her clichéd ideas already,'' Polly said. "She can't tell me anything new.''

A week later, Polly returned to the United States without ever seeing the inside of an Italian brothel.

However, I phoned Senator Merlin and made an appointment with her for myself. We met in a small conference room of the Senate. She did have some new ideas, however, as far as I was concerned, about prostitution in Italy. She was gray haired, aged seventy, and looked like a very prim and old-fashioned grandmother. But she didn't talk that way. She was a fiery Marxist Socialist.

"Prostitution in Italy is an unfair unilateral institution made for men by men,'' Senator Merlin told me. "They make slaves and lepers of these poor women. Why, they are prisoners in these houses with the shutters closed all day and night. They are not allowed out. They have to carry a card that labels them whores for life. If they marry an army officer, he loses his rank. The madams are permitted to exploit them, getting commissions on everything they buy, and the poor girls have to send out for almost everything from food to clothes.

"Besides,'' la Merlin continued, "why should there be bordellos for men only? Women have biological urges, too. I myself might like to go to a whorehouse with male inmates and satisfy myself sexually with one of them, picking him out of a group walking around naked in front of prospective customers. No, the government won't allow males to be official whores because they consider such work unbecoming the dignity of a male. Well, I consider such work unbecoming the dignity of a

268

woman.

"In fact, most women only become whores because they have to support illegitimate children. Their noble lovers abandoned them when they got them pregnant.

"I certainly don't want to abolish prostitution for moral reasons but for social and humanitarian reasons."

I interrupted her to say that Miss Adler had predicted that venereal disease would increase in Italy once prostitution was done away with.

"So what? We should make women whores so that men don't get venereal diseases? Anyway, if we have to choose between syphilis and gonorrhea on one side and nonslavery for women on the other, let's choose venereal disease. At least you can get rid of VD with modern antibiotics."

The last day of brothels and card-bearing streetwalkers was anticlimactic. There was no rush by Italian males to have a last historic fuck on the last night of legal prostitution. Whorehouses merely did business as usual. Italian men didn't believe that whoring would come to an end in sunny Italy, the land of spaghetti and sex. It would continue in another form. And they were right.

# CHAPTER XVII

There was a hiatus of some months between the closing of Italian brothels and the development of a new form of sex for hire. In Rome, the new form was first noticeable to observers of Italian mores in the sudden increase in the number of massage ads in the newspapers, especially in the *Messaggero*. In fact, that highly respected daily suddenly began carrying as much as two columns of this type of advertisement on its back page. The heading was: *Cure Estetiche* — Esthetic Treatments. Because of these ads the newspaper was nicknamed the *Massaggero* and became the official directory of play-massage parlors in the national capital. The offerings were discreetly but suggestively worded, such as:

French masseuse gives personal-style massage . . . . Woman doctor gives electric massage . . . . Young massaggiatore gives all kinds of massage . . . . Relaxing massage in comfortable warm surroundings . . . . Beautiful Milanese, aged twenty-two, specializes in oriental massage . . . etc.

I wired Schuck, who had sent me kudos on my various stories about the demise of legal brothels, asking if he were interested in what was taking their place, namely: erotic massage establishments. He came back asking me to file a spot news item by cable about them. It was given a good play. Within a few days the Sunday feature editor requested a ten-thousand word wrap-up on the subject. I then decided to see what they were really like.

I looked for one of the places advertised as being just off piazza San Silvestro, not far from the Foreign Press Club. On one of the mailboxes in the hallway on the ground floor I read, printed on a piece of paper, the words: TEACHER OF MATHEMATICS AND FRENCH. ALSO MASSAGE. THIRD FLOOR, NO. 12. I went up the steps, found a similar description on the door of apartment twelve and pushed the button. A little gray-haired old lady answered the bell. She was wearing a long white linen coat.

"Are you interested in mathematics, French, or massage?" she asked.

"Who teaches mathematics?"

"I do. I also teach French and give massage."

"What does a massage cost?"

"It depends on the type."

"I'd like to know in advance what the prices are."

"Come inside. We can talk it over."

She opened the door wider, and I walked into a corridor. She led me into a room that contained a blackboard, a table with books on it, and off in a corner a high rubbing table. She locked the door with a key.

"Get undressed," she said. She showed me some hooks on a wall where I could hang my clothes. She took off her white coat. Underneath she was naked except for black stockings and a black garter belt. Despite her age, her body wasn't bad. She had thick, brown-nippled breasts that sagged quite a bit and her crotch was bushy with gray hair. She must have been over fifty-five.

I stretched out on the table, nude. She didn't attempt to cover me up.

"The prices?" I asked again.

"Well if you want a therapeutic massage, it's seven thousand lire. But if you want a play massage, it's five thousand, and an oral massage is three thousand."

"How is the oral massage?" I asked.

"Magnifico. I take out my teeth for that, and suck you dry like a vacuum cleaner."

"That settles it," I laughed. "I'll take that oral massage."

She asked me to pay her before she began. She put the money in the pocket of her white coat hanging on a hook. I lay back on the table, waiting. She started by running her hands over my body from head to toes and then concentrated on making circles around my penis and testicles with her fingers. When my cock stood up, she calmly took her false teeth out and put them in a tumbler filled with a pink liquid on a dresser. She then returned to me and put her mouth over my peter and sucked it in without touching it with her fingers. Her mouth was warm and soft like a cunt only there was a tongue in it that darted about titillating my hardened dick, teasing the cord that held the foreskin to it. Her breasts rubbed against my belly and thighs. I couldn't hold back. The semen came surging forth, searing the inside of my dong. She kept her mouth closed on it for a long time. Then she lifted her head up slowly, walked to the washstand, and spat into it. I lay quietly, feeling exhausted but contented.

"You want to try it again?" she asked. "This time it will be better. It will take you longer to come. It will be like the second coming of Christ. It will be exquisite pain."

I didn't answer.

I got up and walked towards my clothes and started putting on my undershirt. She continued her sales talk.

"I suck you as before, only it's better the second time and only two thousand lire."

She lisped as she still had her teeth out. Oh, hell, I thought. That's a bargain. I took two thousand lire from my pants and handed it to her.

"I'll take the bargain-priced second treatment."

She laughed happily.

"They all do, you know. And you'll be back, too. Don't forget my name is Rosa. Just like the flower."

"But tell me one thing, Rosa. Why is the therapeutic massage the most expensive?"

"Because it takes longer, almost an hour. But with the play massage my hands make you come quickly, while with the oral treatment you come almost immediately."

She mouthed Junior again and immediately proved her point.

The next place I tried a few days later was on the via Nomentana, not so far from the Villa Torlonia, where Mussolini lived while he was dictator. The discreet inscription on the door said: Electric therapy. My ringing was answered by a young brunette with prominent breasts that were noticeable even beneath her loose-fitting white coat. They all wear white coats, I thought. She ushered me into a waiting room that resembled that of almost any family doctor. It contained a few comfortable chairs and a table covered with old magazines. There were a few uninteresting pictures on the wall.

"Take a seat," the girl said. "La dottoressa is occupied at the moment."

I sat down and pulled out one of the Rome afternoon newspapers I had stuck in my pocket so as not to waste time. I always had to keep up with the news. I scanned through the pro-Communist *Paese Sera* and found nothing interesting in it. As I was glancing through the progovernment *Giornale d'Italia,* the young girl came in and said: "La dottoressa will receive you. That will be five thousand lire in advance." I paid her. "Come this way."

She led me into a studio where a stout raven-haired woman, also wearing a white coat, sat at a desk. She must have been about thirty-five. She looked up from writing in a notebook. Indicating a chair in front of her desk, she asked me to sit down. The young girl left the room. There was an impressive diploma hanging on the wall.

"What is your trouble?" the dottoressa began.

"Trouble?" I repeated, bewildered by her question. I wondered if I had made a mistake in the ad. "Don't you give electric massage?"

"Si, signor, but what is your particular complaint?"

I thought I had better play her game.

"Well, I read your ad in *Il Messaggero* this morning, and as I have been feeling rather tired of late, I thought electric massage might be stimulating. Be good for me like a tonic."

"And your heart? Does it give you any trouble?"

"No, my heart is all right."

"Strip and stretch out there," she said, pointing to a leather-covered table that seemed to be bristling with wires. It was in one corner of her office.

I took off my clothes, putting them on a chair, and then got onto the table on which she had placed, in the meantime, a white sheet. She listened to my heart with a stethoscope. She moved it very professionally over my chest and back.

"Your heart is all right, but there is a slight murmur. Nothing serious. I can give you electric therapy for fatigue."

As she said this she lifted up her white coat and dark skirt and fastened a wired steel bracelet just above her left knee. Then she attached another steel bracelet, with a wire connected to it, to my ankle. She switched on a machine at the foot of the table. There was a whirring noise.

"Now I enter into the magnetic field," she said, placing her two hands on my naked chest. Vibrant shocks flowed from them and my flesh clung to her electrified fingertips as they moved slowly from my chest down to my belly and around my thighs, sending thrilling shock waves over me.

"Just touch my cock," I said.

"I can't do that."

"Please do," I begged. Junior was erect, twitching, also pleading to be touched.

"It's impossible. Your pubic hairs are like a million wires. If I touched you there, you would be electrocuted."

"That's the way to die. In the midst of an electrical orgasm. Please touch me. I'll go off as soon as you touch me there. Please, please."

But my obsequious appeals only made her more arrogant.

"All the years I have studied for my degree and now I have it and what am I supposed to do with it? Produce orgasms. I won't do it."

She lifted her left foot onto the seat of a chair, raised up her clothes and removed the bracelet. She called out: "Clara, come and finish this treatment."

She strode out of the room, slamming the door behind her. The young brunette came in and without saying a word removed her white coat. There was nothing underneath except long black stockings held up by elastic ribbons. She wired herself as the dottoressa had done and soon entered the magnetic field with her fingers without mentioning it. Junior had wilted during the interruption but was aroused to stiffness by her digital ministrations around my belly and thighs.

"Is it true," I asked, "if you touch my cazzo, I will be electrocuted?"

She laughed. "Is that what the dottoressa said?"

"Yes, but I'm willing to die happy. In exquisite agony. Please touch me."

With all my banter, I wasn't quite sure whether I was afraid or not, but I didn't believe there would be any danger of death. If the shock would kill me, it would also be fatal to the girl, I reasoned. And she would also die.

"You really want me to do it?"

"Absolutely. If you don't, I'll grab your hairy fig and we'll both die."

I put my hand on her crotch as she encircled my cock inside of her clenched hand. Ker-unch . . . bang . . . thunder . . . blaze . . . It reminded me of Anzio when a railroad shell rumbled overhead and crashed into a munitions ship that exploded in flames. It seemed to me I had never come so long nor so explosively. While I squeezed her cunt with one hand, I pulled her toward me and sucked on a nipple that was also electrified. Then I lay there semiconscious, my eyes closed. Finally, I said: "Grazie" and let her loose from the magnetic field.

Altogether, I must have tried out ten different so-called massage parlors. Each one had its own gimmick of sex play. In one I was given a triple massage. I say triple because there was a trio of three operators who worked on me all at once, turning my body into a sort of xylophone. They consisted of two naked girls and one naked man. Each one of them took turns at sucking me off while the other two pinched my nipples, tickled my testicles, or fingered my anus.

In another establishment, the only operator was a youthful massaggiatore. He was the one who advertised that he gave all kinds of massage.

All I remembered about him was that his cob in repose was smaller than mine, but when he began to pull on it, it was as though he were tugging on a cable that kept lengthening out from inside of him. It became enormous. He pummeled me with it like a truncheon. "I have il piu grande cazzo of all the massaggiatori in Rome," he bragged. We played with each other manually, but he suddenly drew away, saying: "You mustn't make me come! I have to get through the day's work yet, and then my wife will expect me to perform when I get into bed with her tonight."

"In that case, I won't come either."

He said if I would pay him double, he would have an orgasm to please me, but I turned down his offer.

Another place was run by a Milanese woman who went in for anal play. She started out massaging my back, then slapping my buttocks until they were red, muttering all the time in Italian: "Oh, your ass is blushing. It is burning. It's hot." She then began spanking me with a hairbrush. "It stings, it stings," she kept repeating. Then before I knew what she was up to she had slipped a rubbered finger, covered with Vaseline, into my asshole, pushing it smack against my prostate gland. The result was instant ejaculation. She tidily caught the sperm with a small towel.

The last place worth mentioning — in a negative sense, at least — was in via Babuino, not far from the Spanish Steps. My ring was answered by a smartly dressed maid who ushered me into an elegant, lace-curtained bedroom. A naked woman with her hair streaming to her waist rose from the bed to greet me. We shook hands.

"Take your clothes off," she said. The maid came forward to help me.

"Just a moment," I said. "How much do you charge?"

"Ten thousand lire."

"For a massage?"

"Che massaggio! Here we fuck."

"Excuse me, but you did advertise that you are a massaggiatrice from

Bologna?''

"That was the ad. We aren't allowed to use the word *fuck* in it."

Her manner irked me; she struck me as too crude, impersonal, and even hostile. I decided I didn't want to have sex with her even for the sake of a news story.

"I only wanted a massage," I said.

"That takes too long. Screwing is faster."

"Excuse me." I turned and walked toward the front door, giving the maid a thousand-lire tip toward a smooth exit. The naked woman yelled after me: "Stupido. Americano cretino. You don't even know that Bologna means we take it up the ass."

# CHAPTER XVIII

In the beginning of October of 1958, Pius XII showed symptoms of a serious illness, including hiccups. On the third of that month, he received Francis Cardinal Spellman, one of his most intimate friends. After the audience, Spellman expressed anxiety to a few correspondents, of whom Eleanor was one, about the pontiff's condition. The New York archbishop said he found Pius "rather weak." Vatican reporters noticed that at this time the pope frequently referred to death and several times used the phrase: "the joy of eternity."

Suddenly the pope took a severe turn for the worse, but even though most of the newsmen sent the story to their papers, it was given little if any play. There was a saying in the Vatican: "The pope is never ill until he is dead." Editors for one reason or another generally agreed with this adage. But when the eighty-two-year-old leader of the Roman Catholic church had two strokes within forty-eight hours, and his temperature and blood pressure soared, they reluctantly began to realize the pope was gravely ill. By October 7, most Vatican sources were convinced that Pius was dying. He had received Extreme Unction.

Dr. Riccardo Galeazzi-Lisi, an eye doctor, who was the official papal physician, had already called in three eminent Italian specialists. They were Prof. Antonio Gasbarrini, Dr. Ferdinando Corelli, and Prof. Ermano Minazzini. The oculist soon became the villain of the death scene, which took place in the pope's summer palace in Castelgandolfo in the Alban Hills outside of Rome. He was accused of personally taking and selling closeup pictures of Pius in his death agony. The photos were so gruesome that they inspired an Italian newspaper cartoon which depicted a gravely ill man begging his doctor: "But no television, please." Galeazzi-Lisi also wrote a series of articles about Pius's condition containing intimate accounts of the pope's disease and suffering. Most editors deleted the more ghastly descriptions.

Competition was so keen among Italian editors that four Rome newspapers jumped the gun, publishing the death of the pope twenty-four hours before it happened. The false news about the death was due to a signal gone wrong. A tipster for a Rome news agency had selected a certain attic window for the signal. When the pope died, somebody among the entourage of the summer palace in the pay of the news agency — possibly Galeazzi-Lisi — was to open it. That meant the pope was dead. Instead, one of the nuns, feeling warm while she was cleaning the room, opened the window to let in some fresh air.

The official announcement finally came over the Vatican Radio at 4 A.M. (Rome time) on October 9, 1958. It was made by Father Francesco Pellegrino, an Italian Jesuit, who was director of the Holy See's radio newscasts. During the previous two days he had been pouring into the microphone the latest official versions of the pope's condition. It was the first time in the two-thousand-year history of the Catholic church that the dying moments of the pope were so recorded. Between medical bulletins, interspersed with sacred organ music, there were calls for prayers from the then half-billion Catholics throughout the world. In the cobblestoned square of the hilltop village, thousands knelt all day and into the hot muggy night, praying for the pope. Some were schoolchildren, some nuns, some villagers, and some foreigners. Swiss guards, in blue, red, and yellow uniforms, clanged their halberds in salute for cardinals and other high church dignitaries who came from Rome by auto. Diplomats were ushered in an elevator to the third floor, where they signed for their governments.

Pius's apartment consisted of his bedroom, a private chapel, and a library and study overlooking Lake Albano, a water-filled crater of an extinct volcano. There were the pope's patrician relatives, his widowed sister, Countess Elisabetta Pacelli Rossignani, and his three nephews, Prince Giulio, Carlo, and Marcantonio Pacelli. Each would look in on the pope for a few minutes at a time.

Close by the stricken pontiff was tiny Sister Pasqualina, née Josephine Lehnert, aged sixty-three, the German nun who had kept house for Pacelli since before he was elected pope. She had first looked after him when, as a young diplomat, he was threatened with tuberculosis. There had long been irreligious reports current that she was more than just a nurse or housekeeper in the papal household. Malicious tongues claimed she and Pius were romantically attached. Informed sources stressed that in the last six years of his life, it was almost impossible to have a private audience with Pius unless she personally approved of it. *Time* magazine added to these rumors of carnal relations between the once beautiful nun and the aged pope by calling her *la papessa,* literally meaning: *the pope's woman.*

Father Pellegrino gave the official time of death as 3:52 A.M., only eight minutes before his announcement was broadcast to the world.

I was Pibe's legman during this dramatic story. I spent much of my time in Castelgandolfo while Pibe remained in Rome, banging out news copy that she was getting from Vatican tipsters, ANSA, and myself. She slept in the office while I spent at least two nights trying to sleep in our tiny Fiat. I at least had the pleasanter job as I was out in the sun much of the time, eating in nearby restaurants on the shores of Lake Albano. As usual scores of top troubleshooters and religious experts piled into Rome for the story. Only this time we weren't confronted with the problem of getting UP clients laid. Also, the *Daily News* didn't send anybody over to help us. Thank god!

With the six-hour difference in time, Pibe caught the last edition of the *Daily News* with the pope's death. Both our by-lines were prominent beneath gigantic headlines. The paper couldn't get enough on the story.

Pibe ordered me — in a way that would've been approved by women's lib — to stay in Castelgandolfo and view the remains of the pope on his deathbed. I dutifully followed instructions and late in the afternoon, I was among the long line of mourners who walked past the dead pope. The reason for the delay was the villain was still running things. I mean Galeazzi-Lisi, the eye doctor. He had taken over the task of embalming the pope's body with a new system known as "aromatic osmosis." It was reminiscent of the way, he said, that Christ was embalmed without the skin being broken. He said it should preserved the corpse for at least one hundred years.

I struggled and fought with five thousand other people to enter the main portal to the papal villa. Among them were five hundred ruggedly devout American tourists. The crowd broke through a cordon of fifty police stretched hand to hand in front of the main doorway. The Swiss Guards inside closed doors and channeled the human avalanche into an orderly procession. The pope lay on a red velvet-covered catafalque. A television camera was focused on it and those filing by. I passed before the catafalque as part of the procession. The pope was garbed in a white cassock, a short red cape trimmed with ermine, and an ermine-bordered red cap known as the *camauro* — only worn by popes after death. On his feet were red slippers.

His hands were clasped together with a white rosary intertwined between his fingers, which held a black cross.

The pope's face was lifelike, but it had a more severe expression than at any time that I had seen him in audiences and at press conferences during his reign. Perhaps it was because his eyes were closed. They had always struck me as so expressive in life. His face also bore traces of his intense suffering during the last few days.

A sheet of cellophane was wrapped around him over his clothes, covering him completely from head to foot. It was part of Galeazzi-Lisi's aromatic embalming system.

The remains of the two hundred and sixty-first pontiff were brought the next afternoon from Castelgandolfo to Saint Peter's Basilica in majestic solemnity and ancient panoply. Three million mourners crowded the seventeen-mile route of the funeral procession. Men and women wept as the glass hearse, decorated with angels and a gilded tiara, went by them. Passing the Colosseum where Christians were fed to lions centuries ago, the procession continued through the hushed downtown streets of Rome. Mourners crowded every archway of the ancient buildings. Some watched clinging to the ruins of Nero's golden house. Some swayed from the branches of umbrella pines on Colleoppio Hill. The cortege avoided via Laerana, on the direct route to the Vatican, where, according to some accounts the ninth century pontiff — Pope Joan — was revealed as a woman when she gave birth to a child. No pope, it is said, has ever traveled along that route since then.

The hearse entered Vatican City through via della Conciliazione, followed by thousands of onlookers who jammed into Saint Peter's Square, making a total of three hundred thousand persons. Throne bearers lifted the body and slowly climbed the flight of Saint Peter's steps. The portals closed behind it.

That night Galeazzi-Lisi climbed up a ladder to the seven-foot high catafalque on which the pope's body had been placed and renewed his embalming treatment. He did this every night until interment. Pius's face already had darkened and his body had begun to swell. The oculist again covered the remains with cellophane "to subject it to volatile fumes." Galeazzi-Lisi admitted that "the difficulty has been holding the fumes around the corpse so they can penetrate it. That is why we have to envelop the Holy Father for some hours at a time with cellophane. It is replaced each night and removed early in the morning before the public is admitted." Galeazzi-Lisi declared that Pius knew all about the new method and had approved of it.

The morning after the body was transferred to Saint Peter's, the massive portals of the basilica were opened at 6:15 A.M. — forty-five minutes ahead of schedule — because impatient thousands were overflowing the steps. Many persons had camped all night in the chilly air outside the doors. I was among them. Altogether millions filed before the catafalque on which Pius lay in state during the four days before he was entombed in a crypt under the basilica.

Galeazzi-Lisi complained that the heat from the TV lighting and twenty-four giant candles surrounding the bier helped to ruin his embalming experiment. He and his aides were accused of thinking of the sales they would lose for their process of aromatic osmosis in wealthy, funeral-conscious America as a result of the failure of the experiment. Despite the continuous fumigation that Galeazzi-Lisi carried out every night on the pope's remains, several of the Swiss and Noble Guards standing at attention beside the bier fainted from the odor of decomposition.

Finally, the body was placed in a cypress coffin lined with scarlet silk. This coffin was then placed inside a lead liner, which in turn went inside a coffin of elm. As a choir sang a funeral dirge, red rope and pulleys were used to hoist the triple coffin onto the confessional altar. Finally the coffin was lowered into the crypt and entombed near the burial place of the first pope, Saint Peter.

FOOTNOTE: The College of Cardinals dropped Galeazzi-Lisi as a Vatican physician, and the medical profession of Rome took action to expel him.

# CHAPTER XIX

Pope Pius XII was interred. Next came the conclave that would choose his successor. Cardinals from all over the globe poured into Rome to attend it. I helped Eleanor to compose a list of papabili. The only certainty was that a non-Italian would not be elected. That reduced the possibilities to the number of Italian cardinals — seventeen. The *Daily News,* that could do wonders with pictures, printed photos of all seventeen Italian princes of the church on one page under the caption: "One of These Will Be Pope." The photos illustrated the jointly by-lined article that Pibe and I wrote.

We pointed out that although an Italian was sure to be the next pontiff, nevertheless it still wasn't certain what kind of prelate he would be: liberal or radical; conservative or progressive; pastoral or political; or whether he would be relatively young or relatively old; in the latter case, advanced age would make for a transitional pontificate. This was believed to be favored by most of the non-Italian cardinals.

One Italian newspaper commented that Cardinal Spellman, although one of the best-known churchmen in the world, didn't stand a chance because "he speaks Italian and Latin like Oliver Hardy."

The history of Italian priority — Mark Twain called it monopoly — on the papacy is similar to one of Shakespeare's historical dramas of the English kings, being fraught with intrigues, feuds, murders, riots, palace revolutions, and counterrevolutions. In its inception, the so-called priority was simply a matter of geography. The early church had no College of Cardinals. The bishops of Rome (only called popes after 352 A.D.) were nominated by acclamation. The city's priests, along with lesser bishops from neighboring cities, made the choice in something resembling a New England town meeting. They elected somebody they knew, and to be known required being a Roman. Even Saint Peter the Apostle traveled from Galilee to settle in Rome before he was consecrated in 42 A.D. during Nero's reign.

Unable to dominate the papacy while it remained in Rome, King Philip IV of France persuaded Pope Clement V, a Frenchman, to take the papal court to Avignon. For almost seventy years — from 1309 to 1378 — Clement V and six consecutive French popes of Avignon packed the Sacred College of Cardinals with their fellow countrymen. The papacy became a closed corporation.

The pontiff who moved the papacy to France, Bertrand de Goth of Bordeaux, liked wine, women, and song. His six Avignon successors, with the exception of the last, were openly political, and the Avignon papal court was denounced as "a sink of vice." Saint Catherine of Siena joined with poets Dante and Petrarch in despairing that the Holy See would ever be "returned to Rome and freedom." Petrarch, who sired two illegitimate children and certainly was no prude, wrote about Avignon:

"Impious Babylon, hell on earth, sink of vice, sewer of the world . . . where old men plunge headlong into the arms of Venus forgetting their age, their dignity, and their powers. They rush into every shame: gluttony, drunkenness, unchastity, fornication, incest, rape, adultery, and lascivious delights of the pontifical games."

Saint Catherine said "the papal court of Avignon assails my nostrils with the odors of hell itself." Equally shocked, Dante urged the minority of Italian cardinals to flee to Rome.

Heeding the criticism, Gregory IX, the last French pope, revolted against the dynasty in 1378 and returned the papacy to Rome. He died in that year. When the cardinals met to elect his successor, a Roman mob threatened to kill "all cardinals who aren't Italian unless they make an Italian pope."

By a vote of fifteen to one, Archbishop Prignano of Naples became Urban VI. The French dynasty was finished. The next twenty popes comprised fifteen Italians, four Spaniards, and Swiss-born Robert of Geneva, who became Clement VII. The last non-Italian pope was a

Dutchman, Adrian VI. He was elected in the conclave of 1522. The Romans hated him and denounced the cardinals who elected him as "betrayers of Christ's blood and infidels who should be buried alive." On his death a year later, reports spread that Adrian had been murdered. No non-Italian has occupied the papal throne since.

On October 25, 1958, fifty-one cardinals — their number diminished by the sudden death earlier in the day of Edward Cardinal Mooney of Detroit — entered Vatican Palace in the afternoon and were sealed in a conclave to elect a new pope. The two remaining American cardinals, Spellman of New York and Francis McIntyre of Los Angeles, were the last to enter. They came in separate cars directly from the deathbed of Mooney who had been stricken during an afterlunch nap in his room at the North American College.

The fifty-one cardinals conferred and prayed during the night for guidance from the Holy Ghost before the balloting, four times a day, began the next morning. After three days and eleven ballots, a white puff of smoke wafted up in the late afternoon from the slender chimney over the Sistine Chapel. It meant that a successor to Pius XII had been chosen. "Viva il Papa," roared the fifty thousand people gathered in Saint Peter's Square as they saw the white smoke, although they didn't know who the new pontiff was. It was fifty minutes later before he appeared on the floodlit balcony above the main door of the world's largest basilica at 6:02 P.M. By that time the crowd had swollen to three hundred thousand in the square, including Romans and tourists, as a result of the Vatican radio announcement that a pontiff had been elected.

"Viva il Papa," roared the people again as word swept through the crowds that the plump little man with twinkling eyes and jug ears on the balcony — the new leader of the half-billion Roman Catholics in the world — was Angelo Giuseppe Cardinal Roncalli, aged seventy-six, patriarch of Venice, and son of a poor Italian farmer. He was the oldest pope to take office in more than two centuries.

Roncalli's selection of John XXIII as his pontifical name came as a surprise. John XXII, who died in 1334, was the second of the Avignon popes. The Vatican said later that night that Roncalli had chosen the name because of his esteem for John the Baptist. It was also the name of his father and the name of the church in which he was baptized. The new pope's official signature in Latin was *Johannes*.

A few days after his election, John held his first press conference. His special personality immediately became apparent. Pius knew seven languages and spoke them almost without an accent until weakened by illness and then even his German and English, which he spoke the best, bore traces of his native Italian. John spoke Latin, Greek, French, and some Turkish but with an Italian accent. He decided to address the correspondents in French. His French was so bad that we had trouble understanding what he said.

Afterwards, we grouped together and compared notes to make sure we at least had gotten the sense of his remarks. But what was important about the conference was that it showed the differences between himself and his predecessor. Where Pius had been austere, scholarly, and aloof, John was jovial, down-to-earth, and friendly. He also was more human than Pius. For example, he had difficulty keeping to the pontifical ''we'' and frequently said ''I'' and then would correct himself or let the slip go with a shake of his head and a smile. I watched some of the aides around him — they were still the same who had attended Pius. They looked shocked at the lack of formal dignity which John displayed. But most of the correspondents were charmed by his modesty. He even admitted that he only knew French ''comme ci, comme ça,'' but was using the tongue in order to communicate with so many non-Italian reporters who had come to cover the conclave.

He nervously adjusted his skullcap several times during the conference. He confessed that he marveled that one of his humble origin had been elevated so high. He gave us no clue as to what his future policy would be except to pay great tribute to his predecessor, which of course proved nothing. He concluded his talk by saying: ''As reporters of world events, you must remember that truth is sacred.''

The first impression among Vatican observers was that John was going to be a pastoral pope. But that was all wrong. During his short pontificate he became quite political. He changed the nineteen-year-old policy of Pius, who waged a cold war against Communists, to one of coexistence with them. He also smashed some ecclesiastical hornets' nests when he convoked the Ecumenical Council, opening traditionally taboo discussions on such controversial subjects as birth control, marriage for priests, and elevation of women to a higher position in the Catholic church. He proved to be a much beloved revolutionary with a leaning toward the left, holding out an olive branch to Soviet Russia.

# CHAPTER XX

La Dolce Vita, even more than the Vatican, dominated the Rome news scene throughout the years. Only papal deaths, conclaves, and the Ecumenical Council stole the spotlight from Roman scandals that were continually happening. In fact they dated back to when Nero fiddled while Rome burned. At first I wasn't quite sure what the phrase, The Sweet Life, meant. It struck me as meaningless as the proverb, In Vino Veritas. I'd known some inebriates who told the truth, but I also had met an awful lot of prevaricating drunks who claimed they had gone to bed with women they hadn't even kissed. It was the King of the Paparazzi who defined the phrase for me. The paparazzi were the self-proclaimed Boswells of la Dolce Vita; at least they chronicled it in pictures which often misrepresented the facts. But there before you was the scene in black and white on newspaper pages. You had to believe it.

The King of the Paparazzi was as incredible as some of the photos they took. He was Ivan Kroscenko, a misplaced person. He had joined up as a mascot of the Italian Army in its retreat from Soviet Russia during World War II and ended up in Rome. To make a living, he started taking pictures and selling them. He soon found that the more scandalous they were, the better they sold. Because of his cunning and initiative, he soon became the leader of Rome's pack of scooter-borne free-lance photographers — the supersnoopers — who followed the spoor of scandal through the streets of the Eternal City as avidly and usually as noisily as a pack of hounds on the scent of a rabbit. They were chasing celebrities who apparently were trying to keep their sex relations a secret.

Sitting on the terrace of the Cafe de Paris on the via Veneto one night with the self-proclaimed king, I asked Ivan how he defined la Dolce Vita. He meditatively sipped his espresso — he rarely drank alcohol — before answering. Then he said: "I would say that it is the sex life of very prominent people such as international film stars, European noblemen, American millionaires, and people with terrific personalities. It includes the erotic games of the Jet Set as well as the breakup of marriages, the beginning of new romances, preferably involving a scandal but always on high celebrity levels. Unknowns haven't anything to do with la Dolce Vita. Who cares about their sex life? It's got to deal with people like Ingrid Bergman and Roberto Rossellini, Liz Taylor and Richard Burton, ex-Queen Soraya and Prince Raimondo Orsini, Maria Callas and Aristotle Onassis, Jacqueline Kennedy and Onassis, Sophia Loren and Carlo Ponti. At least that's la Dolce Vita as far as newspapers are concerned."

I said to him that I thought he was a bit of a snob when it came to celebrities. "You didn't include Lucky Luciano or Joe Adonis."

"Hell, no. They were crime news."

I first met Kroscenko just a month before Liz Taylor arrived in Rome for the filming of the multimillion dollar colossus, *Cleopatra*. He was already planning another drama that would star Liz Taylor, Eddie Fisher, and a new heartbeat for the famous actress.

"You just wait," the king confidently predicted. "You'll see photographs of Liz, intimate ones, with some handsome actor, fascinating director, or patrician playboy. We are already getting things lined up."

In their dusk-to-dawn prowls for photogenic scandal, the paparazzi did not always wait for something to happen. Sometimes they set it up.

One of their tricks was to select one of themselves to provoke the action. A paparazzo, who had been picked by a draw of matchsticks, would go up to a noted actor squiring some beautiful girl and say something nasty about her. One of their favorite provocative phrases was: "You know that woman with you is a ten-thousand lire whore. She fucks anybody." Bing, bang, wham. The actor's fists would fly out at the insulting photog and knock him down while the other paparazzi would shoot pictures of the actor, his girl friend, and the prostrate cameraman on the pavement. It made an action picture. It also made the newspaper reader think that the couple must be having a serious affair if the male celebrity was willing to fight to keep from being photographed with the girl accompanying him. I saw this type of skulduggery perpetrated against Burt Lancaster, Peter O'Toole, and Rex Harrison on via Veneto.

The romance that the king had predicted for Miss Taylor actually took place. The first inkling of it was late on the night of February 18, 1962. Pibe and I were sitting on the stove-warmed terrace of Cafe de Paris when suddenly all the paparazzi there jumped up and dashed off on their souped-up scooters and tiny Fiats. We followed after them in our own car and arrived at the Salvator Mundi Hospital. There Kroscenko reluctantly told us that Liz Taylor was inside "gravely ill with some kind of mysterious poisoning." Pibe and I, who had both been patients there, went inside and asked for information about Liz. The paparazzi just squatted outside like Indians. The night nurse, an elderly nun, blithely denied that the twenty-nine-year-old actress was a patient.

The next day, fuel was added to reports of a torrid romance. Husband Eddie Fisher was kept waiting seven hours before Liz would receive him in her private room in the Salvator Mundi. Richard Burton, who played Marc Antony to Liz's Cleopatra, interrupted a Paris holiday. The handsome Welsh actor said on arrival at Rome's airport: "I want to see Elizabeth as soon as possible."

A few days later, Burton fired the American handling his public relations because he refused to leak to the press that Burton and Liz were going to bed together. In the meantime, Eddie secretly took off for New York, and the story broke wide open.

While Eddie in New York continued to deny that Liz was having an affair with Burton or anybody else, the paparazzi were taking pictures of Liz and her leading man kissing on the porch of an isolated bungalow at the swank seaside resort of Porto Santo Stefano, in northern Italy, where the Dutch royal family had a villa. The two film stars spent an Easter weekend there. I myself saw them holding hands and kissing, but the photos of the omnipresent paparazzi documented my story. They were good to work with because without their pictures as evidence, editors were afraid of libel suits.

A few weeks later Burton was reported to have moved into Liz's fourteen-room villa on the ancient Appian Way outside Rome. I accompanied a commandolike paparazzi raid on the house. After scaling the wall, the photogs pegged stones on the roof to arouse the household, hoping an enraged Burton would dash out in pajamas followed by an indignant Liz in a brief, transparent nightgown — amid popping flashbulbs. But if Burton was inside, he didn't fall for the ruse. The paparazzi were up against a canny celebrity who was proving tougher to bag than a starlet-chasing prince.

Ivan also was a philosopher. He believed in his craft and the integrity of peddling scandal.

"I am the king and I can speak for my fellow cameramen," he told me. "You know that we don't like the name of paparazzi that has been given us, but we are not ashamed of what we do. We work hard, much harder than most other people. Some of us are frustrated artists. We find taking an exclusive picture of Liz and Richard kissing as exciting as painting a masterpiece.

"I don't think we do harm to anybody. Most of our operations are in public places frequented by many people. If a married man and a married woman decide to romance in public, it's their responsibility, not ours, if they get photographed.

"When people come to Rome," Ivan continued, "they behave differently." He listed a whole string of names which included Ava Gardner, Anita Ekberg, Ingrid Bergman, Linda Christian, Shirley MacLaine, and Maria Callas.

"Something happens to visitors here. Rome is a bewitching city. It casts a spell. It is a city of myths and illusions — the greatest dreams end up being smashed against the walls of the Colosseum."

The paparazzi were given their name by movie director Federico Fellini, who featured them in his film, *La Dolce Vita,* which sensationally portrayed the scandals of Rome's café, cinema, and blue-blooded society. Fellini called the leading night-life photographer in the picture: Signor Paparazzo. The director explained that he wanted a name that suggested a buzzing, stinging insect. The result was that all such lensmen are now called *paparazzi* — plural for *paparazzo.*

The word itself has been variously translated as meaning anything from a flock of ducks to a cockroach. One learned authority on the Italian language said it stemmed from a noun in Neapolitan dialect which means someone who sticks his nose in somebody else's business.

When Jacqueline Kennedy came to Ravello, between Naples and Salerno, to spend a three-weeks summer vacation with her sister, Princess Lee Radziwill, in August of 1962, it was Kroscenko who worked out a truce with the then First Lady of America. She agreed to let the paparazzi photograph her in action during ten minutes a day. They in return promised they wouldn't bother her the rest of the time. It turned out to be a perfect truce.

At the age of forty, Kroscenko became weary of the royal pace and abdicated in favor of Gilberto Petrucci, ten years his junior. Petrucci, a fast-moving scoop artist who had been knocked down once by Rex Harrison, was a handsome womanizer who had great success with female tourists, especially Americans. I wrote a story about the new king, and Schuck wired back with a request for a feature follow-up. The message read:

> 22160 PACKARDS NEED FOR SUNDAYS EDITION
> PERSONALITY SKETCH PETRUCCI AND TELEPHOTO
> OF WHAT HE CONSIDERS HIS GREATEST
> PHOTOGRAPHIC SCOOP
>
> SCHUCK

Gilberto, who was even friendlier than Kroscenko, was glad to oblige, but I was disappointed with what he gave me as his masterpiece. I had expected a curvaceous movie star; instead it was a picture of a bald, toothless old man standing in front of a barbershop.

"Christ, Gilberto," I said when I looked at it. "What the hell is this? The *News* wants cheesecake to illustrate a feature story about you."

"But this is my greatest scoop. That's what you asked for, wasn't it?"

"That's right."

"Well, this is it. It's the only picture taken in fifty years of Alessandro Serenelli. He is now eighty-one years of age and a repentant rapist and murderer. At the age of eighteen he violated and killed Maria Goretti who was only eleven years old. That was in 1902. She became known as the Virgin of the Marshes and was beatified in 1947 and elevated to sainthood in 1950. The old man attended the canonization service in Saint Peter's Basilica without the public knowing he was present. Only the pope and a few prelates knew he was there."

Gilberto said that since Serenelli had been released from prison in 1927, he had been hiding in a Capuchin monastery at Ascoli Piceno on the Adriatic coast in central Italy. He worked as a lay gardener. I checked with Vatican sources and found that Gilberto had his facts right. Serenelli had left Ascoli Piceno a total of four times. Three were to travel to Vatican City to appear before the Holy Congregation of Rites in connection with its investigation into the heroic virtues of Maria Goretti. He testified that Maria resisted his carnal advances with her life. He confessed to the congregation that he only penetrated the young girl's virginal vagina after stabbing her fourteen times in her parents' farmhouse outside of Anzio. On her deathbed a few hours later, she asked God to forgive the man who had assaulted her. The fourth time Serenelli traveled from the monastery was to attend her canonization in Saint Peter's.

"I resorted to all kinds of tricks to get the picture," Gilberto said. "Finally I played the part of a hungry idiot and was taken to a soup kitchen inside the monastery. Attendants there said that Serenelli went out once a month for a haircut at a barbershop just outside the walls. That's where I snapped him. It took more time than any of my Dolce Vita pictures."

Back in New York, the *News* managed to produce cheesecake for the article. It took an old daguerreotype of Maria Goretti, girlish and buxom, from its archives and did things to it that made the saint look like a sexpot.

If the story was big enough the paparazzo was willing to go outside of Italy to get it. One of the biggest coups carried out abroad was masterminded by Settimio Garrittano of Milan. He organized a squad of Italo-Greek scuba-diving photogs. Pretending to be fishermen, they operated patiently for three weeks from an old sailboat off the Greek island of Skorpios. They used powerful East German and Russian telescopic cameras to take pictures of Jackie Onassis on the beach. They finally got a series of photos showing her completely in the nude — bare breasts, hairy triangle, and all. The photos were sold to Italy's sophisticated magazine, *Playmen,* for the record sum of twenty thousand dollars. The woman editor, Adelina Tattilo, held them for more than a year. She published them the same week that an Italian-language edition of Hugh Hefner's *Playboy* made its first appearance on the newsstands of Italy. Her timing was an attempt to keep *Playmen* in front as the most daring publication in the country.

In recent years, newly assigned reporters to Rome frequently have asked me what has happened to la Dolce Vita. They said they hadn't seen much evidence of it anymore. Probably true. La Dolce Vita, however, was still very much alive, but like everything else in the early seventies it became saturated with narcotics. At one time, celebrities weren't so afraid of their high jinks being photographed because there was only champagne and sex — fairly harmless ingredients for a party in Italy — but with the introduction of drugs among members of the Jet Set, la Dolce Vita was compelled to go underground. Italian law and Italian police being implacable about narcotics, made secrecy a must. For some years now the Sweet Life has not been unfolding before the eyes of tourists seated on the sidewalk cafés of via Veneto, but in private apartments, villas, and palaces where drug-sparked sex games have become top secret, with not even paparazzi being able to crash them. If anything the orgies have become more hardcore than ever, including group fucking and homosexual exhibitions.

I took a friend of mine not long ago to a Dolce Vita party tossed by a wealthy American in a luxury apartment in the center of Rome. My friend committed the unforgivable sin of thinking sex was funny. The host had just started to set the pace by getting down on his knees, entirely naked, and taking turns with a lesbian in cunt-lapping the most beautiful girl at the party. Many of the guests were high on drugs. As the girl being worked on appeared to be on the verge of an orgasm, my friend began roaring with laughter.

"Throw out that laughing hyena," commanded the host, raising his head from between the girl's thighs. "This is a serious orgy."

Two husky waiters carried out his order and my friend found himself on the sidewalk wearing only a woman's nightgown.

# CHAPTER XXI

The Elf wired me that she was coming to Rome and would be arriving by the wayward bus at piazza Cinquecento around 2 P.M. I showed the message to Pibe. It ended with the noncommittal phrase: "Love and kisses."

There was no clue as to why the Elf was making the trip.

"Well, we can put her up at our place if you want," Pibe said. "She is no worse than your other girl friends and she's intelligent."

"We'll see," I said. "I'll play it by ear. You don't mind if I meet her alone and take her out to lunch?"

"Fair enough. But get to the office before six. I have to attend Alessandrini's press conference."

Frederico Alessandrini was now the offical Vatican spokesman. Pibe punctiliously attended all his conferences trying to keep up with Vatican developments and to maintain her contacts. She could even call him up on the phone and ask him to answer late-night queries from New York. There was so much wasted motion in covering the Vatican.

I reached the bus station ten minutes ahead of arrival time. My bête noire was there too. The Italian count. He was handsome and dapper as usual. The bastard! He looked at me. I looked at him. We didn't speak. The bus arrived and we both waited behind the five or six others who were also meeting it. He seemed to be as reluctant as myself to show enthusiasm or concern. Finally the Elf appeared in the doorway, and she slowly descended looking among the crowd. Then she spotted the two of us. She tried to greet us both simultaneously without showing any preference.

"Hi there," she called, looking between us, engulfing us both with her eyes.

Being impulsive, I couldn't resist surging forward, but even as I reached her before the count, I remembered that she had frequently mentioned him in her last few letters to me although she still described herself as living with the blind boy. But her passing references to the count were so cryptic that I had become suspicious. She seldom lied but she was capable of important omissions. I tried to kiss her on the mouth, but my lips only brushed her cheek.

"Anything wrong?" I asked.

"Not a thing," she said. "I am really happy. Oh, here's the count."

He also only succeeded in kissing her on the cheek.

"You must both help me get my luggage."

We went with her, one on each side of her, to the back of the bus. A man on top of the vehicle was handing bags and suitcases down to the driver who said: "Ciao" to both the count and myself. When the Elf had identified four pieces of baggage as hers, saying "E tutto," I tipped the driver and started picking up her belongings. The count quickly grabbed the two remaining suitcases.

"Here's a taxi," I said hailing a cab. The count put the two pieces he was carrying into the front seat next to the driver. I piled the other two bags on top of them.

"I was hoping to take you to lunch, kid," I said, trying to edge out my rival.

"Yes, have lunch with him, cara," the count said. "You have a lot to tell him. Meet me around five at my place. I'll take your baggage home in this taxi, and you can get another one."

Acting like Trilby under the influence of Svengali, she replied submissively: "Yes, dear. That's fine. I'll be there at five."

"Shit," I said.

Without saying good-bye to him, I took the Elf by the arm and steered her to another cab. I told the driver: "Andiamo al Ristorante Valadier. Nel Pincio."

It was spring and the trees were already green. Blooming mimosa and bougainvillaea added color to the Pincio. We rode in silence for the first few minutes through heavy traffic. Then I burst out:

"That goddamn whoremonger has certainly hypnotized you."

"That's not true," the Elf replied quietly. "I love him very much and just want to be with him. And with him alone. You are the one who hypnotized me."

"Me!"

"Yes, you. You got me to make love to you in front of all our friends in Cairo. You talked me into going to bed with the Greek and having a threesome with the two of you. It was you who talked me into wanting to come to Positano and wrote the whole script unloading me onto the blind boy. Well, I'm not having any more of your hypnotism. You've masterminded me enough. Now I'm going to do what I want to do." She was silent for a moment, then she said: "If I didn't know you, I'd believe you were jealous."

"Jealous? Me?"

"Yes, just like anybody else despite all your big talk."

"Listen, kid. I only want to protect you against him. Honestly, I do. Fuck him all you want, but don't go away with him. You'll never see Rome nor Positano again if you become his mistress. He's a possessive Italian. You will be under lock and key."

"That's fine with me. I don't want anybody else."

"You mean you don't want to screw the Greek, the blind boy, or me anymore?"

"That's right."

"He must be wonderful in bed."

"He is. You know what they call his prick in Positano?"

"No. What?"

"The golden cock."

"Who told you that?"

"He did."

The cab stopped at Valadier's. I found a free table on the terrace.

After we had ordered lunch, including white Chianti to go with the swordfish steaks, I repeated as though stunned: "He told you. He himself told you he has a golden cock. Un cazzo d'oro! What a braggart. Don't you know these Italian men yet? They always talk like that. And girls, goddamn it, fall for it."

"But it's the truth."

"Oh, shit."

I stopped eating and just drank. I ordered another bottle of Chianti, and before we finished it, I asked for the bill. It was nearly three-thirty. That only left me about an hour and a half with her before she met the count. After paying the bill, I took her to my place in a taxi. The goose was still strutting around in the courtyard. The Elf didn't even notice it. She seemed in a daze. When we got inside the apartment, there was only the tuttofare.

"Olga," I told the maid, "take the rest of the day off."

"But I have so much to do. There's a whole mountain of laundry to wash."

"Come back at six. But get going now. Subito!"

When the maid had left, the Elf remarked that I didn't waste time.

"I don't have any to waste," I replied.

I sat down on the divan she once had slept on as our guest and pulled her down next to me. "Shall we have a last go?"

"If you want." Her voice was listless.

"Let's get undressed and try to make it a good one."

I started taking off her clothes but, looking at her watch, she said she would do it herself and for me to undress myself. She wanted to be on time for that five o'clock appointment. I began removing my clothes quickly — like a fireman in reverse. Soon both of us were naked. But we were so embarrassed that we hardly knew where or how to start. I began to talk — compulsively.

"You know he's married and has two children?" I said.

"Of course. He told me all about them. He even admitted he has no intention of divorcing his wife although they are legally separated. He is a good Catholic."

"And you're willing to be only a mistress?"

"Certainly."

"He's just a skunk. I didn't warn you against him for fear my warning would make you interested in him. He is more of a whoremonger than I am. He took a woman away from me in Positano." I was referring to the millionairess. "Now you're the second."

"You see, you are jealous."

"I'm not. It's just that I feel responsible for you."

"He'll look after me."

"I hear he has vast vineyards, so perhaps he can," I admitted, trying to placate her and get her in a better mood for sex. "I'm sorry I've been so petty. Kiss me and forgive me."

She kissed me softly on the mouth. A platonic kiss. I forced my tongue between her lips. My hands felt her breasts. Soon we were fondling each other's genitals.

"Oh, darling Elf," I whispered into her ear. "You always arouse me. Please be good to me this last time. Let's make it a wonderful farewell fuck."

"I'll do my best, Pack. For old time's sake."

Our mouths vacuumed together, our tongues dueling each other. I eased into her. We were hyphenated in sex. All of a sudden her cunt became prehensile. Its sphincter began squeezing my prick. The insides of her loins wriggled like a mess of worms, tantalizing the entire length of my staff. It felt as though myriads of tiny, convulsive hands inside of her were strangling my rod, jerking it off. I extricated myself from her membranous pergola so as not to ejaculate too soon.

"Christ, darling," I said. "I can't keep it in there without shooting. A clutching, clenching cunt! I have never felt anything like it."

"Muff me for awhile. Then we'll come together."

I slid my head down between her thighs and pushed my tongue deep inside of her twitching quim. Even my tongue was squeezed by its velvet muscles. I found the enflamed boil of her clit and gave it a light lingual honing. She soon was whimpering and murmuring, "Put it in. Quickly. I can't hold it."

I rose up and flung myself on top of her, thrusting my pulsating peter into the quicksand of her cleft. It sank in fast and deep. What an exotic cunt, I thought as it began garroting my cock with its frantic orgiastic grip while I darted back and forth inside her, my foreskin covering and uncovering the bulging knob of my virility. With an explosion of passion, the seminal fluid surged from my testicles flooding the depth of her belly.

"I can feel you coming," she keened. "I'm coming too."

Her fingernails drew thin paths of blood along both sides of my spinal column, as she scratched at my back in the abandon of her climax.

We lay still, our limbs intertwined for a few minutes.

"Long live Queen Cunt," I said gaily, disentangling my hot and sweating body from hers. As I gave her dripping slit a final kiss, I thought what a disciplined slave of the deadline I am. At this critical ecstatic moment in the relationship of the Elf and me, I am worried about getting back to the office to file copy in time for the first edition.

"Long live King Cock," the Elf laughed but looked at her watch, thinking probably of her own deadline with the count. "Well, we finally did it, didn't we?" She gave my cock a quick kiss, wetting her lips with the silver strings of afterlove dangling from it.

"Did what?" I asked.

"Reached a rapport. Got together."

"I'll say we did, but listen, Elf, where did you learn that clutching-cunt technique? You didn't have it in Cairo or when I left you in Positano."

"I learned it from the blind boy. You said he was sensitive. Well, he discovered I had latent prehensile qualities and taught me to develop them. I feel awful about it."

"Why? It's great. You're a much better screw than before."

"I hate to hurt people. I hate the way I've wounded the blind boy. He taught me that trick and because of it the count fell in love with me and then I with him. I am sure without that new technique of mine the count wouldn't have gone overboard for me." Then being practical, she said, "Do you mind if I wash first in the bathroom? It's getting late."

"Go ahead. I'll use the kitchen."

When we were both dressed, I phoned for two taxicabs. We didn't have much time to talk, but we were both happy that we had ended our relationship on a note of sex and friendship. We kissed with open mouths, but without any tongue play, and shook hands. I felt very sophisticated and understanding. I had finally taken my defeat by the count with good grace and with philosophical aplomb, I thought. The mutual orgasm had helped me to save face.

We waved to each other as we got into the separate taxis and went our separate ways. That was the last time we met.

Some years later, I learned the count and the Elf had both grown gray. They had been crippled when the Jaguar he was driving skidded and turned turtle on the Bologna-Venice highway while they were speeding through a rainstorm. The once whimsical Elf used a cane while the count's aristocratic face was marked by a dull blue streak across his left cheek as a result of the accident. But like a Heidelberg dueling scar, it enhanced his appearance. His two sons, now grown up, lived with them, and everybody who met them said it was a happy menage, not needing the sanctity of marriage to make it good. And I who am against marriage could see nothing wrong with that except that I missed her clutching cunt.

When we quarreled, Pibe would sometimes say: "You see, you have no judgment. The count was a pretty good fellow after all."

298

# CHAPTER XXII

After thirty-five years in Italy, I am still not certain what I think of the Italians. Sometimes I love them, admire them; other times I despise and almost hate them — except I don't really hate anyone. Having worked in Rome for such a long time — through periods of Fascist dictatorship, a world conflict, and postwar democracy — it is obvious that I haven't tried too hard to get away from the Italians. So at least I must like living among them although they can be the most exasperating, elbowing, loud-mouthed, ill-mannered, melodramatic, and irresponsible people in the world. Whenever I return to Rome after having been away on assignment, I spontaneously murmur: "It's great to be back."

The truth probably is that I like the defects of the Italians. Even their corrupt methods and acts of violence, passion, and murder seem so human, or at least to have a personal motive behind them. Vendetta! The good of the family! They are an amoral rather than an immoral people, capable of flirting with a girl gallantly one moment and raping her the next, laughing and joking with you while cheating you in any transaction from collecting a restaurant bill to selling you a house.

Pibe and I soon found that the Italian way of life was very infectious; we soon became diseased ourselves. We weren't alone. Everything foreign in this country becomes Italianized. The Foreign Press Club is more Italian than the Italian Press Club. We soon went along with the traditional but illegal Italian procedure of signing two leases for an apartment we took in via Margutta: one which listed the rent as extremely low and the other, giving the actual figure. Naturally the low-rent lease went to the authorities so that both sides had less taxes to pay and copies of the real contract were kept secretly by the owner and us.

Newcomers to Italy soon cease going to a tabaccaio where you have to pay a large government tax on cigarettes, both domestic and foreign. Cigarette smuggling is a big racket in Italy in which sailors from the U.S. Sixth Fleet help supply the underground commodity which is then sold by fat old women in the side streets of Rome, Naples, Milan, and other big cities. They hide the merchandise beneath their skirts and between their breasts. They also can produce whole cartons from behind nearby locked doors.

One time I bought two cartons of Chesterfields for a visiting fireman from the *News*. A uniformed policeman indifferently watched the transaction.

"Why didn't that cop arrest you and that black-market woman?" the visitor asked. He had pretended, incidentally, that he wasn't with me while I paid and collected the illicit goods.

"That's not his department," I said. "He's not a customs policeman, and if he were he probably wouldn't do anything about it because she would give him a cut."

The black marketeers also made deliveries to your home and office.

Speaking of the Sixth Fleet, I often wondered if Lucky Luciano didn't use its sailors to help him in his alleged international drug trafficking. After he had been expelled from America at the end of the war and sent back to Italy, he spent most of his time in Naples. He used to lunch every day at the waterfront restaurant of Zi' Teresa. There scores of U.S. sailors would come up to his table while he ate and ostensibly ask him for his autograph. He always nervously obliged, looking carefully around him as though afraid somebody might shoot him down. In good old gangster style, he always sat with his back to the wall. He was frequently accompanied by a blonde. She was Igea Lissoni, a nightclub dancer, whom he had told friends, "is the only woman I ever loved." He married her in 1949. After her death from cancer in 1958, he wore a black tie and a mourning armband for two years.

The Sixth Fleet moved all over the Mediterranean from its home port in those days of Naples. Special units attached to the fleet were constantly returning to the United States at the end of their tour of duty and being

300

replaced by other ships. I saw some of the autographed notes Lucky wrote for the sailors. They were cryptic and could easily have contained secret messages and instructions about pickups and deliveries of narcotics.

I had a hard time at first putting up with the way many Italians cheated at cards and just generally lied, sometimes for no particular reason, or just to make things run more smoothly. Cheating and lying are part of the make-believe that causes Italy to tick and if you stay here long enough you are apt to do the same things yourself. I learned to play scopone with the fishermen of Positano. They would tell each other in dialect what cards they had or suggest to each other what to play. At first I objected and they left me out of their games. Finally I begged in, and this time Pibe and I began exchanging similar information in American slang which they couldn't understand. The Italians loved it, and the mutual cheating seemed to add zest to the game.

The lying part is more complicated to explain but it seems to start with the Italians liking to be pleasant and polite. Italians will compliment each other on their appearance, exaggerating how well they look sartorially or healthwise; what lovely children they have when the little monsters are really quite terrible.

Then lying is very convenient in the home and avoids a lot of family unpleasantness. One of the reasons for many divorces in the United States is honesty. One of the American spouses just truthfully admits to being in love or having an affair with somebody else. The problem is then frankly discussed. An Italian husband would never admit to his wife that he has a mistress nor would the wife tell the truth about a lover she may have on the side. To most Italians, telling the truth in such marital matters would be cruel, causing unhappiness by the confrontation of brutal facts. It might even lead to multiple killings: murder of the lover or the wife or both and suicide by the cornuto (cuckold) himself. In Italy, lies are the oil for a smoothly running marital life; a married partner would only admit infidelity if caught in the act.

Even in business deals lying is more or less accepted, and labels on bottles and cans describing the contents are often dangerous misstatements of fact, risking the health of consumers.

There is an atmosphere of prevarication about the country from declarations of love to government communiqués. And when a person is caught in a lie, he is regarded generally as having committed a mere peccadillo, hardly anything meriting serious criticism. A lie is only an untruth; it could even be a pleasant idea like Santa Claus, the Easter

Bunny, and heaven. If an industrialist should be arrested — which rarely happens — for misrepresentation of his merchandise, he would be considered unlucky and deserving of sympathy. In recent years wine has been on the market that never even contained a grape or the juice of a grape. Instead, the ingredients consisted of alcohol, sugar, banana peels, ox blood, and dyes.

Many Italians couldn't grasp the excitement in America over Watergate and considered it much ado about nothing. Didn't all political parties spy on each other and try to discredit each other? Wasn't it a natural form of political life? Why develop electronics if you don't use the resultant progress to bug political rivals? Why be president if you can't manipulate taxes? Machiavelli is still esteemed a great thinker by most Italian statesmen.

In the morning when I walk to the Stampa Estera, I have to pass through narrow, alleylike streets. The sidewalks are about two feet wide with only enough space for a single pedestrian. An Italian is coming towards me. A duel has started. Is he going to make me step aside into the gutter? Or am I going to force him off the pavement? I move close to the wall so that I have the inside track. I then look down at the ground pretending not to see him. Not expecting such a maneuver, he generally steps aside. But if he is really tough and bangs right into me, I bring up my knee forcefully into his groin, bouncing him off the sidewalk. I say very politely: "Scusi." I keep on going, preparing myself for another encounter.

After winning several of these contests, I say to myself: "Pack, you are a rough bastard. Why don't you relax and let the Italians use their own sidewalks for which they pay taxes and which, incidentally, are littered with dog shit?" According to Italian superstition it is good luck if you accidentally step in it. I begin to feel ashamed of myself. I change my tactics. I step into the gutter on my own initiative. Nobody says: "Grazie." Then I begin getting sore all over again.

And if you are driving a car, you run into a similar bluffing problem every five minutes. Are you going to let the Italian driver force you from your right-of-way? There's never a tranquil moment in just going from one place to another in Italy.

But the post office! That is the worst of all. I have a registered, airmail, special-delivery letter to mail. I take my place at the end of a long line of people in front of the proper window. Suddenly an Italian steps in front of me.

"Hey, cornuto, get at the end of the line," I yell at him.

He shrugs his shoulders as a gesture of contempt for me and moves away, but instead of going to the rear he goes forward and steps in front of somebody else. Oddly enough, this person doesn't object. So I shout out: "Hey, cornuto, get at the end of the line. This is a civilized country."

He doesn't answer but the people in line glare at me. They are on his side. He is doing the natural thing, trying to get ahead of others. I am crude, making a scene about it, instead of doing the same thing myself.

The Italian knows how to work on one's vanity. I used to fool myself that I disliked the false titles that waiters, barmen, barbers, and clerks would bestow on me. It was never just: "Buon giorno, signor," but "Buon giorno, commendatore. . . . Buon giorno, dottore. . . Buon giorno, professore." When I first came to Italy it was "Buon giorno, dottore," but now that my age is showing I am given the most respected rank, that of professore — I who never have taught anything to anybody in my life. It's pleasant. I must admit it titillates the ego; it's nice to have somebody go out of his way to promote me academically.

Obsequiousness comes easy to an Italian but so does arrogance. I am never sure which I prefer. You never feel that the Italian really considers himself humble when he praises you but that in actuality he knows your human weakness and is just cunningly playing up to your conceit, really making a monkey of you if you stop to analyze it. The arrogant Italian, on the other hand, is really capable of insulting you sincerely. You admit he is being more honest but less simpatico. Even his arrogance is not political or national. It is personal. When he talks about his country, he runs it down the same as the fawning type of Italian, describing it as *povera Italia* — poor Italy. Both the arrogant and subservient Italian constantly refer to Italy as a second-rate country in almost everything except soccer. When you talk about soccer you are involving the Italian's national pride. Then they all become rabidly patriotic.

Although they may disagree as to interpretations, most students of Italy regard the family as the foundation of the entire nation. It is also more economically efficient than almost any other family unit in the world. In Positano and other small villages, I talked to scores of people who had no other income than what their children and grandchildren sent from the United States, Argentina, or Venezuela. The Italian family enables the survival of both the very poor and the very rich. Everybody in it helps everybody else. In wintertime, thousands of southern Italians go to winter resorts in the North to work in hotels owned or operated by their relatives. In summertime, the mountain people come down to the beaches and work in the tourist-jammed sea resorts in jobs produced by relations.

But one of the great tricks of instinctive protectiveness of the family is to mix its political affiliations for commercial reasons. Even under Mussolini, there was always an anti-Fascist son, daughter, or nephew premeditatedly or subconsciously developed in preparation for the eventuality that Il Duce would someday be overthrown. When Alfredo in Rome, the King of Fettucine, for example, was not allowed by Allied martial law to continue to run his famous restaurant because he had served banquets for such leading Nazis as Marshal Goering, he merely handed it over to his son who wore the red scarf of the Italian partisans. It was the same in almost every business concern throughout postwar Italy: the Fascist parents transferred their establishments to their left-wing sons or daughters.

If the Reds should take over the country now, every anti-Communist father, including a Christian Democrat or a right-wing Liberal, would produce a dyed-in-the-wool Commie offspring to handle the family's property and business interests. The family is a practical commercial concern offering insurance against a changing political world.

And the many children of the average Italian family mean the parents are almost certain to be looked after in their old age.

Each family is also a tribunal with its own laws and its own code of honor and enforcement officers, comprising fathers, uncles, and brothers. In traditionalist areas of the country, modernism has been coming slowly, ever so slowly. If a girl's virginity has been taken from her by a man and it becomes known to the family, there will be a council meeting, and the father or some brother or all of them together may be appointed to kill the seducer or castrate him. As a rule, those who take justice in their own hands are caught but given very light sentences because, despite all the talk of enlightenment in this country, the ancient code of honor is still an extenuating factor and taken into consideration by the courts.

One of the best examples of such an honor killing occurred not so long ago in Catania, Sicily. The shooting was dramatic. Accompanied by his beautiful, twenty-year-old daughter, high school teacher Gaetano Funari marched into a student-filled classroom of the University of Catania and pumped five bullets into the chest of Professor Francesco Speranza. The professor died instantly. As the teacher fired he said in a cold voice: "He seduced my daughter who was his student. Family honor demands I kill him."

Funari was found guilty of "homicide for reasons of honor" and sentenced to two years and eleven months imprisonment.

The family is not always so honorable, particularly in poverty-stricken areas where ten and twelve members sleep in only a few rooms. Such crowded conditions lead to incest and newspapers are full of accounts of such scandals, especially when the police become involved, which is almost inevitable when the girl stabs or shoots a father or a brother. But social workers believe that these overcongested homes lead to many more incestuous relations than ever are published in the press.

# CHAPTER XXIII

I worked as an extra alongside of Sophia Loren and her mother in mob scenes in the film *Quo Vadis,* shot at Cinecittá in 1949. My red beard and bulging belly made me a movie type. Even then, at seventeen, Sophia was a gorgeous, bosomy creature but was only making three thousand lire (five dollars) a day — the same as me. She hadn't been discovered yet by balding, paunchy producer Carlo Ponti, twenty-one years her senior.

Sophia was born on the outskirts of Naples in a slum area called Pozzuoli, known locally as the Gateway to Hell because it perched on the rim of a volcano. She and her younger sister, Maria, were the illegitimate daughters of Romilda Villani and Riccardo Scicolone, a ne'er-do-well traveling salesman who was estranged from his wife. They were supported by the meager earnings of grandfather Villani.

Sophia described her childhood to me this way: "I was a sickly girl. The other kids called me il stecchetto [the matchstick], and I had only two dresses: one for summer, one for winter. They hung loose and flapping around my skinny frame."

At sixteen she still had trouble with her clothes but by then, popping out of them was her trouble. Logically enough, her mother who had been a red-haired beauty queen entered Sophia in a Naples beauty contest. The girl came in second, winning twenty-five thousand lire, a roll of wallpaper, and the vote of Carlo Ponti who was one of the judges. Legend

306

has it that he told her at the time: "You should become a movie actress."

That was all the encouragement Romilda Villani needed. She took her blossoming daughter to Rome and looked for film jobs for both of them. Eventually she got Sophia and herself work as extras in *Quo Vadis*. It was the first big American production made in Italy after the war. Romilda acted as Sophia's manager, shoving her shapely daughter into any bit part she could find.

Meantime, Sophia earned more consistent pay by posing for romance magazines known to Italians as *fumetti* because the written-in dialogue looked like smoke coming from the speakers' mouths. Editors changed her name from Sophia Scicolone to Sophia Lazzaro and cast her in photographs as everything from a high-class courtesan to an Arab princess that eventually won her a featured role in a long-forgotten film, *Africa under the Sea*.

Then as if on cue, Ponti popped up again and changed her name to Sophia Loren and cast her in a series of Ponti-De Laurentiis films. Carlo's insistence that Sophia get all the leading roles soon irritated his partner, Dino De Laurentiis, and the latter's wife, Silvana Mangano, still remembered for her shapely figure in *Bitter Rice*. Dino and Silvana thought Carlo was pushing his protégée too fast. Finally, the company was dissolved in a bitter clash over whether to cast Silvana or Sophia in *The Wall*.

Soon after Dino and Carlo parted in the early fifties, Sophia hit international stardom and Ponti's marriage to Giuliana Fiastri, one of Italy's first women lawyers, hit a snag. There was a lot of publicity about Ponti's discovery and his plans to make the beautiful waif from a Naples slum into a world celebrity. There were also pictures of Carlo kissing his new star.

In 1953, Giuliana won a legal separation in a Roman civil court, getting custody of the two children, a handsome financial settlement, and two villas. Carlo got visiting rights.

Three years later, Ponti obtained a Mexican divorce and married Sophia in a proxy ceremony in which two Mexican lawyers acted as stand-ins for the principals. Three moralistic souls — a housewife in Genoa, a male hairdresser in Milan, and a lawyer in Arezzo — exercised their right under Italian law and filed bigamy charges against Carlo and Sophia.

The case immediately caught popular imagination, probably because it summed up in the glamorous actress and the prosperous producer all the legal woes that could befall loving couples in a land where the law at the time decreed that marriages must last forever. It threatened to bring about the fall of the shaky coalition government of then Premier Giuseppe Saragat.

In an attempt to prevent arrest, Ponti, with his ex-wife's cooperation, sought to have his first marriage annulled on the grounds that neither he nor Giuliana, back in 1946, expected it to last. Roman ecclesiastical courts rejected all their applications. Under Italian law the crime of bigamy, which carried a jail sentence of up to five years, could be wiped out only if one of the two marriages is declared null and void. For eight long years the legal battle waged and for eight years Ponti and Sophia had to be wary of visits to their native country. Sophia once said: "We are married when we go to America but not when we return to Italy."

The marital mix-up was not the only thing to plague the actress. Another was the embarrassing situation of her almost equally luscious younger sister, Maria, whose natural father had not gotten around to recognizing her as his daughter although he had previously established in court that he had begotten Sophia. As a star witness in a libel trial brought by Maria against her stepmother, Nella Rivolta Scicolone, Sophia courageously admitted that she was a bastard as well as Maria and that free-loving Riccardo Scicolone fathered both of them. The trial brought out that when Maria started working as a starlet, she found she had to have a name. In Italy the name of the father can be granted to his natural children only with the consent of the father's wife. Nella, a Rome cinema usherette, refused to give her consent to Riccardo in the case of Maria because by this time he had gone back to living with Sophia's mother.

"I know that my father, Riccardo Scicolone, is also Maria's father," Sophia weepingly told the court. "I always knew it as a small child, and there never has been any doubt about it."

Scicolone himself testified that he wanted to give his name to Maria but "somehow I didn't seem to be able to do it right. There has been so much conflict." He glared at Nella, who was in the courtroom as were Maria and her mother. All three women were weeping as well as Sophia. Maria finally won the legal battle for the right to use her father's name.

Shortly after this litigation, Sophia found herself coming to the defense of her sister once again. This time it involved a battle in the press with Donna Rachele Mussolini, the late dictator's seventy-nine-year-old widow.

Newspapers had printed interviews with Rachele in which she was asked what she thought of her youngest son's engagement to Maria Scicolone. The white-haired First Lady of Fascism minced no words. She said she had hoped her son Romano — a banjo-eyed jazz musician — would ''make a more important marriage.''

''Any son of a Fascist dictator is very lucky indeed to have a chance to marry Maria,'' Sophia snorted indignantly as reporters scribbled down her words. ''They are very much in love, and what more do they need for a happy marriage?''

Sophia and Donna Rachele had a long talk and when it was over, Il Duce's widow gave her blessing to the forthcoming marriage. She said: ''Maria is a nice girl, sweet and good. She is also beautiful, but what pleases me most is her love of the home. She can cook too, which is a rare thing these days and will make a wonderful housewife for my son.''

At the time they became engaged, Romano was thirty-three and Maria, twenty-three. Romano had always loved jazz, but his father was against it as ''an American importation.'' As a boy, Romano had to wait until his father went to his office in Palazzo Venezia before he dared practice his favorite music on the piano. When I asked if he believed in Fascism, he snapped back: ''I am not a Fascist. But don't expect me to run down Fascism. That would be repudiating my own father.'' He said he wanted to be married on February 11 because that was the anniversary of the date his father signed the Lateran Treaty in 1929, regulating relations between Italy and the Holy See.

''That was my father's most lasting achievement,'' Romano said.

The wedding actually took place, however, on March 3, 1962. More than six thousand people attended the ceremony that was held in the Catholic church of Predappio, in northern Italy. It was almost a riot with everybody pushing and shoving to get in. Romano fainted as he walked down the aisle while Maria swooned at the altar. The chauffeur-driven car taking Sophia from the church to the wedding party in Donna Rachele's home hit a man and killed him.

The following month, edgy Italian officials, wary of Sophia Loren's dubious marital situation, shied away from presenting her with the Oscar she had won for her work in the film, *Two Women*. The statuette went back to Hollywood, and Sophia, deeply hurt, had to go there to collect it several months later. It was presented to her at the Beverly Hills Hotel in Hollywood during a ten-thousand-dollar supper party in the grand manner which had been denied her by her native Italy, apprehensive of the disapproval of the Catholic Church.

All through her strenuous movie career, Sophia hoped to have a child, but she was prone to miscarriages. She had four of them. The fifth time she became pregnant, she took a plane to Switzerland and virtually locked herself in a Geneva hotel penthouse for six months in an attempt to fulfill her maternal wish. Her determination won out and on December 29, 1968, she gave birth to a seven-pound twelve-ounce boy. Ponti had flown into Geneva from Milan the day before to be by Sophia's beside. Carlo was fifty-five at the time and Sophia, thirty-four.

"I am so happy, the boy is wonderful," Ponti said as soon as he saw his dark-haired, blue-eyed baby. "Sophia and myself already have decided to name him Carlo, Jr."

Dr. Hubert de Watteville, a noted gynecologist, said delivery was made by Cesarean operation because the baby was in an abnormal position.

By the time the baby was born, Sophia and Carlo had managed to straighten out their marital tangle. Ponti had become a French citizen in 1965, then divorced his first wife under French law, and remarried Miss Loren in a secret Paris ceremony. Then a Rome penal court ruled they were not guilty of bigamy but merely of having gone through what it described as an irregular procedure. Later the Italian Parliament passed a divorce law.

Sophia completed her rise from rags to riches when she and Carlo bought an eighteenth-century palace in the Alban Hills, renovating and modernizing all of its fifty-three rooms and landscaping the vast, walled grounds around it. They bought art treasures in many parts of the world, turning one of the wings into a priceless museum. They also went in for hosting international celebrities. Sophia even found time to write a cookbook in which she mixed recipe-giving with personalities and happenings.

But the countryside calm didn't last for long. She and Carlo began receiving threats to kidnap their tiny son, nicknamed Cipi. The palace was converted into an armed fortress. Guards were seen carrying machine guns as they patrolled the grounds. Elaborate protection arrangements included a modern burglar-alarm system especially in the area where Cipi slept and played. According to friends, the wealthy movie couple began reinforcing security in their home after they returned from New York where Sophia was robbed of jewels valued at six hundred thousand dollars. One of the gunmen threatened to take revenge on the baby if something went wrong.

Following hormone treatments, Sophia gave birth to a second baby, Eduardo, in January of 1973.

Because dispatches by cable and radio were costly, Schuck was always riding us to make them shorter. In one of his air-mail reprimands about wordy cables, he wrote in his special style:

Dear Packs,

The Big Boss came over to the Foreign News Desk today and saw one of your wallpaper-long wires unfolding itself from the Teletype. He yelped:

"Jesus! The Pope must have fucked Sophia Loren. Otherwise there wouldn't be any excuse for sending such a long story from Rome."

Just remember, Packs, keep your stuff SHORT. We're a tabloid. Not the *Times*. Regards,

Hugh

# CHAPTER XXIV

John XXIII, the peasant pope, who won the hearts of Catholics and non-Catholics alike, died in the same sort of twilight as he had been elected supreme pontiff, four years, seven months, and six days before — a notably short reign — but his rustic simplicity, his fat man's joviality, and his obvious sincerity had made him one of the most beloved leaders in history. Death came at 8 P.M. on June 3, 1963. It came barely ten minutes after tearful crowds had ended an extraordinary outdoor mass celebrated in Saint Peter's Square beneath his window. It came with his three farmer brothers and his one sister at his bedside. It came after four days of terrible agony on the threshold of death. He was eighty-one. Catholic President Kennedy and atheist Premier Khrushchev both wired condolences.

A precedent breaker, Pope John studded his pontificate with landmarks in every area of papal activity, but the high point of all was his convocation of the Ecumenical Council, the gathering in the Vatican of Roman Catholic bishops from all over the world. It was a bold venture that other recent popes had contemplated but only contemplated since the last Ecumenical Council was held in 1869-1870. He conceived the idea within three months of his coronation. For two months the council fathers labored through their initial session, their words and feelings attentively heeded by his open mind. More than once he added his own voice to simplify a procedure, to speed things up, but always insisting on free expression for the bishops. The meetings were attended by non-Catholic observers, bringing together — as not since the Reformation — representatives of Roman Catholic and non-Catholic churches.

He won the nickname of Johnny Walker, when he boarded a train at dawn, embarking on a sixteen-hour rail pilgrimage across Italy to pray at shrines in Loreto and Assisi. The four-hundred mile journey was the first train trip by a pope in one hundred years. It carried the pontiff to hundreds of thousands of small-town people in the distant countryside. It marked above all, the final break from the idea that the papacy was a self-imposed imprisonment, keeping a pope always within the shadow of the tiny Vatican state. The seclusion began in 1870 when Italian nationalists wrested Rome from papal rule to make it the capital of modern Italy. Even after the Lateran Accord of 1929, no pope put the new agreement between the Vatican and Italy to the full test until John XXIII.

He also departed from the centuries-old tradition that a pope should eat his meals alone, in solitary dignity. He not only began having business lunches with high-ranking members of the curia, but he also invited in personal friends, even humble Vatican employees. Once he looked out a window of his private apartment as he was about to be served and saw a Vatican gardener working in the hot sun. He sent his secretary to invite him to lunch.

"I like eating," John told newsmen, "but not alone. Vatican protocol in the past required a pope to dine by himself at a table under the impassive gaze of a member of the papal suite. Loneliness ruins my appetite so I have changed all that. The other day, for example, I called in one of my gardeners to lunch with me. It was a pleasant simple meal consisting of vegetable soup, fish, fruit, and red wine, and I found the conversation very interesting."

No pope had ever had so many anecdotes recounted about him as John. Once on a visit to the Vatican carpentry shop, he remarked to his secretary, "That looks like thirsty work." He then ordered red wine all around.

On visiting Rome's Queen of Heaven Prison — the one I spent a week in just after Mussolini declared war on the United States — he told the inmates with a chuckle: "Since you couldn't come to see me, I've come to see you." He added for good measure that one of his relatives had once served a jail sentence for poaching.

One time he received a group of Italian bishops which included Arrigo

Pintonello, who as chief chaplain of the Italian army wore the insignia of a general. The pope walked among the bishops so that each might kiss his ring, but when he came to Pintonello, John, who had been a chaplain-sergeant in World War I, stood at attention, saluted smartly, and rapped out: "General, Sergeant Roncalli at your command."

Soon after he learned of his mortal illness, John personally changed the rules for the papal death chamber. Remembering the grisly photographs taken of his predecessor by eye doctor Galeazzi-Lisi, John left instructions in a manu proprio — this is ecclesiastical Latin meaning "by his own hand" and refers to the pope's personal instructions which are less authoritative than his encyclicals or papal bulls — prohibiting the taking of photos of a dying pope or of a pope in his bed after death. He also banned any sound recordings in the death chamber.

But on his own deathbed, John appeared calm and tranquil as usual, showing no signs of the pain he had suffered during the last four days and nights of his life. The strong character of his brief pontificate was etched on his granite-gray face.

With prelates, diplomats, and members of the Italian government, I passed in single file by the red velvet-draped catafalque where the pontiff lay in his apartment before being borne to Saint Peter's Basilica. He was resplendent in his pontifical regalia of gold-embroidered red velvet. On his head was the golden miter signifying his episcopal authority. The room was dimly lit with its three windows partially shuttered. Light came from a crystal chandelier and four giant candles, one at each corner of the catafalque. As we passed the bier, nearly everybody, including President Antonio Segni and outgoing Premier Amintore Fanfani, genuflected and kissed the tip of the pope's red slipper. Tall, sword-carrying Noble Guards in high knee boots, doeskin trousers and plumed helmets stood at attention on either side of the catafalque.

That evening the body was carried under gray skies from the Vatican Palace to lie in state in the adjoining Saint Peter's Basilica. Two days later, after more than two million mourners had shuffled past his remains, John was buried in the grotto below the main altar of Saint Peter's.

Already preparations were being made for the election of a new pope. "The pope is dead. Long live the pope." History was repeating itself quickly. We were running out of adjectives. Thank god, tabloids don't object to clichés, I thought.

We pulled out of the mothballs the old saw: "Whoever enters the conclave a pope leaves it a cardinal." Only this time it wasn't true; any more than it hadn't been true when Eugenio Pacelli was elected pope in 1939.

On the morning of June 21, 1963, I stood in the broiling sunlight of Saint Peter's Square. All of a sudden there was a puff of smoke from the silver-hued stovepipe above Sistine Chapel. I looked at my watch. It was 11:22, on the second day of balloting in the conclave. Nobody was sure whether the smoke was black or white, but by some telepathy or other, the word spread through the crowd: "Bianca! Bianca!" It was picked up by radio and television stations around the world. It meant: a new pope had been elected. Within fifty minutes the crowd of thirty thousand in the sunbaked square swelled into three hundred thousand as Romans, tourists, and pilgrims converged into it from all parts of the city. Women fainted in the crush. At ten minutes past noon, the three cardinal chiefs of the conclave made their appearance on Saint Peter's balcony. Finally, the bass voice of Alfredo Cardinal Ottaviani, as senior cardinal deacon, boomed over the loudspeakers: "Annuncio vobis gaudium magnum, habemus Papam." — "I announce with great joy to you, we have a pope."

He then began to give the new pontiff's name — "Giovanni Battista . . . "— when the crowds interrupted with shouts of "Montini! Montini!" Gradually the pandemonium ended and Ottaviani repeated Cardinal Montini's full name, adding that he had chosen the name of Paul VI after the Apostle Paul.

A delighted frenzy of cheering and clapping broke out. The shouts were: "Viva il Papa!" Then Pope Paul, wearing the smallest of the three sizes of robes that had been made in advance for the occasion, appeared on the balcony. His white garb sparkled in the sun. A frail figure, he raised his arms for silence. A hush descended on the square. He gave his first Urbi et Orbi benediction — To the City and to the World. The bells of Rome's five hundred churches pealed out the news joyously: the half billion Roman Catholics again have a supreme pontiff. As he withdrew, newsboys were already in the square, shouting: "Extra! Extra! Montini elected pope."

# CHAPTER XXV

The Roman Catholic church and Italy as a country are almost one and the same in their political thinking. When a few slight changes occur, they take place along parallel lines. They both, for example, have turned even more leftward during the past fifteen years. Pope John XXIII, from the very start of his four-year-long pontificate, tried to improve the atmosphere with Communist countries, without compromising, however, on belief. On one occasion, he even canceled previously scheduled audiences with prominent Catholics to receive Khrushchev's son-in-law, Andrei Adjubei, who was interviewed at the time by almost all Italian newspapers. They played up his remarks beneath front-page headlines, stressing that he said: "I don't believe in religion. I am an athiest." Many Italian Catholics didn't like the red carpet — and it was a Communist-hued red — that Pope John unrolled for Adjubei at the Vatican.

Before that, Amintore Fanfani, a Christian Democrat leader, broke the political ice by forming a coalition government in March of 1962 that received the necessary backing from the Marxist Socialists of Pietro Nenni in Parliament. The Marxists weren't, however, members of the government. Then Aldo Moro, a perennial foreign minister, and a big wheel in the Christian Democrat party brought Nenni's Marxist Socialists into the government. That was on December 4, 1963. Moro gave them six key portfolios. This was considered smart politics because it drove a wedge between the Nenni Socialists and the Communists who had cooperated in the years immediately after the war as a left-wing common front. Until 1975, the center-left combination was still the current formula for the formation of a cabinet. The Marxist-Socialists did well. Through their governmental reforms almost everything in Italy became state-run, including electricity, gas, railways, telephones, shipping, and bus lines. Left-wing unions have supreme power and through frequent strikes gain their objectives. Some observers here said it would be better to have the Communists in the government; then strikes might be outlawed as in Russia. But that would put an end to American collaboration with Italy.

When Fascism was wiped out at the end of World War II, there were no young non-Fascist leaders to spring up and take the places of the Blackshirt Podestà. The present lot of politicians — Saragat, Scelba, Fanfani, Rumor, Colombo, Andreotti, Moro — all lack charisma. They are all second-rate statesmen still smelling of political mothballs.

Even the Communists can't produce anybody to equal Palmiro Togliatti, who died in 1964. He was the best the Reds had to offer, and he never did more than take orders from Moscow. He has been replaced by Enrico Berlinguer, who is a zero outside of his own party. One of the most able speakers of the modern politicians has been Giorgio Almirante, head of the neo-Fascist MSI party, whose parliamentary immunity was recently removed so he could stand trial, charged with attempting to revive Fascism. In a country that was once associated with Nazi Germany and is now ashamed of it, a man like Almirante hasn't much chance. He is clobbered on all sides. His only claim to fame at best was that he was an undersecretary of propaganda to Mussolini when Il Duce, already gaga, was head of the Salò Republic at the end of the war.

Italy's greatest asset is that some power, like the United States, or some international group, like the United Nations or the European Community, may come to its aid. A bankrupt Italy would endanger the rest of the world economically, so she must be rescued.

The Church has not had an easy time of it since Pope John XXIII, the Beloved Reformer, convoked the Ecumenical Council. That vast gathering of bishops from all parts of the world soon made it clear that many priests wanted to marry and a great number of prelates favored the contraceptive pill. The result was that marrying-minded priests have lost out to date but have hope that the way is being paved for them to wed the same as Protestant ministers within another decade or so.

As for the pill, Pope Paul VI, who had to make the final decision after John died, worked out a solution in typical Italian style. The Church disapproved the pill, with the pontiff issuing an encyclical against it. But many Catholic women soon started using the pill just the same and certainly were not being excommunicated for it. The way the Church, without officially saying so, worked out the formula was more or less like this: those women who for reasons of health, economy, or because of being unmarried and not able to wed, had dire need of not bearing a child were forgiven if they used the pill, but the pope himself, the Church itself, never came forward and said so officially. In fact, just the contrary. In other words, in the double-talk of ecclesiastical rhetoric the Church denounced the use of the pill but forgave those who felt constrained by compelling needs of special circumstance to take it.

No greater authority on Italy than Luigi Barzini erred on the question of divorce. Writing in his book, *The Italians*, first published in 1964, the author-senator declared: "Of course there is still no divorce on the lawbooks, and there never will be, but the people themselves rightly consider it a barbarous and ruinous institution; the necessity to preserve some solid bulwark against the impermanence of things will always prevent its adoption. Not even the wildest anarchists and left-wing revolutionaries dared to propose it in the past. The Communists today angrily deny they are contemplating it."

But six years later, a bill making divorce legal in officially Catholic Italy was passed by the Chamber of Deputies on December 1, 1970. It already had been approved by the Senate. A few hours later, President of the Republic Giuseppe Saragat signed the document making it law within the next two weeks. Immediately many thousands of unhappy spouses began taking advantage of the new legislation.

But the opponents of divorce, including primarily the Catholic church, the pro-Vatican Christian Democrats, and the neo-Fascists immediately unleashed a joint movement for a referendum. At first glance the neo-Fascists and the Christian Democrats seemed strange political bedfellows, but in reality they weren't. The 1929 concordat between Mussolini and Pope Pius XI gave Roman Catholic marriage rules the force of law in Italy. As a result, only the Vatican's Sacred Rota Court could annul Italian marriages until December 15, 1970. The referendum against divorce was overwhelmingly defeated in the summer of 1974.

Actually not so many Italians have taken advantage of the divorce law. The reason being that the men have become accustomed to the idea of having at least two families — one legal, one illegal, plus a number of girl friends and an occasional streetwalker. Divorce involved more complications for an Italian than an American, for example. To many Italian men, it meant he must marry his former mistress, then start looking for a new mistress while still going with prostitutes on the side who suddenly were jockeying among each other to become the mistress.

The Italian male is so sex-minded that even impotence doesn't interfere with his having a sex life. There's a story about the eighty-year-old Italian roué who called on his doctor. He said: "Professore, I would like you to examine me. To see if I am sexually fit."

"Very well. Let me see your sex organs, please."

The aged patient replied, "Eccoli," and stuck out his index finger and his tongue.

The hierarchy of the Church is gradually becoming more foreign, but many foreign cardinals are influenced by Italian thinking. American and Irish Princes of the Church, for example, are more conservative than Dutch, Belgian, or Swiss Catholics. But what nettles me the most is that all Catholics, dissident or conformist, liberal or conservative, accept the Italian idea that women must not hold high positions in the Church, not even a post as humble as that of a clergyman. A woman cannot even be a simple parish priest. Women are second-rate citizens both in Italy and the Holy See. The Madonna of the Church or the mamma mia of Italy are both venerated as glorious figureheads whose role is to serve the male. The Virgin Mary is the Divine Incubator who conceived Christ without carnal relations — just a shadowing over her by the Holy Ghost. The mother of the Italian family sits on the right-hand side of her husband, being his complacent whore, baby producer, and domestic slave.

The Italians are probably the least devout Catholics in the world. They have their own way of interpreting gospel, doctrine, and encyclicals. If I were a murderer or just a common thief, I should prefer to confess to an Italian priest than to one of any other nationality. He would be more understanding, perhaps because he is accustomed to dealing with so much crime in his own country. All Italians seem to take Catholicism in their stride. I find this to be true when I least expect it. One dawn, going home after working on an all-night news story in the office, I ran into an attractive streetwalker. She agreed to take me to her place for a ten-thousand lire blow job if I would wait while she attended early-morning mass. I accompanied her and went through all the religious motions she performed.

Then we left the church for a session of paid sex in her apartment with an illuminated crucifix on the wall just over the bed. I remembered that Mary Magdalene was a saint.

# CHAPTER XXVI

It took me a few seconds to recall the name of the slender woman who spoke to me in the working section of the Foreign Press Club. She had been looking at notices on the bulletin board. She seemed to know me well, calling me: "Caro Pack," and asking "How is Pibe?" Then I remembered. It was the Gondola. She had been nicknamed that because she was afraid of automobiles. She had come to Rome from Venice where there were no cars. Answering an ad in the *Rome Daily American*, she got a job as secretary and translator for a U.S. correspondent. She was a sexy number, and soon went to bed with her distinguished-looking, white-haired boss, who was generally believed to be a spy, but nobody knew for which country.

The reports in the Club were that she was very adept at fellatio — some called her the best blow job in Rome — and was willing to be sodomized. She eventually married her employer. A few years after the wedding, he died of a heart attack. He had the reputation of being a lavish host at home and at high-priced restaurants, with most of his colleagues believing that the tabs he picked up were coverd by expense accounts connected either with journalism or espionage. But when he died he left the Gondola only a small, furnished penthouse in Trastevere, a brown-and-white fox terrier, and a meager income from a life-insurance policy.

A few months after his death, the Gondola asked Pibe and me for a job, but we had no opening for her. For a while she occasionally came into the Press Club bar, and she was taken on from time to time as a translator by transient or newly assigned correspondents. She spoke Italian with a Venetian accent and English like an American.

I told her Pibe was out of town for a few days covering a story and asked her to have a drink downstairs at the bar. She accepted and we went down by an inside staircase to the floor below. The Foreign Press Club was still in the same building, but it had been pushed up a flight. We lost the ground floor because the management of the building told the Club that there were artesian springs under the foundation, and the building would topple over if the water wasn't canalized into the SPQR sewers by powerful pumps. The downstairs part was needed, the management claimed, for installation of the pumps. After the Club had been transferred to its new location for more than a year, the hydraulic machinery not only hadn't been installed, but the premises had been leased to a big bookstore at a much higher rent. There were a few protests, but not really serious ones. After all, that was the Italian way of doing business. The Club merely had been outmaneuvered.

The Gondola and I sat down at a table in a corner of the bar trying to find some point of contact over Scotch and soda. She turned me on. There was a thin, exhausted quality about her as though she had been worn out by too many orgasms, probably from masturbation.

"You've lost weight," I said, "but it makes you look more exciting."

"Thanks. I wish it did."

"Are you still doing translation work?"

"Occasionally, but you know what that pays. Quasi niente. That's why I was looking at the bulletin board. To see if there might be something for me. There wasn't."

"Don't you have a lover?"

"I'm not young anymore. Italian men only want pretty young things. I'm almost thirty-five."

"And Americans?"

"All the ones I meet these days seem to be queers or sexless."

"But you look as though you're getting plenty of sex."

"Yes and no." She blushed, seeming embarrassed.

"You either are or you aren't."

"I'll explain it to you sometime. É triste."

"You intrigue me. How about dinner? Tomorrow night? I'll fatten you up on steak alla fiorentina."

322

"That would be nice."

We agreed to meet at the Press Club for drinks and then dine at Mario's on via della Vite, just a block away.

"Perhaps you'll invite me to your place afterwards," I said hopefully.

"Ma si. Con piacere." She gave me a promising smile.

And so, the following night I found myself in an elevator ascending to the Gondola's tiny attic apartment in Trastevere. It consisted of a living and dining room combined, a bedroom, a bathroom, and a kitchenette, which opened onto a small tiled terrace. The fox terrier greeted her deliriously. It jumped up, barked happily, and rubbed contentedly against her legs.

"Basta, basta, Brownie," she said patting its head.

The dog sprang onto an easy chair that was covered with an old green bath towel. It whimpered softly as though asking for attention.

I sat down on a sofa and the Gondola pulled a small table in front of me. Then she put a bottle of grappa, a carafe of water, some sliced lemons, and two glasses on it.

"That dog really loves you," I said.

"I love Brownie, too."

"I'm sorry I haven't any Scotch or Cognac," she apologized, "but I can't afford it."

"There's nothing wrong with grappa. It puts hair on your chest."

I poured out some grappa in one of the the glasses for her. She asked for some water and a bit of lemon juice in it. I obliged and did the same for myself. She sat down next to me on the sofa. We sipped the potent Alpine drink. I already had one hand on her thigh. She didn't object.

"Your mouth is like a beautiful goblet," I said. "Let me drink some grappa from it." I thought how corny I sounded.

She took a big drink from her glass. Her cheeks swelled out as she held the liquor in her mouth. I leaned my head back on a cushion. She placed her lips on top of mine. I opened my mouth. First her tongue pushed its way in. Then the grappa came pouring in, almost making me choke, there was so much of it. I swished the grappa back and forth in our mouths as we both swallowed it little by little until there wasn't any left. But our tongues still afire with alcohol and passion, continued to lick one another.

"You do it to me this time," the Gondola said as our mouths finally drew apart.

The grappa flowed slowly from my mouth into hers. I could feel her unzipping my fly and gently pulling out my cock. I pushed my hand up her skirt and beneath her silk panties, running my fingers through the hair between her legs.

"Let's get undressed," I murmured.

I stood up and threw off my clothes, scattering them on the floor, I didn't care where just so they didn't land on the electric stove she had turned on when we came in. She stripped slowly, provocatively, carefully draping her things over a chair. Then she threw herself naked onto the bed.

"Let's start with soixante-neuf," she said, using the French phrase to make it sound more refined, I imagined.

I slid on top of her with my mouth nuzzling the pelt of her pubis. My tongue found her clit as she called out: "Brownie, lie down. Stai buona." I heard the dog jump back onto its chair whining jealously. The Gondola began sucking. She was terrific. She pushed my foreskin back and forth with her thick lips, teasing the delicate cord with her serpentining tongue.

"Easy," I called out. "I'm about to pop."

"I'm ready too. Get into me. Get that cazzo into me."

I awkwardly but quickly changed position, hurling my scepter into her. The dog bounded onto the sofa. Then I felt its saliva-soaked tongue.

"Gondola! Gondola!" I cried. "Call off Brownie. That goddamn dog of yours is licking my asshole."

"She doesn't bite. Her mouth is clean. She loves it. Don't you like it?"

"Her mouth clean? God knows where it has been."

"She never leaves this floor. She does her business on the terrace. You don't need to worry. Brownie's mouth is as pure as yours."

"I'm sorry. I've lost my rail-on."

In the midst of my germ anxiety, my tallywacker had shriveled into a small thing like a piece of burnt bacon.

"Let Brownie suck it. She'll bring it up."

Animal contact. This was it. The world's worst perversion, I thought. I remembered when I was a kid in Atlantic City High School, there was a fellow who was known as cock happy. He even had cut a hole in his left trouser pocket so he could masturbate any time he wanted to: while in a movie, walking along the boardwalk, or in the schoolroom. He used to like to jerk off in front of me. He wanted us to do it together: mutual masturbation; but I refused because I wanted to be a great athlete, especially a great pole-vaulter and a sprintman. I even aspired to be a great quarterback. In the days of the bamboo pole, I was only six inches under Sabin Carr's world record. Orgasms were bad for training, I reasoned. I must sublimate. And I did. But I was an enthusiastic scopophiliac. I loved to watch the sex play of others. My schoolmate had a dog, a collie. I suggested to him one day that he let the collie lick his john. He didn't seem to worry about germs.

"You want to see it? Would it excite you?"

"I think so."

"I'll try it then."

He let down his trousers, sprawled out on a chair, and the dog came over to him. He waved the hardening member as though it were a stick. The collie licked it with its tongue. The cock shot up in the air, the dog lowered its mouth and lapped my friend's balls. He pushed himself out still farther from the chair and hoisted up his buttocks so the dog could get at his anus. When my friend's orgasm came, the collie slurped up the spermatozoa as though it were cream and wagged his tail for more. If I weren't afraid of germs or of harming my athletic prowess, I would let a dog do that to me, I mused at the time.

Now was the chance, I thought. Brownie never went out into the street and smelled canine excrement. Her mouth and tongue were clean. She didn't bite. Am I am a Marco Polo or a coward?

"Viva Marco Polo," I said.

"Marco Polo?"

"Yes, Marco Polo. Let Brownie lick me."

La Gondola went into the kitchenette. She came back with some margarine and smeared it on my cock. Brownie began licking, ravenously. Junior reared up.

La Gondola kissed me on the mouth and pinched my nipples. It was too exciting.

"I can't hold it," I said.

She pushed Brownie onto the floor and threw herself on her back.

"Get into me. Quickly."

I penetrated her. My buttocks bobbed up and down. Brownie was back, tonguing my balls and rectum, buggering me lingually.

"I'm going to shoot," I cried. "I can't stop it. It's too good. Jesus! Here it goes."

"Shoot into me, Pack. Let it flow warm and creamy."

Her patter was another aphrodisiac, hastening the climax. I reached it quickly and collapsed on top of her. She pushed me to one side and, patting her dripping crotch, called out: "Vieni qui, Brownie. Prendi. É buona."

The dog went after her honeypot as though it were a bowl of cream. Its long red tongue pushed its way inside the pink depth and swabbed out the white sap I had left there. I put my lips on the Gondola's tightly closed mouth. She opened it and our tongues tangled lustfully. Down below, Brownie snuffed away madly but tenderly, sending the Venetian into paroxysms. She shrilled: "Brownie, I love you. I love you. Oh you're killing me, Brownie. I'm coming."

La Gondola bridged up her backside and spread her legs wide apart to help the terrier lap her more intimately, even rectally. She fell back on the sofa with a cry of exhaustion. "Basta! Basta!" She and I stopped kissing.

"Brownie, Pack, you're terrific."

"You might put my name first," I said, half laughing.

"You're not jealous of Brownie?"

"No, but that's because I'm not jealous of anybody, including dogs. But you really love Brownie. I'm sure of that. Perhaps it's a great love. Remember Leda? She fell in love with a swan and fucked it. I saw the painting of them screwing. It hangs in the Florence Museum. Maybe you and Brownie could make the Metropolitan."

"Don't make a joke of it. Brownie is the only sex I've had since my husband died and now you. Is it so awful to love a dog?"

"Of course not. I figure it's love that counts, not its object."

Only, I thought I don't believe in love. I believe in affection and sex, and the intimacy of sex that brings minds together in a rapport that could never be attained without the conjoining of cock and cunt.

I got up and refilled our glasses with grappa, lemon juice, and water. We had another round of triple sex, with Brownie being very much a part of it, her canine tongue sweeping lasciviously over all my private parts. La Gondola and I had another drink, and the sweet little four-legged bitch was given a plate of horsemeat and spaghetti. Then I left. I explained that I had to spent the night at home, especially with Pibe away, in case the New York office phoned me there during the night. I didn't want to hurt the Gondola's feelings; also the excuse was halfway true. I had found sharing the Venetian with Brownie, a biped with a quadruped, a great anthropological adventure, but I didn't want to make a meaningful pattern of it as I had done with the Elf and the Greek. It was something I had played with in my subconscious, something I had always wanted to do since I was a youngster and now I had done it. Pibe laughed it off when I told her about the episode on her return to Rome.

"You crazy undeveloped kid," she said. "Don't you ever grow up?"

326

I could end this story here except the Gondola, I think, deserves a few more words. She sometimes received invitations to embassy cocktail parties because her late husband's name still hadn't been removed from all the lists of press attachés in Rome. The invitations were always addressed to signor and signora. At one of these parties — at the French embassy, I recall — she met an elderly career diplomat, but not of ambassadorial rank. He was an American widower, very proper, Harvard graduate, and everything comme il faut. She made a play for him, getting him to come to her tiny penthouse. They had sex, conventional sex, without Brownie. He became infatuated with her.

One evening while I was working late in the office, the Gondola phoned. She was hysterical.

"Please come immediately," she said. "I just can't stand it here alone any longer. I've committed murder. You're the only one I can talk to about it. Please come."

Pibe was out on a Vatican story. As soon as I finished the dispatch I was typing, I grabbed a taxi and drove to Trastevere. La Gondola opened the door almost as soon as I rang the bell. There was no barking in welcome from Brownie.

"What's it all about?" I asked.

"I've murdered Brownie," she said breaking into a torrent of tears. On the small table before the divan there was a bottle of Scotch, two glasses, a bucket of ice, and some mineral water. I poured us both drinks. I sat down next to her and offered her a cigarette. We both lit up.

"Why did you do it?"

"This diplomat is in love with me," she said. "He has asked me to marry him, but he is such a proper cold-pisser. He wants me to go to Switzerland and get culturally polished during the next two years. He wants me to learn perfect French, get rid of my Venetian accent in Italian, and speak English like a Bostonian. I must learn how to play bridge. Then he will announce our engagement, introduce me to his friends, and marry me. In the meantime, he is keeping me. I'm a kept woman. Generously kept. That's why we have Scotch tonight, and that's why I haven't called you up for months."

"Yes but why did you kill our sweet little Brownie?"

"Well, I'm coming to that. One night the diplomat and I were having sex, and Brownie, who I thought I had locked out on the terrace, came bouncing in and began licking his balls and asshole. He pushed her away and she kept coming back. Finally he kicked her and said to me: 'I think this bitch is used to doing this sort of thing. It's disgusting.' I denied it and he said in his frigid manner: 'You must destroy it. I won't have a mongrel dog around that nuzzles anuses and testicles. And don't give it to anybody because it might do the same thing to the new owner and then what would people say? That you go in for animal contacts. No. I insist that you destroy it. If you don't I won't marry you.'

"So this afternoon I took poor Brownie to the vet and had her chloroformed. She's already buried in a dog cemetery at Pomezia and will have a nice tomb. What else could I do?"

I put my arm around her and kissed her, saying, "Brownie was a very sweet creature. No wonder you loved her."

"She meant so much to me. She gave me so much happiness. Please fuck me, Pack. Bugger me. I'll do anything you want me to do. I'll suck your ass, let you piss in my mouth. I just want to get back at that diplomat bastard."

# CHAPTER XXVII

I didn't realize I was growing old until Eleanor began taking more interest in food than sex. Pibe, who was two years younger than me, was a fantastic cook and had no trouble teaching our tuttofare of the moment — Assunta — how to prepare gourmet meals. At the same time, I found myself doing more and more legwork for Pibe. I would go to the Vatican to cover Alessandrini's press conferences and give her my notes from which she would write her stories. Later, she began telling me on the phone how to write the dispatches and she would stay at home. Gradually, she became bedridden and only left our apartment to go to a hospital during periods when her body swelled up like a blowfish.

For the past several years, we had been sleeping not only in separate beds but in separate bedrooms. We had moved out of our via Margutta studio because it was damp, so damp in fact that mosslike verdigris grew on our clothes that were kept in closets, and slimy slugs crawled out of the drains and made phosphorescent tracks across the carpets. We also were a target for thieves.

A new barman in the Stampa Estera masterminded two holdup attempts on Pibe while I was away covering the death and gangster-style funeral of Lucky Luciano in Naples. She won the first attack, kicking her assailant in the vulnerables, in the face and jumping on his stomach. He finally rolled away from her and escaped. She held onto her bag throughout the combat and didn't lose any money.

But two nights later, the same young Italian, probably indignant that a woman had gotten the better of him, struck again. He lay in wait for her in the darkness, as she was unlocking our studio door at 2 A.M. He dashed out of the shadows and hit her over the head with a length of metal. She fell down unconscious. After kicking her in the stomach and face, he made off with her handbag containing three hundred dollars plus three times more than that in Italian lire which was intended to pay the Stampa Estera trimester rent. At the time Pibe was treasurer of the Foreign Press Club and chairman of the bar committee. The barman knew she was carrying a large sum of cash in her bag because she carelessly exposed its contents as she drank and talked with colleagues. The police who were called in, quickly suspected the barman. He and his strongarmed accomplice who made the actual assaults, were arrested, tried, and given jail sentences.

We then moved to via Pompeo Magno in the tree-studded, old residential section of Prati. Pibe's bedroom balcony overlooked the Tiber. The building was a real palazzo with ceilings so high that you couldn't see them except in daylight. It was here that Pibe began staying more and more in bed.

There was an old saying among the foreign colony in Rome: if you get seriously ill in Italy, take an airplane and leave the country immediately. I made the terrible mistake of not getting Pibe on a plane. Instead we stayed on in Rome. Pibe's parents were dead and so were mine. Even my only sister had died. Pibe had no sisters or brothers. We owned no property in America. Rome was more like home than New York, Alantic City, or Yakima.

Pibe's onetime million-dollar legs bloated; they were as shapeless as tree trunks. She was listless, had no energy, and I couldn't coax her out of bed. Her decline, almost imperceptible at first, began after she was beaten up during the via Margutta holdup. Something had happened to her body, but the doctors didn't know what it was, perhaps a Middle East disease.

She came back from the Holy Land where she had reported Pope Paul's first of eight jet plane trips outside of Italy. He already had proclaimed himself "an Apostle on the move." She seemed to improve somewhat and with my help as her legman she resumed covering the Vatican, including all the sessions of the Ecumenical Council with its debates on such controversial subjects as birth control, priestly celibacy, and the council's solemn declaration that the Jews shouldn't be held responsible for the crucifixion of Christ.

Covering the Vatican was nerve-wracking. You could never relax. The tiniest incident had to be checked for ulterior meanings. For example, one day in 1966, Paul VI paid what seemed to be an innocent visit to Castle Mount Fumone, fifty miles south of Rome, as a homage to Pope Saint Celestine V. Well, if you didn't know who Celestine V was, then you missed the significance of the trip. Celestine V — as Pibe with her weird historical background knew — had been a Benedictine monk before being elected pope and was never happy on the papal throne. He wanted to return to the simple life of a pious hermit. In 1214, Celestine resigned and became the only pontiff in history to abdicate. And so that brief visit to Castle Mount Fumone, where the thirteenth-century pope died, sparked reports that Paul also was planning to hand in the keys of Saint Peter. Paul's possible abdication became a favorite theme of speculation for years afterwards.

It also was the daily grind of running down vague Vatican rumors and dealing always in the double-talk of ecclesiastical Italian and Latin that really knocked out Pibe. Her back curved more and more; her strange illness was accompanied with pains and aches and caused her heart to flutter and almost stop beating at times. Her black hair had become salted with gray. Despite medical orders she continued to drink White Horse and smoke Chesterfields, at least three packs a day. She also took more and more sleeping pills, finally totaling two Perequils and two Veronals a night. Sometimes she woke up and couldn't remember whether she had fallen off to sleep without taking any barbiturates or not. So she would swallow another round of them. I was always afraid she would give herself an overdose.

When she went to hospital, she would insist on my bringing her Scotch in a Listerine bottle and packs of cigarettes which she hid in a hollowed-out dictionary on the table next to the bed. I also had to slip her a razor blade, so she could slash her wrists in case she decided that life wasn't worth continuing.

With our philosophy of abandon, it was impossible for me not to comply with such requests. I brought Pibe the Scotch and the cigarettes. I gave her the razor blade. If you believe in abandon, then you don't believe in carefully planned security measures and, consequently, you grow old without any insurance or Medicare. The only way in our case to cope with adversity, including ill health and poverty, was to commit suicide. Suicide took the place of health insurance, costly operations, and made eleemosynary care unnecessary. The sum total of a life is the square root of the intensity with which you have lived for x number of years.

I remember when the old UP colleague of ours, Aldo Forte, stretched himself out comfortably on a mattress on the floor of the kitchen after shutting all the doors and windows and turning on all the gas. He waited comfortably for death to come. Pibe and I went to the funeral held in the tiny chapel of Rome's Verano Catholic Cemetery. Poor Aldo's coffin was not even allowed all the way inside the chapel. It was stuck halfway in and halfway out the door. Interment took place in an unsanctified part of the burial ground. What a revenge for a religion that believed in souls. It punished the body from which the soul — if you believed in one — had departed and held the body up to shame because the mind, also no longer existent, had tried to seek relief from pain by its own volition and not wait for a more natural and probably more painful end. Not even the right to die when you want to! What slaves the Church wanted to make of its followers!

Whenever Pibe came back to our via Pompeo Magno apartment from her sessions in the Salavator Mundi Hospital, I always tried to get her interested in sex. My belief was that sexual activity in any form was a panacea for all illness. The first time I came back with her in an ambulance and tucked her in bed, I took off my clothes and slipped under the covers beside her. I kissed her on the mouth and put her hand on my cock.

"What's the idea?" she said. "It's limp. I don't want any duty fucking from you or anybody else. If it isn't sticking up like a tent pole, don't pretend you're horny. Besides, sex doesn't turn me on anymore."

The next morning, I decided to make another attempt to arouse Pibe carnally. When Assunta brought me my coffee, and the newspapers, I told the maid I was expecting a very important letter and wanted her to go by bus to the Stampa Estera and pick up my mail. That would get rid of her for at least an hour and a half thanks to Rome's midmorning traffic jams. As soon as I heard her shut the door behind me, I got out my hidden porno pictures, which I had brought from Cairo on one of my trips to Egypt, and selected my favorite photo. It was that of a trio making love. One naked girl was sitting with her pussy on the face of a man, unclothed except for socks and shoes, with his pecker pushed into a woman sitting astride his belly. The two women were inhaling each other's tongue and caressing each other's breasts. Just looking at them produced an erection. I then Vaselined a candle and poked it into my rectum, way up in there pressing against my prostate gland. This put steel into my fleshy rod. Giving it a few final strokes, I rushed into Pibe's bedroom.

"I'm horny," I said, kissing her. "Feel it."

She touched my cock and found it convincing.

"But I don't feel horny," she said. "I'm sorry."

"You'll like it once it's inside of you. Just try it. Open your legs."

"I tell you, I just don't feel horny. Maybe another day."

Her lack of enthusiasm killed my hard-on. Junior nose-dived, drooping down like a length of flax. I kissed Pibe affectionately, platonically on the cheek.

"It's all right, darling. I love fucking and muffing you. There's no duty involved. Only desire."

"Thanks, Pack. If you're as randy as you seem, call up a masseuse and have yourself an orgasm. I don't mind. You know that."

Pibe not only didn't want to have sex herself, but she didn't even want me to tell her about my own erotic adventures anymore.

"But our goldfish-bowl agreement," I said to her once when she interrupted one of my accounts of a boudoir episode.

"You have all the sex you want," she said. "Have your fox terriers, your baboons, play-massage women, bugger boys, old queens, whores, and my best friends, but don't tell me about them any more. Your Casanova experiences bore me. I'd rather read a good history book than listen to them."

"Fair enough. But you shouldn't drive me away from you completely. Sexually, I mean. I'm always with you, my darling, with or without sex."

Then I began to wonder if perhaps she might not be interested in sex if she could find another man who might turn her on. One night I asked her about this idea as she expertly, despite her consuming illness, prepared thick Tuscan steaks — *filetti di bue ai ferri* — on an electric grill which I had set up beside her bed. Pibe sat on the edge of the bed wearing a sky-blue bathrobe, poking at the spluttering meat with a yard-long fork.

"Listen, perhaps you would like sex with somebody besides me?" I said, in a questioning tone. She didn't answer and poked harder at the two steaks. "That little fag you like so much," I continued, "the one you went to Greece with a few years ago. Wouldn't you like to try him? I wouldn't mind. In fact, if you want, I'd even let him bugger me. We could have a threesome. Would you like that?"

"My steak is ready," she said. "I like it bloody. It will take a few minutes longer for yours."

The fat flared up in flames as she adroitly transferred a steak from the grill to a plate. She helped herself to some mashed potatoes and put a blob of butter on top of them.

"You didn't answer my question, darling," I said. "What about some other male for you? A change from me."

"Sex doesn't interest me anymore," she said. "I just don't want anybody that way. That's all there is to it."

I pretended the tears that came to my eyes were due to the smoke from the grill. It was terrible, I thought. It reminded me of a phrase that Dr. Barnard, the transplant expert had used during a televised roundtable discussion in Rome with Italian doctors. "The donor was clinically dead," the South African surgeon had said. Pibe was sexually dead. It was a real death, I thought. After all, our lives together had contained so much sex, a cornucopia — still my favorite word — of physiological, biological ecstasy and intimacy. Sex had welded us together. Copulation, fellatio, cunnilingus, and confession of our extramarital relations to each other were all part of our mutual understanding and affection for one another. There were still the memories of those rampaging days. I recalled some of them sadly. Pibe interrupted me to hand me a plate of red-hot filetto.

"Eat this instead of me. It's even better."

I forced a laugh. And trying to keep up the comedy, I said, "I'll wear a black ribbon around my cock in mourning for your late, lamented cunt."

"Promise me that when I'm really dead, you'll have an orgy to remember me by. A sort of fucking wake. You promise?"

"I'll think about it," I said hesitantly. The tears flowed down my cheeks. "Please don't talk like that, Pibe darling."

Two months later, Pibe was back in the Salvator Mundi Hospital. Again I brought her White Horse in a Listerine bottle and hid Chesterfields in the hollowed-out dictionary. The Veronal and a razor blade she kept in a cough-drop box. I visited her every day, no matter how important the news of the day may have been; and I always brought her flowers. She loved red roses and yellow tulips. She shocked the Catholic sisters with her strong four-letter language. When a nurse would try to make her go to bed before she felt like going to sleep, she would yell out: "Oh, shit. Bugger off. This is a hospital not a fucking prison."

When Pibe pressed her bedside button, calling a nurse, and the response wasn't immediate, Pibe would curse: "You lazy son of a bitch" or "you Communist bastard" and berate the shocked nun for lax service.

The doctor told me I must try to stop Eleanor from swearing at the nurses or else the management, composed of German-Swiss Catholic sisters, would not allow her to remain there. But Pibe by this time had become very much of a misanthrope. She didn't seem to like anybody, not even me, but she insisted I stay with her as much time as I could spare from the office.

"You're not such a bad son of a bitch," she told me one afternoon as I sat by her bedside. "I've gotten used to you through all the years of our ups and downs. You're like a goddamn Italian. You're at your best in adversity. A punk in prosperity."

The next morning I was awakened by the phone ringing. I turned on the lamp beside the table and, looking at my watch, I saw it was about 8 A.M. The curtains were still pulled down.

"Il Signor Packard?" the female voice asked in a German-accented Italian. I said: "Si," immediately realizing that it was the Salvator Mundi calling me.

The woman recited in well-memorized phrases: "La Signora Packard died peacefully during the night. The time of death was two-thirty A.M. The night nurse phoned your home, but there was no answer."

I was too stunned to answer at first. Then I managed to say: "I'll come immediately. Thank you."

Assunta was moving around in the kitchen. I could just barely hear her slippered steps. I called to her. She came into my bedroom.

"Buon giorno, Signor Packard," she said.

"You heard the phone ringing? It was the Salvator Mundi. The head nurse told me that la signora died during the night. She said death came peacefully."

Assunta let out a shriek. She began weeping and wringing her hands. "Dio mio," she cried. "Che tristezza! Che grande donna!" You might have thought she cared more for Pibe than I did the way she cried and carried on.

"The nurse told me she phoned here early this morning, and there was no answer. You didn't hear the phone?"

"Madonna mia, no. I was asleep in my room upstairs. I never hear the phone once I am asleep."

I poured myself a big slug of whisky. "Get me some ice quickly."

I dashed into the bathroom, shaved and showered and was back in my bedroom in ten minutes. A bowl of ice was there. I dropped two cubes into the glass. Drinking as I dressed, I was soon ready to leave for the hospital.

Assunta wanted to come with me but I said no, that I wanted her to buy some black armbands and sew them onto some suits. I selected three jackets for her.

I phoned for a cab; in another twenty minutes I was at the Salvator Mundi. I took the elevator to the first floor and hurried to Pibe's room. I went in without knocking. The woman in the bed turned to look at me. At the movement, I let out a cry. I thought it must be Pibe. She wasn't dead after all. It had all been a mistake on the phone. Then I realized that the woman was younger than Pibe and didn't really look anything like her except that she had dark hair.

A nurse hurriedly came in the room.

"Oh, Signor Packard," she cried, "la signora is in the chapel." You might have thought from the way the nurse spoke that Pibe had gone to the chapel to attend a religious service. "Please follow me."

I excused myself to the baffled woman in the bed and followed the white-starched uniform down the hall. The head nurse made her appearance and led me into her office. I asked her how Pibe died.

She was very frank and forthright in her account of the death.

"Well, your wife had turned off the oxygen tank so she could smoke," the sister said. "In fact, the cigarette was still lit when the night nurse happened to come in to see how Signora Packard was doing. It had just begun to set fire to the counterpane, which was smoldering. On the table beside her was a glass of straight whisky. It had come from a Listerine bottle that was almost empty. There was a smile on her face. I honestly believe she died without even knowing she was dying. God be praised. The night doctor was called and confirmed that she had been dead for only a few minutes."

"I'd like to see her."

"She is in the morgue. In the chapel. I'll take you there. Oh, here, this package is for you."

She handed me some objects wrapped in a paper napkin. I opened it up. There were Pibe's two bejeweled rings and her wristwatch. There was no wedding ring because I had never given her one. "There is her suitcase with her books and other belongings." The nun pointed to it in a corner of her office.

The nurse led the way through the main doorway into a garden where the morgue-chapel was located in a small building. Pibe was stretched out like a dead pope on a catafalque; she was draped in a white shroud with only her head and face visible. An electric fan was beamed on the upper part of her body. The artificial breeze made her hair ripple. One eye was slightly open, almost as though in an impish wink. I imagined there was a slight smile on her face. I kissed her on one cheek, then the other, and finally on her mouth. Her flesh felt irrevocably cold. The nun said: "If you would like to stay alone with your wife, here is the key. Be sure to lock the door when you leave."

She gave me the key, and I thanked her. As soon as she left, I went to the door and locked myself in. I wanted to be alone with Pibe, without any fear of interruption.

Kneeling down, I kissed Pibe's cold mouth, letting my tongue slip in between her lips.

"Darling, darling," I whispered. "I love you even in death. Your poor swollen legs remind me of the million-dollar shapeliness they once had. You still excite me, darling Pibe, with the memory of all we enjoyed together. You and I were companions in adventure. We were correspondents, incorporated. We were sex partners extraordinary. I never really enjoyed fucking anybody unless you took part in it. We should have had so many threesomes and foursomes in which the two of us screwed as one."

I let my hand slip beneath the shroud and found her breasts. I pulled down the white cloth and kissed one after the other of them, sucking each erect nipple. I opened my fly and began masturbating. My rod stood up as stiff as in rigor mortis. I pulled off the shroud, with my unoccupied hand, letting my incubus mouth meander downwards, licking her navel and muffing the frigid gash like a wound between her legs.

"Darling, darling Pibe, you arouse me even in death," I muttered. "I'm coming. I'm coming, I tell you. Really coming. It's wonderful jerking off and lapping you at the same time. I'm no necrophile. You are still alive to me. What edible pussy! What hair pie! What a gourmet dish!" My clenched hand rubbed up and down my shaft. There was no stopping it now. Liquid fire was pouring through the urethra, squirting into the palm of my right hand, making it sticky with the pasty fluid. Some of it fell on the shroud, wetting it. I slid my dripping hand between her legs and fingered the sperm into her vagina. This is the communion of our passion and affection, it is the transubstantiation of the juices of sex into the life-force of the world, I thought. I licked the translucent honey off my fingers and from her curly brown triangle. Darling, I thought, darling Pibe, you have become swallowed into the eternity of nothingness, the peaceful magnificent oblivion of death. No hell, no heaven, just the calm of nothingness.

I carefully put the shroud back in place, unlocked the door, and went out in the warm sun to face the remainder of life alone — without god, without Pibe.